THE
PILGRIMAGE
TO MECCAH

EYEWITNESS ACCOUNTS

THE PILGRIMAGE TO MECCAH

AMBERLEY

First published 2015

Amberley Publishing
The Hill, Stroud
Gloucestershire, GL5 4EP

www.amberley-books.com

British Library Cataloguing in Publication Data.
A catalogue record for this book is available from the British Library.

ISBN 978 1 4456 4421 9 (print)
ISBN 978 1 4456 4434 9 (ebook)

Typeset in 10.5pt on 13pt Sabon.
Typesetting and Origination by Amberley Publishing.
Printed in the UK.

CONTENTS

Editor's Note

This is an abridged version of Richard Burton's original two-volume travel classic detailing his pilgrimage to Mecca in 1853, originally published as *Personal Narrative of a Pilgrimage to El Medinah and Meccah*. It details the main sites visited on his journey, up to his arrival in Mecca itself. The original language has been retained as it appeared in the 1855 edition of the book, which displays Burton's inimitable style, but also a very different way of thinking from the modern day. At times, views expressed in the text may appear rather shocking, but it is important to remember that at the time of writing certain (no-longer held) views regarding various populations of countries of the world prevailed. Although sometimes surprising, this volume nevertheless offers the reader an important historical and cultural insight into a journey few outside Islam have made.

To Alexandria

A Few Words Concerning What Induced Me To A Pilgrimage

In the autumn of 1852, through the medium of General Monteith, I offered my services to the Royal Geographical Society of London, for the purpose of removing that opprobrium to modern adventure, the huge white blot which in our maps still notes the Eastern and the Central regions of Arabia. Sir Roderick Murchison, Colonel P. Yorke and Dr. Shaw, a deputation from that distinguished body, with their usual zeal for discovery and readiness to encourage the discoverer, honored me by warmly supporting, in a personal interview with the chairman of the Court of Directors to the Honorable East India Company, my application for three years' leave of absence on special duty from India to Muscat. But they were unable to prevail upon Sir James Hogg, who, remembering the fatalities which of late years have befallen sundry soldier-travellers in the East, refused his sanction, alleging as a reason that the contemplated journey was of too dangerous a nature. In compensation, however, for the disappointment, I was graciously allowed by my honorable masters the additional furlough of a year, in order to pursue my Arabic studies in lands where the language is best learned.

What remained for me but to prove, by trial, that what might be perilous to other travellers is safe to me? The 'experimentum crucis' was a visit to El Hejaz, at once the most difficult and the most dangerous point by which a European can enter Arabia. I had intended, had the period of leave originally applied for been granted, to land at Muscat – a favourable starting-place – and there to apply myself, slowly and surely, to the task of spanning the deserts. But now I was to hurry, in the midst of summer, after a four years' sojourn in Europe, during which many things Oriental had fallen away from my memory, and – after passing through the ordeal of Egypt, a country where the police is curious as in Rome or Milan – to begin with the Moslem's Holy Land, the jealously guarded and exclusive Haram. However, being liberally supplied with the sinews of travel by the Royal Geographical Society; thoroughly tired of 'progress' and of 'civilisation', curious to see with my eyes what others are content to 'hear with ears', namely, Moslem inner life in a really Mohammedan country; and longing, if truth be told, to set foot on that mysterious spot which no tourist has yet described, measured, sketched and daguerreotyped, I resolved to resume my old character of a Persian wanderer, and to make the attempt.

The principal object with which I started was this – to cross the unknown Arabian Peninsula, in a direct line from either El Medinah to Muscat, or diagonally from Meccah to Makallah on the Indian Ocean. By what 'circumstance the miscreator' my plans were defeated, the reader will discover in the course of these volumes.

The secondary objects were numerous. I was desirous to find out if any market for horses could be opened between Central Arabia and India, where the studs are beginning to excite general dissatisfaction; to obtain information concerning the Great Eastern wilderness, the vast expanse marked Ruba El Khali (the Empty Abode) in our maps; to inquire into the hydrography of the Hejaz, its water-shed, the disputed slope of the country, and the existence or non-existence of perennial streams; and finally, to try, by actual observation, the truth of a theory proposed by the learned Orientalist, Colonel W. Sykes, namely, that if history speak truth, in the population of the vast Peninsula there must exist certain physiological differences sufficient to warrant our questioning the common origin of the Arab family. As regards horses, I am satisfied that from the Eastern coast something might be done, – nothing on the Western, where the animals, though thoroughbred, are mere 'weeds' of a foolish price and procurable only by chance. Of the Ruba el Khali I have heard enough, from credible relators, to conclude that its horrid depths swarm with a large and half-starving population ; that it abounds in Wadys, valleys, gullies and ravines, partially fertilised by intermittent torrents; and therefore, that the land is open only to the adventurous traveller. Moreover, I am satisfied, that in spite of all geographers, from Ptolemy to Jomard, Arabia, which abounds in Fiumaras, possesses not a single perennial stream worthy the name of river; and the testimony of the natives induces me to think, with Wallin, contrary to Ritter and others, that the Peninsula falls instead of rising towards the south. Finally, I have found proof, to be produced in a future part of this publication, for believing in three distinct races. 1. The aborigines of the country, driven, like the Bheels and other autochthonic Indians, into the eastern and south-eastern wilds bordering upon the ocean. 2. A Syrian or Mesopotamian stock, typified by Shem and Joktan, that drove the Indigenae from the choicest tracts of country; these invaders still enjoy their conquests, representing the great Arabian people. And 3. An impure Egypto-Arab clan – we personify it by Ishmael, his son Nebajoth and Edom (Esau, the son of Isaac) – that populated and still populates the Sinaitic Peninsula. And in most places, even in the heart of Meccah, I met with debris of heathenry, proscribed by Mohammed, yet still popular, though the ignorant observers of the old customs assign to them a modern and a rationalistic origin.

I have entitled this account of my summer's tour through El Hejaz, a Personal Narrative, and I have laboured to make its nature correspond with its name, simply because 'it is the personal that interests mankind'. Many may not follow my example; but some perchance will be curious to see what measures I adopted, in order to appear suddenly as an Eastern upon the stage of Oriental life; and as the recital may be found useful by future adventurers, I make no apology for the egotistical scemblance of the narrative. Those who have felt the want of some 'silent friend' to aid them with advice, when it must not be asked, will appreciate what may appear to the uninterested critic mere outpourings of a mind full of self.

On the evening of April 3. 1853, I left London for Southampton. By the advice of a brother officer – little thought at that time the adviser or the advised how valuable was the suggestion! – my Eastern dress was called into requisition before leaving town, and all my 'impedimenta' were taught to look exceedingly Oriental. Early the next day a 'Persian Prince' embarked on board the Peninsular and Oriental Company's magnificent screw steamer 'Bengal'.

A fortnight was profitably spent in getting into the train of Oriental manners. For what polite Chesterfield says of the difference between a gentleman and his reverse, – namely, that both perform the same offices of life, but each in a several and widely different way – is notably as applicable to the manners of the Eastern as of the Western man. Look, for instance, at an Indian Moslem drinking a glass of water. With us the operation is simple enough, but his performance includes no less than five novelties. In the first place, he clutches his tumbler as though it were the throat of a foe; secondly, he ejaculates, 'In the name of Allah the Compassionate, the Merciful!' before wetting his lips; thirdly, he imbibes the contents, swallowing them, not drinking, and ending with a satisfied grunt; fourthly, before setting down the cup, he sighs forth, 'Praise be to Allah!' – of which you will understand the full meaning in the Desert; and, fifthly, he replies, 'May Allah make it pleasant to thee!" in answer to his friend's polite 'Pleasurably and health!'. Also he is careful to avoid the irreligious action of drinking the pure element in a standing position, mindful, however, of the three recognised exceptions, the fluid of the Holy Well, Zem Zem, water distributed in charity, and that which remains after Wuzu, the lesser ablution. Moreover, in Europe one forgets the use of the right hand, the manipulation of the rosary, the abuse of the chair,–your genuine Oriental looks almost as comfortable in it as a sailor upon the back of a high-trotting horse – the rolling gait with the toes straight to the front, the grave look and the habit of pious ejaculations.

Our voyage over the 'summer sea' was eventless. In a steamer of two or three thousand tons you discover the once dreaded, now contemptible, 'stormy waters' only by the band – a standing nuisance be it remarked – performing

'There we lay
All the day,
In the Bay of Biscay, O!'

The sight of glorious Trafalgar excites none of the sentiments with which a tedious sail used to invest it. 'Gib', the familiar name of Gibraltar, is, probably, better known to you, by Gautier and Warburton, than the regions about Cornhill; besides which, you anchor under the Rock exactly long enough to land and to breakfast. Malta, too, wears an old familiar face, which bids you order a dinner and superintend the icing of claret (beginning of Oriental barbarism), instead of galloping about on donkey-back through fiery air in memory of St. Paul and White-Cross Knights. But though our journey was monotonous, there was nothing to complain of. The ship was in every way comfortable; the cook, strange to say, was good, and the voyage lasted long enough, and not too long. On the evening of the thirteenth day after our start, the big-trowsered pilot, so lovely in his deformities to western eyes, made his appearance, and the good screw 'Bengal' found herself at anchor off the Headland of Figs.

Having been invited to start from the house of a kind friend, John Larking, I disembarked with him, and rejoiced to see that by dint of a beard and a shaven head I had succeeded, like the Lord of Geesh, in 'misleading the inquisitive spirit of the populace'. The mingled herd of spectators before whom we passed in review on the landing-place, hearing an audible 'Alhamdulillah whispered 'Muslim!' The infant population spared me the compliments usually addressed to hatted heads; and when a little boy, presuming that the occasion might possibly open the hand of generosity, looked in my face and exclaimed 'Bakhshish,' he obtained in reply a 'Mafish,' which convinced the bystanders that the sheep-skin contained a real sheep. We then mounted a carriage, fought our way through the donkeys, and in half an hour found ourselves, chibouque in mouth and coffee-cup in hand, seated on divans in my friend's hospitable house.

Wonderful was the contrast between the steamer and that villa on the Mahmudiyah canal! Startling the sudden change from presto to adagio life! In thirteen days we had passed from the clammy grey fog, that atmosphere of industry which kept us at anchor off the Isle of Wight, through the liveliest air of the inland sea, whose sparkling blue and purple haze spread charms even on Africa's beldame features, and now we are sitting silent and still, listening to the monotonous melody of the East – the soft night-breeze wandering through starlit skies and tufted trees, with a voice of melancholy meaning.

And this is the Arab's Kayf. The savouring of animal existence; the passive enjoyment of mere sense; the pleasant languor, the dreamy tranquillity, the airy castle-building, which in Asia stand in lieu of the vigorous, intensive, passionate life of Europe. It is the result of a lively, impressible, excitable nature, and exquisite sensibility of nerve, – a facility for voluptuousness unknown to northern regions; where happiness is placed in the exertion of mental and physical powers; where 'Ernst ist das Leben'; where niggard earth commands ceaseless sweat of brow, and damp chill air demands perpetual excitement, exercise, or change, or adventure, or dissipation, for want of something better. In the East, man requires but rest and shade: upon the bank of a bubbling stream, or under the cool shelter of a perfumed tree, he is perfectly happy, smoking a pipe, or sipping a cup of coffee, or drinking a glass of sherbet, but above all things deranging body and mind as little as possible; the trouble of conversations, the displeasures of memory, and the vanity of thought being the most unpleasant interruptions to his Kayf. No wonder that Kayf is a word untranslatable in our mother-tongue!

Let others describe this once famous capital of Egypt, the city of misnomers, whose dry docks are ever wet, and whose marble fountain is eternally dry, whose 'Cleopatra's Needle" is not Cleopatra's; whose 'Pompey's Pillar' never had any connection with Pompey; and whose Cleopatra's Baths are, according to veracious travellers, no baths at all. Yet is it a wonderful place, this 'Libyan suburb' of our day, this outpost of civilisation planted upon the skirts of barbarism, this Osiris seated side by side with Typho, his great old enemy. Still may be said of it, 'it ever beareth something new'; and Alexandria, a threadbare subject in Bruce's time, is even yet, from its perpetual changes, a fit field for modern description.

The better to blind the inquisitive eyes of servants and visitors, my friend lodged me in an outhouse, where I could revel in the utmost freedom of life and manners. And although some Armenian Dragoman, a restless spy like all his race, occasionally remarked that 'voilà un Persan diablement dégagé', none, except those who were entrusted with the secret, had any idea of the part I was playing. The domestics, devout Moslems, pronounced me to be an Ajomi, a kind of Mohammedan, not a good one like themselves, but, still, better than nothing. I lost no time in securing the assistance of a Shaykh, and plunged once more into the intricacies of the Faith, revived my recollections of religious ablution, read the Koran, and again became an adept in the art of prostration. My leisure hours were employed in visiting the baths, and coffee-houses, in attending the bazars, and in shopping, – an operation which hereabouts consists of sitting upon a chapman's counter, smoking, sipping coffee, and telling your beads the while, to show that you are not of the slaves for whom time is made; in fact, in pitting your patience against that of your adversary, the shopman. I found time for a short excursion to a country village on the banks of the canal; nor was an opportunity of seeing "El-nahl" neglected, for it would be some months before my eyes might dwell on such pleasant spectacle again.

Careful also of graver matters, I attended the mosque, and visited the venerable localities in which modern Alexandria abounds. Pilgrimaging Moslems are here shown the tomb of El-nabi Daniyal (Daniel the Prophet), discovered upon a spot where the late Sultan Mahmud dreamed that he saw an ancient man at prayer. Sikandar El-Rumi, a Moslem Alexander the Great, of course left his bones in the place bearing his name, or – as he ought to have done so – bones have been found for him. Alexandria also boasts of two celebrated Walis – holy men. One is Mohammed El-Busiri, the author of a poem called El-Burdah, universally read throughout the world of Islam, and locally recited at funerals, and on other solemn occasions. The other is Abu Abbas El-Andalusi, a sage and saint of the first water, at whose tomb prayer is never breathed in vain.

It is not to be supposed that the people of Alexandria could look upon my phials and pill-boxes, without a yearning for their contents. An Indian doctor, too, was a novelty to them; Franks they despised, but a man who had come so far from the West! Then there was something infinitely seducing in the character of a magician, doctor, and fakir, each admirable of itself, thus combined to make 'great medicine'. Men, women, and children besieged my door, by which means I could see the people face to face, and especially the fair sex, of which Europeans, generally speaking, know only the worst specimens. Even respectable natives, after witnessing a performance of 'Mandal' and the Magic mirror, opined that the stranger was a holy man, gifted with supernatural powers, and knowing everything. One old person sent to offer me his daughter in marriage – he said nothing about dowry – but on this occasion I thought proper to decline the honor. And a middle-aged lady proffered me the sum of 100 piastres, nearly one pound sterling, if I would stay at Alexandria, and superintend the restoration of her blind eye.

But the reader must not be led to suppose that I acted 'Carabin', or 'Sangrado' without any knowledge of my trade. From youth I have always been a dabbler in medical and mystical study. Moreover, the practice of physic is comparatively easy amongst dwellers in warm latitudes, uncivilised people, where there is not that complication of maladies which troubles more polished nations. And further, what simplifies extremely the treatment of the sick in these parts is, the undoubted periodicity of disease, reducing almost all to one type – ague. Many of the complaints of tropical climates, as medical men well know, display palpably intermittent symptoms unknown to colder countries; and speaking from individual experience, I may safely assert that in all cases of suffering, from a wound to ophthalmia, this phenomenon has forced itself into my notice. So much by way of excuse. I therefore considered myself as well qualified for the work as if I had taken out a 'buono per l'estero' diploma at Padua, and not more likely to do active harm than most of the regularly graduated young surgeons who start to 'finish themselves' upon the frame of the British soldier.

After a month's hard work at Alexandria, I prepared to assume the character of a wandering Dervish, after reforming my title from 'Mirza' to 'Shaykh' Abdullah. A reverend man, whose name I do not care to quote, some time ago initiated me into his order, the Kadiriyah, under the high-sounding name of Bismillah Shah: and, after a due period of probation, he graciously elevated me to the proud position of a Murshid in the mystic craft. I was therefore sufficiently well acquainted with the tenets and practices of these Oriental Freemasons. No character in the Moslem world is so proper for disguise as that of the Dervish. It is assumed by all ranks, ages, and creeds; by the nobleman who has been disgraced at court, and by the peasant who is too idle to till the ground; by Dives, who is weary of life, and by Lazarus, who begs bread from door to door. Further, the Dervish is allowed to ignore ceremony and politeness, as one who ceases to appear upon the stage of life; he may pray or not, marry or remain single as he pleases, be respectable in cloth of frieze as in cloth of gold, and no one asks him – the chartered vagabond – Why he comes here? or Wherefore lie goes there? He may wend his way on foot or alone, or ride his Arab steed followed by a dozen servants; he is equally feared without weapons, as swaggering through the streets armed to the teeth. The more haughty and offensive he is to the people, the more they respect him; a decided advantage to the traveller of choleric temperament. In the hour of imminent danger, he has only to become a maniac, and he is safe; a madman in the East, like a notably eccentric character in the West, is allowed to say or do whatever the spirit directs. Add to this character a little knowledge of medicine, a 'moderate skill in magic and a reputation for caring for nothing but study and books', together with capital sufficient to save you from the chance of starving, and you appear in the East to peculiar advantage. The only danger of the 'Path' is, that the Dervish's ragged coat not unfrequently covers the cut-throat, and, if seized in the society of such a 'brother' you may reluctantly become his companion, under the stick or on the stake. For be it known, Dervishes are of two orders, the Sharai, or those who conform to religion, and the be-Sharai, or Luti whose practices are hinted at by their own tradition that 'he we daurna name' once joined them for a week, but at the end of that time left them in dismay, and returned to whence he came.

I Leave Alexandria

The thorough-bred wanderer's idiosyncrasy I presume to be a composition of what phrenologists call 'inhabitiveness' and 'locality' equally and largely developed. After a long and toilsome march, weary of the way, he drops into the nearest place of rest to become the most domestic of men. For awhile he smokes the 'pipe of permanence' with an infinite zest; he delights in various siestas during the day, relishing withal a long sleep at night; he enjoys dining at a fixed dinner-hour, and wonders at the demoralisation of the mind which cannot find means of excitement in chit-chat or small talk, in a novel or a newspaper. But soon the passive fit has passed away; again a paroxysm of ennui coming on by slow degrees, Viator loses appetite, he walks about his room all night, he yawns at conversations, and a book acts upon him as a narcotic. The man wants to wander, and he must do so or he shall die.

After about a month most pleasantly spent at Alexandria, I perceived the approach of the enemy, and as nothing hampered my incomings and outgoings, I surrendered. The world was 'all before me', and there was pleasant excitement in plunging single-handed into its chilling depths. My Alexandrian

Shaykh, whose heart fell victim to a new 'jubbeh', which I had given in exchange for his tattered zaabut offered me, in consideration of a certain monthly stipend, the affections of a brother and religious refreshment, proposing to send his wife back to her papa, and to accompany me, in the capacity of private chaplain, to the other side of Kaf. I politely accepted the 'Bruderschaft', but many reasons induced me to decline his society and services. In the first place, he spoke the detestable Egyptian jargon. Secondly, it was but prudent to lose the 'spoor' between Alexandria and Suez. And, thirdly, my 'brother' had shifting eyes (symptoms of fickleness), close together (indices of cunning); a flat-crowned head, and large ill-fitting lips; signs which led me to think lightly of his honesty, firmness, and courage. Phrenology and physiognomy, be it observed, disappoint you often amongst civilised people, the proper action of whose brains and features is impeded by the external pressure of education, accident, example, habit, and necessity. But they are tolerably safe guides when groping your way through the mind of man in his natural state, a being of impulse in that chrysalis state of mental development which is rather instinct than reason.

Before my departure, however, there was much to be done.

The land of the Pharaohs is becoming civilised, and unpleasantly so: nothing can be more uncomfortable than its present middle-state between barbarism and the reverse. The prohibition against carrying arms is rigid as in Italy; all 'violence' is violently denounced, and beheading being deemed cruel, the most atrocious crimes, as well as those small political offences, which in the days of the Mamelukes would have led to a beyship or a bowstring, receive fourfold punishment by deportation to Faizoghli, the local Cayenne. If you order your peasant to be flogged, his friends gather in threatening hundreds at your gates; when you curse your boatman, he complains to your consul; the dragomans afflict you with strange wild notions about honesty; a government order prevents you from using vituperative language to the 'Natives' in general; and the very donkey boys are becoming cognisant of the right of man to remain unbastinadoed. Still the old leaven remains behind: here, as elsewhere in 'Morning-Land', you cannot hold your own without employing your fists. The passport system, now dying out of Europe, has sprung up, or rather revived in Egypt, with peculiar vigour. Its good effects claim for it our respect; still we cannot but lament its inconvenience. *We,* I mean real Easterns. As strangers – even those whose beards have whitened in the land – know absolutely nothing of what unfortunate natives must endure, I am tempted to subjoin a short sketch of my adventures in search of a Tezkirch at Alexandria.

Through ignorance which might have cost me dear but for my friend Larking's weight with the local authorities, I had neglected to provide myself with a passport in England, and it was not without difficulty, involving much unclean dressing and an unlimited expenditure of broken English, that I obtained from the consul at Alexandria a certificate, declaring me to be an Indo-British subject named Abdullah, by profession a doctor, aged thirty, and not distinguished – at least so the frequent blanks seemed to denote – by any remarkable conformation of eyes, nose, or cheek. For this I disbursed a dollar. And here let me record the indignation with which I did it. That mighty Britain – the mistress of the seas – the ruler of one-sixth of mankind – should charge five shillings to pay for the shadow of her protecting wing! That I cannot speak my modernised 'civis sum Romanus' without putting my hand into my pocket, in order that these officers of the Great Queen may not take too ruinously from a revenue of 56 millions! O the meanness of our magnificence! The littleness of our greatness!

My new passport would not carry me without the Zahit or Police Magistrate's counter-signature, said the consul. Next day I went to the Zabit, who referred me to the Muhafiz (Governor) of Alexandria, at whose gate I had the honor of squatting at least three hours, till a more compassionate clerk vouchsafed the information that tho proper place to apply to was the Diwan Kharijiych (the Foreign-Office). Thus a second day was utterly lost. On the morning of the third I started, as directed, for the palace, which crowns the Headland of Figs. It is a huge and couthless shell of building in parallelogrammic form containing all kinds of public offices in glorious confusion, looking with their glaring white-washed faces upon a central court, where a few leafless wind-wrung trees seem struggling for the breath of life in an eternal atmosphere of clay, dust, and sun-blaze.

The first person I addressed was a Kawwas or police officer, who, coiled comfortably up in a bit of shade fitting his person like a robe, was in full enjoyment of the Asiatic 'Kayf'. Having presented the consular certificate and briefly stated the nature of my business, I ventured to inquire what was the right course to pursue for a visá.

They have little respect for Dervishes, it appears, at Alexandria!

M'adri – 'Don't know', growled the man of authority without moving any thing but the quantity of tongue necessary for articulation.

Now there are three ways of treating Asiatic officials, – by bribe, by bullying, or by bothering them with a dogged perseverance into attending to you and your concerns. The latter is the peculiar province of the poor; moreover, this time I resolved, for other reasons, to be patient. I repeated my question in almost the same words. Ruh! 'Be off', was what I obtained for all reply. But this time the questioned went so far as to open his eyes. Still I stood twirling the paper in my hands, and looking very humble and very persevering, till a loud Ruh ya Kalb! 'Go O dog!' converted into a responsive curse the little speech I was preparing about the brotherhood of El-Islam and the mutual duties obligatory on true believers. I then turned away slowly and fiercely, for the next thing might have been a cut with the Kurbaj, and, by the hammer of Thor I British flesh and blood could never have stood that.

After which satisfactory scene – for satisfactory it was in one sense, proving the complete fitness of the Dervish's dress – I tried a dozen other promiscuous sources of information – policemen, grooms, scribes, donkey boys, and idlers in general. At length, wearied of patience, I offered a soldier some pinches of tobacco, and promised him an oriental sixpence if he would manage the business for me. The man was interested by the tobacco and the pence; he took my hand, and inquiring the while he went along, led me from place to place, till, mounting a grand staircase, I stood in the presence of Abbas Effendi, the governor's Naib or deputy.

It was a little, whey-faced, black-bearded Turk, coiled up in the usual conglomerate posture upon a calico-covered divan, at the end of a long bare large-windowed room. Without deigning even to nod the head, which hung over his shoulder with transcendent listlessness and affectation of pride, in answer to my salams and benedictions, he eyed me with wicked eyes, and faintly ejaculated 'Min ent!' Then hearing that I was a Dervish and doctor – he must be an Osmanli Voltairian, that little Turk – the official snorted a contemptuous snort. He condescendingly added, however, that the proper source to seek was 'That' which meaning simply 'below', conveyed rather imperfect information in a topographical point of view to a stranger.

At length, however, my soldier guide found out that a room in the custom-house bore the honorable appellation of 'Foreign Office'. Accordingly I went there, and, after sitting at least a couple of hours at the bolted door in the noon-day sun, was told, with a fury which made me think I had sinned, that the officer in whose charge the department was, had been presented with an olive branch in the morning, and consequently that business was not to be done that day. The angry-faced official communicated the intelligence to a large group of Anadolian, Caramanian, Boshniac, and Roumelian Turks – sturdy, undersized, broad-shouldered, bare-legged, splay-footed, horny-fisted, dark-browed, honest-looking mountaineers, who were lounging about with long pistols and yataghans stuck in their broad sashes, head-gear composed of immense tarbooshes with proportionate turbans coiled round them, and two or three suits of substantial clothes, even at this season of the year, upon their shoulders. Like myself they had waited some hours, but they were not patient under disappointment: they bluntly told the angry official that he and his master were a pair of idlers, aud the curses that rumbled and gurgled in their hairy throats as they strode towards the door, sounded like the growling of wild beasts.

Thus was another day truly orientally lost. On the morrow, however, I obtained permission, in the character of Dr Abdullah, to visit any part of Egypt I pleased, and to retain possession of my dagger and pistols.

And now I must explain what induced me to take so much trouble about a passport. The home reader naturally inquires, why not travel under your English name?

For this reason. In the generality of barbarous countries you must either proceed, like Bruce, preserving the 'dignity of manhood', and carrying matters with a high hand, or you must worm your way by timidity and subservience; in fact, by becoming an animal too contemptible for man to let or injure. But to pass through the Holy Land, you must either be a born believer, or have become one; in the former case you may demean yourself as you please, in the latter a path is ready prepared for you. My spirit could not bend to own myself a Burma, a renegade – to be pointed at and shunned and catechised, an object of suspicion to the many and of contempt to all. Moreover, it would have obstructed the aim of my wanderings. The convert is always watched with Argus eyes, and men do not willingly give information to a 'new Moslem', especially a Frank: they suspect his conversion to be feigned or forced, look upon him as a spy, and let him see as little of life as possible. Firmly as was my heart set upon travelling in Arabia, by Heaven! I would have given up the dear project rather than purchase a doubtful and partial success at such a price. Consequently, I had no choice but to appear as a born believer, and part of my birthright in that respectable character was toil and trouble in obtaining a Tezkireh.

Then I had to provide myself with certain necessaries for the way. These were not numerous. The silver-mounted dressing-case is here supplied by a rag containing a Miswak, a bit of soap and a comb, wooden, for bone and tortoiseshell are not, religiously speaking, correct. Equally simple was my wardrobe; a change or two of clothing. The only article of canteen description was a Zemzemiyah, a goat-skin water-bag, which, especially when new, communicates to its contents a ferruginous aspect and a wholesome, though hardly an attractive, flavour of tanno-gelatine. This was a necessary; to drink out of a tumbler, possibly fresh from pig-eating lips, would have entailed a certain loss of reputation. For bedding and furniture I had a coarse Persian rug – which, besides being couch, acted as chair, table, and oratory– a cotton-stuffed chintz-covered pillow, a blanket in case of cold, and a sheet, which did duty for tent and mosquito curtains in nights of heat. As shade is a convenience not always procurable, another necessary was a huge cotton umbrella of Eastern make, brightly yellow, suggesting the idea of an overgrown marigold. I had also a substantial housewife, the gift of a kind friend; it was a roll of canvas, carefully soiled, and garnished with needles and thread, cobblers'-wax, buttons, and other such articles. These things were most useful in lands where tailors abound not; besides which, the sight of a man darning his coat or patching his slippers teems with pleasing ideas of humility. A dagger, a brass inkstand and pen-holder stuck in the belt, and a mighty rosary, which on occasion might have been converted into a weapon of offence, completed my equipment. I must not omit to mention the proper method of carrying money, which in these lands should never be entrusted to box or bag. A common cotton purse secured in a breast pocket, (for Egypt now abounds in that civilised animal the pickpocket) contained silver pieces and small change. My gold, of which I carried twenty-five sovereigns, and papers, were committed to a substantial leathern belt of Maghrabi manufacture, made to be strapped round the waist under the dress. This is the Asiatic method of concealing valuables, and one more civilised than ours in the last century, when Roderic Random and his companion 'sewed their money between the lining and the waistband of their breeches, except some loose silver for immediate expense on the road'. The great inconvenience of the belt is its weight, especially where dollars must be carried, as in Arabia, causing chafes and discomfort at night. Moreover, it can scarcely be called safe. In dangerous countries wary travellers will adopt surer precautions.

A pair of common native Khurjin or saddle-bags contained my wardrobe, the bed was readily rolled up into a bundle, and for a medicine chest I bought a pea-green box with red and yellow flowers, capable of standing falls from a camel twice a day.

The next step was to find out when the local steamer would start for Cairo, and accordingly I betook myself to the Transit Office. No vessel was advertised; I was directed to call every evening till satisfied. At last the fortunate event took place: a 'weekly departure,', which, by the by, occurred once every fortnight or so, was in orders for the next day. I hurried to the office, but did not reach it till past noon – the hour of idleness. A little, dark gentleman, so formed and dressed as exactly to resemble a liver-and-tan bull-terrier, who with his heels on the table was dosing, cigar in mouth, over the last 'Galignani', positively refused, after a time – for at first he would not speak at all – to let me take my passage till three in the afternoon. I inquired when the boat started, upon which he referred me, as I had spoken bad Italian, to the advertisement. I pleaded inability to read or write, whereupon he testily cried 'Alle nove! alle nove!' – at nine! at nine! Still appearing uncertain, I drove him out of his chair, when he rose with a curse and read 8 a.m. An unhappy Eastern, depending upon what he said, would have been precisely one hour too late.

Thus were we lapsing into the real good old Indian style of doing business. Thus Indicus orders his first clerk to execute some commission; the senior, having 'work' upon his hands, sends a junior; the junior finds the sun hot, and passes on the word to a 'peon'; the 'peon' charges a porter with the errand, and the porter quietly sits or doses in his place, trusting that Fate will bring him out of the scrape, but firmly resolved, though the shattered globe fall, not to stir an inch.

The reader, I must again express a hope, will pardon the egotism of these descriptions – my object is to show him how business is carried on in these hot countries – business generally. For had I, instead of being Abdullah the Dervish, been a rich native merchant, it would have been the same. How many complaints of similar treatment have I heard in different parts of the Eastern world! and how little can one realise them without having actually experienced the evil! For the future I shall never see a 'nigger' squatting away half a dozen mortal hours in a broiling sun patiently waiting for something or for someone, without a lively remembrance of my own cooling of the calces at the custom-house of Alexandria.

At length, about the end of May all was ready. Not without a feeling of regret I left my little room among the white myrtle blossoms and the oleander flowers. I kissed with humble ostentation my kind host's hand in presence of his servants, bade adieu to my patients, who now amounted to about fifty, shaking hands with all meekly and with religious equality of attention, and, mounted in a 'trap' which looked like a cross between a wheel-barrow and a dog-cart, drawn by a kicking, jibbing, and biting mule, I set out for the steamer.

The Nile Steam Boat

In the days of the Pitts we have invariably a 'Relation' of Egyptian travellers who embark for a place called 'Roseet' on the 'River Nilus'. Wanderers of the Brucian age were wont to record their impressions of voyage upon land subjects observed between Alexandria and Cairo. A little later we find every one inditing rhapsodies about, and descriptions of, his or her Dahabiyeh (barge) on the canal. After this came the steamer. And after the steamer will come the railroad, which may disappoint the author tourist, but will be delightful to that sensible class of men who wish to get over the greatest extent of ground with the least inconvenience to themselves and others. Then shall the Mahmudiyah – ugliest and most wearisome of canals – be given up to cotton boats and grain barges, and then will note-books and the headings of chapters clean ignore its existence.

I saw the canal at its worst, when the water was low, and have not one syllable to say in its favour. Instead of thirty hours, we took three mortal days and nights to reach Cairo, and we grounded with painful regularity four or five times between sunrise and sunset. In the scenery on the banks sketchers and describers have left you nought to see. From Pompey's Pillar to the Maison Carrie, Kariom and its potteries, el Birkah of the night birds, Bastarah with the alleys of trees, even unto Atfeh, all things are perfectly familiar to us, and have been so years before the traveller actually sees them. The Nil El Mubarak itself – the Blessed Nile – as notably fails too at this season to arouse enthusiasm. You see nothing but muddy waters, dusty banks, a sand mist, a milky sky, and a glaring sun: you feel nothing but a breeze like the flues from a potter's furnace. You can only just distinguish through a veil of reeking vapours Shibr Katt from Kafr el Zayyat, and you steam too far from Wardan to enjoy the Timonic satisfaction of enraging its male population with 'Haykal! ya ibn Haykal!' – O Haykal! O son of Haykal! You are nearly wrecked, as a matter of course, at the Barrage; and as certainly dumb-foundered by the sight of its ugly little Gothic crenelles. The Pyramids of Cheops and Cephren, 'rearing their majestic heads above the margin of the desert', only suggest the remark that they have been remarkably well-sketched; and thus you proceed till with a real feeling of satisfaction you moor alongside of the tumble-down old suburb Bulak.

To me there was double dulness in the scenery: it seemed to be Sindh over again – the same morning mist and noon-tide glare; the same hot-wind and heat clouds, and fiery sunset, and evening glow; the same pillars of dust and 'devils' of sand sweeping like giants over the plain; the same turbid waters of a broad, shallow stream studded with sand-banks and silt-isles, with crashing earth slips and ruins nodding over a kind of cliff, whose base the stream gnaws with noisy tooth. On the banks, saline ground sparkled and glittered like hoar-frost in the sun; and here and there mud villages, solitary huts, pigeon-towers, or watch turrets, whence little brown boys shouted and slung stones at the birds, peeped out from among bright green patches of palm-tree, tamarisk, and mimosa, maize, tobacco, and sugar-cane.

Beyond the narrow tongue of land on the river banks lay the glaring, yellow desert, with its low hills and sand slopes bounded by innumerable pyramids of nature's architecture. The boats, with their sharp bows, preposterous sterns, and lateen sails, might have belonged to the Indus. So might the chocolate-skinned, blue-robed peasantry; the women carrying progeny on their hips, with the eternal waterpot on their heads; and the men sleeping in the shade, or following the plough, to which probably Osiris first put hand. The lower animals, like the higher, are the same; gaunt, mange-stained camels, muddy buffaloes, donkeys, sneaking jackals, and fox-like dogs. Even the feathered creatures were perfectly familiar to my eye – paddy birds, pelicans, giant ernnes, kites, and wild water-fowl.

I had taken a third-class or deck passage, whereby the evils of the journey were exasperated. A roasting sun pierced the canvas awning like hot water through a gauze veil, and by night the cold dews fell raw and thick as a Scotch mist. The cooking was abominable, and the dignity of Dervish-hood did not allow me to sit at meat with infidels or to cat the food they had polluted. So the Dervish squatted apart, smoking perpetually, with occasional interruptions to say his prayers and to tell his beads upon the mighty rosary, and he drank the muddy water of the canal out of a leathern bucket, and he munched his bread and garlic with a desperate sanctimoniousness.

The 'Little Asthmatic', as the steamer is called, was crowded, and discipline not daring to mark out particular places, the scene on board of her was motley enough. There were two Indian officers, who naturally spoke to none but each other, drank bad tea, and smoked their cigars like Britons. A troop of Kurd Kawwas, escorting treasure, was surrounded by a group of noisy Greeks;

these men's gross practical jokes sounding anything but pleasant to the solemn Moslems, whose saddlebags and furniture were at every moment in danger of being defiled by abominable drinks and the ejected juices of tobacco. There was one pretty woman on board, a Spanish girl, who looked strangely misplaced – a rose in a field of thistles. Some silent Italians, with noisy interpreters, sat staidly upon the benches. It was soon found out, through the communicative dragoman, that their business was to buy horses for H.M. of Sardinia: they were exposed to a volley of questions delivered by a party of French tradesmen returning to Cairo, but they shielded themselves and fought shy with Machiavellian dexterity. Besides these was a German – a 'beer-bottle in the morning and a bottle of beer in the evening', to borrow a simile from his own nantion – a Syrian merchant, the richest and ugliest of Alexandria, and a few French house-painters going to decorate the Pacha's palace at Shoobra. These last were the happiest of our voyagers – veritable children of Paris, Montagnards, Voltairiens, and thorough-bred Sans-Soucis. All day they sat upon deck chattering as only their lively nation can chatter, indulging in ultra-gallic maxims, such as 'on ne vicillit jamais à table'; now playing écarté for love or nothing, then composing 'des ponches un peu chiques'; now reciting adventures of the category 'Mirabolant', then singing, then dancing, then sleeping and rising to play, to drink, talk, dance, and sing again. They being new comers, free from the western morgue so soon caught by Oriental Europeans, were particularly civil to me, even wishing to mix me a strong draught; but I was not so fortunate with all on board. A large shopkeeper threatened to 'briser' my 'figure' for putting my pipe near his pantaloons; but seeing me finger my dagger curiously, though I did not shift my pipe, he forgot to remember his threat. I had taken charge of a parcel for one M. P – a student of Coptic, and remitted it to him on board; of this little service the only acknowledgment was a stare and a petulant inquiry why I had not given it to him before. And one of the Englishmen, half publicly, half privily, as though communing with himself, condemned my organs of vision because I happened to touch his elbow. He was a man in my own service; I pardoned him in consideration of the compliment paid to my disguise.

Two fellow-passengers were destined to play an important part in my comedy of Cairo. Just after we had started, a little event afforded us some amusement. On the bank appeared a short, fat, pursy kind of man, whose efforts to board the steamer were notably ridiculous. With attention divided between the vessel and a carpetbag carried by his donkey boy, he ran along the sides of the canal, now stumbling into hollows, then climbing heights, then standing shouting upon the projections with the fierce sun upon his back, till every one thought his breath was completely gone. But no! game to the backbone, he would have perished miserably rather than lose his fare: 'perseverance' say the copy-books, 'accomplishes great things': at last he was taken on board, and presently he lay down to sleep. His sooty complexion, lank black hair, features in which appeared beaucoup de finesse, that is to say, abundant rascality, an eternal smile and treacherous eyes, his gold ring, dress of showy colours, fleshy stomach, fat legs, round back and a peculiar manner of frowning and fawning simultaneously, marked him an Indian. When he awoke he introduced himself to me as Miyan Khudabakhsh Namdar, a native of Lahore: he had carried on the trade of a shawl merchant in London and Paris, where he lived two years, and after a pilgrimage intended to purge away the sins of civilised lands, had settled at Cairo.

My second friend, Haji Wali, I will introduce to the reader in a future chapter.

Long conversations in Persian and Hindostani abridged the tediousness of the voyage, and when we arrived at Bulak, the polite Khudabakhsh insisted upon my making his house my home. I was unwilling to accept the man's civility, disliking his looks, but he advanced cogent reasons for changing my mind. His servants cleared my luggage through the custom-house, and a few minutes after our arrival I found myself in his abode near the Ezbekiych Gardens, sitting in a cool Mashrabiyah that gracefully projected over a garden, and sipping the favourite glass of pomegranate syrup.

As the Wakalchs or caravanserais were at that time full of pilgrims, I remained with Khudabakhsh ten days or a fortnight. But at the end of that time my patience was thoroughly exhausted. My host had become a civilised man, who sat on chairs, ate with a fork, talked European politics, and had learned to admire, if not to understand liberty – liberal ideas! and was I not flying from such things? Besides which, we English have a peculiar national quality, which the Indians, with their characteristic acuteness, soon perceived, and described by an opprobrious name. Observing our solitary habits, that we could not, and would not, sit and talk and sip sherbet and smoke with them, they called us 'Jungli' – wild men, fresh caught in the jungle and sent to rule over the land of Hind. Certainly nothing suits us less than perpetual society, an utter want of solitude, when one cannot retire into oneself an instant without being asked some puerile question by a friend, or look into a book without a servant peering over one's shoulder; when from the hour you rise to the time you rest, you must ever be talking or listening, you must converse yourself to sleep in a public dormitory, and give ear to your companions' snores and mutterings at midnight.

The very essence of Oriental hospitality, however, is this family style of reception, which costs your host neither coin nor trouble. You make one more at his eating tray, and an additional mattress appears in the sleeping-room. When you depart, you leave if you like a little present, merely for a memorial, with your entertainer; he would be offended if you offered it him openly as a renumeration, and you give some trifling sums to the servants. Thus you will be welcome wherever you go. If perchance you are detained perforce in such a situation – which may easily happen to you, medical man, – you have only to make yourself as disagreeable as possible, by calling for all manner of impossible things. Shame is a passion with Eastern nations. Your host would blush to point out to you the indecorum of your conduct; and the laws of hospitality oblige him to supply the every want of a guest, even though he be a détenu.

But of all orientals, the most antipathetical companion to an Englishman is, I believe, an Indian. Like the fox in the fable, fulsomely flattering at first, he gradually becomes easily friendly, disagreeably familiar, offensively rude, which ends by rousing the 'spirit of the British lion'. Nothing delights the Indian so much as an opportunity of safely venting the spleen with which he regards his victors. He will sit in the presence of a magistrate, or an officer, the very picture of cringing submissiveness. But after leaving the room, he is as different from his former self as a counsel in court from a counsel at a concert, a sea captain at a hunt dinner from a sea captain on his quarter deck. Then he will discover that the English are not brave, nor clever, nor generous, nor civilised, nor anything but surpassing rogues; that every official takes bribes, that their manners are utterly offensive, and that they are rank infidels. Then he will descant complacently upon the probability of a general Bartholomew's day in the East, and look forward to the hour when enlightened young India will arise and drive the 'foul invader' from the land. Then he will submit his political opinions nakedly, that India should be wrested from the Company and given to the Queen, or taken from the Queen and given to the French. If the Indian has been a European traveller, so much the worse for you. He has blushed to own – explaining, however, conquest by bribery – that 50,000 Englishmen hold 150,000,000 of his compatriots in thrall, and for aught you know, republicanism may have become his idol. He has lost all fear of the white face, and having been accustomed to unburden his mind in

'The land where, girt by friend or foe,
A may man speak the thing he will'

he pursues the same course, in other lands where it is exceedingly misplaced. His doctrines of liberty and inequality he applies to you personally and practically, by not rising when you enter or leave the room – at first you could scarcely induce him to sit down – by not offering you his pipe, by turning away when you address him – in fact, by a variety of similar small affronts which none know better to manage skilfully and with almost impalpable gradations. If – and how he prays for it! – an opportunity of refusing you any thing presents itself, he does it with an air.

'In rice strength,
In an Indian manliness'

say the Arabs. And the Persians apply the following pithy tale to their neighbours. 'Brother', said the leopard to the jackal, 'I crave a few of thy cast-off hairs; I want them for medicine; where can I find them?' 'Wallah!' replied the jackal, 'I don't exactly know – I seldom change my coat–I wander about the hills. Allah is bounteous, brother! hairs are not so easily shed.'

Woe to the unhappy Englishman, Pacha, or private soldier, who must serve an Eastern lord! Worst of all, if the master be an Indian who, hating all Europeans, adds an especial spite to oriental coarseness, treachery, and tyranny. Even the experiment of associating with them is almost too hard to bear. But a useful deduction may be drawn from such observations; and as few have had greater experience than myself, I venture to express my opinion with confidence, however unpopular or unfashionable it may be.

I am convinced that the natives of India cannot respect a European who mixes with them familiarly, or especially who imitates their customs, manners, and dress. The tight pantaloons, the authoritative voice, the pococurante manner, and the broken Hindostani impose upon them – have a weight which learning and honesty, which wit and courage, have not. This is to them the master's attitude: they bend to it like those Scythian slaves that faced the sword but fled from the horsewhip. Such would never be the case amongst, a brave people, the Afghan for instance. And for the same reason it is not so, we read, with the North American tribes. 'The free trapper combines in the eye of an Indian (American) girl, all that is dashing and heroic, in a warrior of her own race, whose gait and garb and bravery he emulates, with all that is gallant and glorious in the white man.' There is but one cause for this phenomenon; the 'imbelles Indi' are still, with few exceptions, a cowardly and slavish people, who would raise themselves by depreciating those superior to them in the scale of the creation. The Afghans and American aborigines, being chivalrous races, rather exaggerate the valour of their foes, because by so doing they exalt their own.

The Ramazan

This year the Ramazan befel in June, and a fearful infliction was that 'blessed month'. For the space of sixteen consecutive hours and a quarter, we were forbidden to eat, drink, smoke, snuff, and even to swallow our saliva designedly. I say forbidden, for although the highest orders of Turks may break the ordinance in strict privacy, popular opinion would condemn any open infraction of it with uncommon severity. In this, as in most human things, how many are there who hold that 'Pecher en secret n'est pas pecher, Ce n'est que l'èclat qui fait le crime'.

The middle and lower ranks observe the duties of the season, however arduous, with exceeding zeal: of the many who suffered severely from such total abstinence, I found but one patient who would eat even to save his life. And among the vulgar, sinners who habitually drink when they should pray, will fast and perform their devotions through the Ramazan.

Like the Italian and Greek fasts, the chief effect of the 'blessed month' upon True Believers is to darken their tempers into positive gloom. Their voices, never of the softest, acquire, especially after noon, a terribly harsh and creaking tone. The men curse one another and beat the women. The women slap and abuse the children, and these in their turn cruelly entreat and use bad language to the dogs and cats. You can scarcely spend ten minutes in any populous part of the city without hearing some violent dispute. The 'Karakun', or station-houses, are filled with lords who have administered an undue dose of chastisement to their ladies, and with ladies who have scratched, bitten, and otherwise injured the bodies of their lords. The Mosques are crowded with a sulky, grumbling population, making themselves offensive to one another on earth, whilst working their way to heaven; and in the shade, under the outer walls, the little boys who have been expelled the church attempt to forget their miseries in spiritless play. In the bazars and streets, pale long-drawn faces, looking for the most part intolerably cross, catch your eye, and at this season a stranger will sometimes meet with positive incivility. A shopkeeper, for instance, usually says when he rejects an insufficient offer, yaftah Allah, 'Allah opens!': in the Ramazan, he will grumble about the bore of Ghashim ('Johnny raws'), and gruffly tell you not to stand there wasting his time. But as a rule the shops are either shut or destitute of shopmen, merchants will not purchase, and students will not study. In fine, the Ramazan, for many classes, is one twelfth of the year wantonly thrown away.

The following is the routine of a fast day. About half an hour after midnight, the gun sounds its warning to faithful men that it is time to prepare for the Sahur, or morning meal. My servant then wakes me, if I have slept, brings water for ablution, spreads the Sufrah, and places before me certain remnants of the evening's meal, it is some time before the stomach becomes accustomed to such early hours, but in matters of appetite, habit is everything, and for health's sake one should strive to eat as plentifully as possible. Then sounds the Salam, or Blessings on the Prophet, an introduction to the call of morning prayer. Smoking sundry pipes with tenderness, as if taking leave of a friend, and until the second gun, fired at about half past two in the morning, gives the Imsak – the order to abstain from food – I wait the Azan, which in this month is called somewhat earlier than usual. Then, after a ceremony termed the Niyat of fasting, I say my prayers, and prepare for repose. At 7 a.m. the labors of the day begin for the working classes of society; the rich spend the night in revelling, and rest from dawn to noon.

The first thing on rising is to perform the Wuzu, or lesser ablution, which invariably follows sleep in a reclining position; without this it would be improper to pray, to enter the Mosques, to approach a religious man, or to touch the Koran. A few pauper patients usually visit me at this hour, report the phenomena of their complaints – which they do, by the by, with unpleasant minuteness of detail – and receive fresh instructions. At 9a.m. Shaykh Mohammed enters, with 'lecture' written upon his wrinkled brow, or I pick him up on the way, and proceed straight to the Mosque El Azhar. After three hours' hard reading with little interruption from bystanders – this is long vacation – comes the call to mid-day prayer. The founder of Islam ordained but few devotions for the morning, which is the business part of the Eastern day, but during the afternoon and evening they succeed one another rapidly, and their length increases. It is then time to visit my rich patients, and afterwards, in order to accustom myself to the sun, to wander through the bookshops for an hour or two, or simply to idle in the street. At 3 a.m. I return home, recite the afternoon prayers, and re-apply myself to study.

This is the worst part of the day. In Egypt the summer nights and mornings are, generally speaking, pleasant, but the forenoons are sultry, and the afternoons serious. A wind wafting the fine dust and furnace heat of the desert blows over the city, the ground returns with interest the showers of caloric from above, and not a cloud or a vapour breaks the dreary expanse of splendor on high. There being no such comforts as Indian tatties, and few but the wealthiest houses boasting glass windows, the interior of your room is somewhat more fiery than the street. Weakened with fasting, the body feels the heat trebly, and the disordered stomach almost affects the brain. Every minute is counted with morbid fixity of idea as it passes on towards the blessed sunset, especially by those whose terrible lot is manual labor at such a season. A few try to forget their afternoon miseries in slumber, but most people take the Kaylulah, or Siesta, shortly after the meridian, holding it unwholesome to sleep late in the day.

As the Maghrib, the sunset hour, approaches – and how slowly it comes! – the town seems to recover from a trance. People flock to the windows and balconies, in order to watch the moment of their release. Some pray, others tell their beads, while others, gathering together in groups or paying visits, exert themselves to while away the lagging time.

O gladness! at length it sounds, the gun from the citadel. Simultaneously rises the sweet cry of the Muezzin, calling men to prayer, and the second cannon booms from the Abbasiyeh Palace – 'Al Fitar! al Fitar!' fast-breaking! fast-breaking! shout the people, and a hum of joy rises from the silent city. Your acute ears waste not a moment in conveying the delightful intelligence to your parched tongue, empty stomach, and languid limbs. You exhaust a pot full of water, no matter its size. You clap hurried hands for a pipe, you order coffee, and, provided with these comforts, you sit down, and calmly contemplate the coming pleasures of the evening.

Poor men eat heartily at once. The rich break their fast with a light meal – a little bread and fruit, fresh or dry, especially water-melon, sweetmeats, or such digestible dishes as 'Muhallabah' – a thin jelly of milk, starch, and rice-flour. They then smoke a pipe, drink a cup of coffee or a glass of sherbet, and recite the evening prayers; for the devotions of this hour are delicate things, and while smoking a first pipe after sixteen hours' abstinence, time easily slips away. Then they sit down to the Fatur (breakfast), *the* meal of the twenty-four hours, and eat plentifully, if they would avoid an illness.

There are many ways of spending a Ramazan evening. The Egyptiuns have a proverb, like ours of the Salernian school – 'After El-Ghada rest, if it be but for two moments: After El-asha walk, if it be but two steps'.

The streets are now crowded with a good-humoured throng of strollers, the many bent on pleasure, the few wending their way to mosque, where the Imam recites 'Tarawih' prayers. They saunter about, the accustomed pipe in hand, shopping, for the stalls are open till a late hour, or they sit in crowds at the coffee-house entrance, smoking Shishas, chatting, and listening to storytellers, singers and itinerant preachers. Here, a barefooted girl trills and quavers, accompanied by a noisy tambourine and a "scrannel pipe" of abominable discordance, in honor of a perverse saint whose corpse insisted upon being buried inside some respectable man's dwelling-house. The scene reminds you strongly of the Sonncurs of Brittany and the Zampognari from the Abruzzian Highlands bagpiping before the Madonna. There, a ball gaunt Maghrabi displays upon a square yard of dirty paper certain lines and blots, supposed to represent the venerable Kaabah, and collects coppers to defray the expenses of his pilgrimage. A steady stream of loungers

sets through the principal thoroughfares towards the
Ezbekiyeh, which skirts the Frank quarter, where they
sit in the moonlight, listening to Greek and Turkish
bands, or making merry with cakes, toasted grains,
coffee, sugared-drinks, and the broad pleasantries of
Kara Gyuz. Here the scene is less thoroughly oriental
than within the city, but the appearance of Frank dress
amongst the varieties of Eastern costume, the moon-lit
sky, and the light mist hanging over the deep shade
of the Acacia trees – whose rich scented yellow white
blossoms are popularly compared to the old Pacha's
beard – make it passing picturesque. And the traveller
from the far East remarks with wonder the presence
of certain ladies, whoso only mark of modesty is the
Burka, or face veil: upon this laxity the police looks
with lenient eyes, inasmuch as, until very lately, it paid
a respectable tax to the state.

Returning to the Moslem quarter, you are bewildered
by its variety of sounds. Everyone talks, and talking
here is always in extremes, either in a whisper, or in a
scream; gesticulation excites the lungs, and strangers
cannot persuade themselves that men so converse
without being or becoming furious. All the street cries,
too, are in the soprano key. 'In thy protection I in thy
protection!' shouts a Fellah to a sentinel, who is Hogging
him towards the station-house, followed by a tail of
women, screaming 'O my calamity! O my shame!' The
boys have elected a Pacha, whom they are conducting in
procession, with wisps of straw for Mashals, or cressets,
and outrunners, all huzzaing with ten-schoolboy
power. 'O thy right! O thy left! O thy face! O thy
heel! O thy back, thy buck!' cries the panting footman,
who, huge torch on shoulder, runs before the grandee's
carriage; 'bless the Prophet, and get out of the way!'
'O Allah bless him!' respond the good Moslems, some

shrinking up to the walls to avoid the stick, others rushing across the road, so as to give themselves every chance of being knocked down. The donkey boy beats his ass with a heavy palm-cudgel – he fears no treadmill here – cursing him at the top of his voice for a 'pander', a 'Jew', a 'Christian', and a 'son of the one-eyed, whose portion is eternal punishment'. 'O chick pease! O pips!' sings the vender of parched grains, rattling the unsavoury load in his basket. 'Out of the way, and say, "there is one God,"', pants the industrious water-carrier, laden with a skin, lit burden for a buffalo. 'Sweetwater, and gladden thy soul, O lemonade!' pipes the seller of that luxury, clanging his brass cups together. Then come the beggars, intensely Oriental. 'My supper is in Allah's hands, my supper is in Allah's hands! whatever thou givest, that will go with thee !' chaunts the old vagrant, whose wallet perhaps contains more provision than the basket of many a respectable shopkeeper. 'Naal 'abuk – curse thy father – O brother of a naughty sister!' is the response of sonic petulant Greek to the touch of the old man's staff. 'The grave is darkness, and good deeds are its lamp!' sings the blind woman, rapping two sticks together: 'upon Allah ! upon Allah ! O daughter!' cry the bystanders, when the obstinate 'hint' of sixty years seizes their hands, and will, not let go without a farthing. 'Bring the sweet and take the full', cry the long-mustachioed, fierce-browed Arnauts to the coffee-house keeper, who stands by them charmed by the rhyming repartee that flows so readily from their lips.

'Hanien,' may it be pleasant to thee! is the signal for encounter. 'Thou drinkest for ten' replies the other, instead of returning the usual religious salutation. 'I am the cock and thou art the *hen*!' is the rejoinder – a tart one. 'Nay, I am the thick one and thou art the *thin*!' resumes the first speaker, and so on till they come to equivoques which will not hear a literal English translation.

And sometimes, high above the hubbub, rises the melodious voice of the blind muezzin, who, from his balcony in the beetling tower rings forth, 'Hie ye to devotion! Hie ye to salvation! Devotion is better than sleep! Devotion is better than sleep!' Then good Moslems piously stand up, and mutter, previous to prayer, 'Here am I at thy call, O Allah! here am I at thy call!'

Sometimes I walked with my friend to the citadel, and eat upon a high wall, one of the outworks of Mohammed Ali's mosque, enjoying a view which, seen by night, when the summer moon is near the full, has a charm no power of language can embody. Or escaping from 'stifled Cairo's filth', we passed, through the Gate of Victory, into the wilderness beyond the city of the dead. Seated upon some mound of ruins, we inhaled the fine air of the desert, inspiriting as a cordial, when starlight and dew-mists diversified a scene, which, by day, is one broad sea of yellow loam with billows of chalk rock, thinly covered by a spray of sand floating in the fiery wind. There, within a mile of crowded life, all is desolate; the town walls seem crumbling to decay, the hovels are tenantless, and the paths untrodden; behind you lies the wild, before, the thousand tomb-stones, ghastly in their whiteness, and beyond them the tall dark forms of the Mameluke Sultan's towers rise from the low and hollow ground like the spirits of kings guarding ghostly subjects in the shadowy realm. Or we spent the evening at some Takiyeh, generally preferring that called the 'Gulshani', near the Muayyid Mosque outside the Mutawallis' saintly door. There is nothing attractive in its appearance. You mount a flight of ragged steps, and enter a low verandah enclosing an open stuccoed terrace, where stands the holy man's doomed tomb; the two stories contain small dark rooms in which the Dervishes dwell, and the ground-floor doors open into the verandah. During the fast-month, zikrs are rarely performed in the Takiyehs; the inmates pray there in congregations, or they sit conversing upon benches in the shade. And a curious medley of men they are, composed of the choicest vagabonds from every nation of Islam. Beyond this I must not describe the Takiych or the doings there, for the 'path' of the Dervish may not he trodden by profane feet.

Curious to see something of my old friends the Persians, I called with Haji Wali upon one Mirza Husayn, who by virtue of his dignity as 'Shahbandar', – he calls himself 'consul-general', – ranks with the dozen little diplomatic kings of Cairo. He suspends over his lofty gate a signboard in which the Lion and the Sun, (Iran's proud ensign,) are by some Egyptian limner's art metamorphosed into a preternatural tabby-cat grasping a scimitar, with the jolly fat face of a 'gay' young lady, curls and all complete, resting fondly upon her pet's concave back. This high dignitary's reception room was a court-yard 'sub dio' fronting the door were benches and cushions composing the Sadr or high place, with the parallel rows of Divans spread down the less dignified sides, and a line of naked boards, the lowest seats, ranged along the door wall. In the middle stood three little tables supporting three huge lanterns – as is their size so is the owner's dignity – each of which contained three of the largest spermaceti candles.

The Haji and I entering took our seats upon the side benches with humility, and exchanged salutations with the great man on the Sadr. When the Darbar or levee was full, in stalked the Mirza, and all arose as he calmly divested himself of his shoes and with all due solemnity ascended his proper cushion. He is a short thin man about thirty-five, with regular features and the usual preposterous lamb-skin cap and beard, two peaked black cones at least four feet in length, measured from the tips, resting on a slender basement of pale yellow face. After a quarter of an hour of ceremonies, polite mutterings and low bendings with the right hand on the left breast, the Mirza's pipe was handed to him first, in token of his dignity – at Teheran be was probably an under-clerk in some government office. In due time we were all served with Kaliuns and coffee by the servants, who made royal congees whenever they passed the great man, and more than once the janissary, in dignity of belt and crooked sabre, entered the court to quicken our awe.

The conversation was the usual oriental thing. It is, for instance, understood that you have seen strange things in strange lands. 'Voyaging – is – victory', quotes the Mirza; the quotation is a hackneyed one, but it steps forth majestic as to pause and emphasis. 'Verily', you reply with equal ponderousness of pronunciation and novelty of citation, 'in leaving home one learns life, yet a journey is a bit of Jehannum'.

Or if you are a physician the 'lieu commun' will be,

> 'Little-learned doctors the body destroy:
> Little-learn'd parsons the soul destroy.'

To which you will make answer, if you would pass for or a man of belles lettres, by the well-known lines,

> 'Of a truth, the physician hath power with drugs,
> Which, long as the sick man hath life, may relieve him;
> But the tale of our days being duly told,
> The doctor is daft, and his drugs deceive him'

After sitting there with dignity, like the rest of the guests, I took my leave, delighted with the truly Persian 'apparatus' of the scene. The Mirza, having no salary, lives by fees, which he extorts from his subjects, who pay him rather than lack some protection, and his dragoman for a counter-fee will sell their interests shamelessly. He is a hidalgo of blue blood in pride, pompousness and poverty. There is not a sheet of writing paper in the 'consulate' when they want one a farthing is sent to the grocer's – yet the consul drives out in an old carriage with four out-riders, two tail-capped men preceding and two following the crazy vehicle. And the Egyptians laugh heartily at this display, being accustomed by Mohammed Ali to consider all such parade obsolete.

About half an hour before midnight sounds the Abrar or call to prayer, at which time the latest wanderers return home to prepare for the Sahur, their morning meal. You are careful on the way to address each sentinel with a 'peace be upon thee!' especially if you have no lantern, otherwise you may chance to sleep in the guard-house. And, 'chemin faisant', you cannot but stop to gaze at streets as little like what civilised Europe understands by that name as an Egyptian temple to the new Houses of Parliament.

There are certain scenes, cannily termed 'Kenspeckle', that print themselves upon memory, and endure as long as memory endures – a thunder-cloud bursting upon the Alps, a night of stormy darkness off the Cape, and, perhaps, most awful of all, a solitary journey over the sandy desert.

Of this class is a stroll through the streets of old Cairo by night. All is squalor in the brilliancy of noon-day. In darkness you see nothing but a mere silhouette. But when the moon is high in the heavens, with the summer stars raining light upon God's world, there is something not of earth in the view. A glimpse at the strip of pale blue sky above scarcely reveals 'three ells of breadth': in many places the interval is less; here the copings meet, and there the outriggings of the houses seem to be interlaced. Now they are parted by a pencil, then by a flood of silvery splendor, while under the projecting cornices and the huge hanging-windows of fantastic wood-work, supported by gigantic corbels, and deep verandahs, and gateways huge enough for Behemoth to pass through, and blind wynds and long cul-de-sacs, lie patches of thick darkness, made visible by the dimmest of oil lights: the arch is a favourite figure: in one place you see it a mere skeleton of stone opening into some huge deserted hall; in another it is full of fretted stone and curved wood. Not a line is straight, the huge dead walls of the mosques slope over their massy buttresses, and the thin minarets seem about to fall across your path. The cornices project crookedly from the houses, and the great gables stand merely by force of cohesion. And that the line of beauty may not be wanting, the graceful bending form of the palm, on whose topmost feathers, quivering in the breeze, the moon-beam glistens, springs from a gloomy mound, or from the darkness of a mass of houses almost level with the ground. Briefly, the whole view is so drear, so fantastic, so ghostly, that it seems rather preposterous to imagine that in such places human beings like ourselves can be born, and live through life, to carry out the command 'increase and multiply', and die.

The Mosque

When the Byzantine Christians, after overthrowing the temples of Paganism, meditated re-building and remodeling them, poverty of invention and artistic impotence reduced them to group the spoils in a heterogeneous mass. The sea-ports of Egypt and the plains of Syria abounding in pillars of granite, basalt, and precious marbles, in Pharaonic, Greek, and Roman statuary, and in all manner of structural ornaments, the architects were at no loss for material. Their Syncretism, the result of chance and precipitancy, of extravagance and incuriousness, fell under eyes too ignorant to be hurt by the irregularity of the hybrid: it was perpetuated in the so-called Saracenic style, a plagiarism from the Byzantine, and reiterated in the Gothic, which is an off-shoot from the Saracenic. This fact accounts in the Gothic style for the manifold incongruities in the architecture, and for the phenomenon – not solely attributable to the buildings having been erected piece-meal – of its most classic period being that of its greatest irregularity.

Such 'architectural lawlessness', such disregard for symmetry – the result, I believe, of an imperfect 'amalgamation and enrichment' – may doubtless be defended upon the grounds both of cause and of effect.

Architecture is one of the imitative arts, and Nature, the myriomorphous, everywhere delighting in variety, appears to abhor nothing so much as perfect similarity and precise uniformity. To copy her exactly we must therefore seek that general analogy compatible with individual variety ; in fact, we should avoid the over-display of order and regularity. And again, it may be asserted that, however incongruous these disorderly forms may appear to the conventional eye, we find it easy to surmount our first antipathy to them. Perhaps we end in admiring them the more, as we love those faces in which irregularity of feature is compensated for by diversity and piquancy of expression.

There is nothing, I believe, new in the Arab Mosque; it is an unconscious revival of the forms used from the earliest ages to denote by symbolism the worship of the generative and the creative gods. The reader will excuse me if I only glance at a subject of which the investigation would require a volume, and which, discussed at greater length, would be out of place in such a narrative as this.

The first mosque in El-Islam was erected by Mohammed at Kuba near El Medinah: shortly afterwards, when he entered Meccah as a conqueror, he destroyed the idols of the Arab pantheon, and purified that venerable building of its abominations. He had probably observed in Syria the two forms appropriated by the Christians to their places of worship, the cross and the Basilica; he therefore preferred a square to a parallelogram, some authors say, with, others, without a cloister, for the prayers of the 'Saving Faith'. At length in the reign of El Walid (about A.H. 90) the capola, the niche, and the minaret made their appearance, and what is called the Saracenic style became the order of the Moslem world.

The Hindoos I believe to have been the first who symbolised by an equilateral triangle their peculiar cult, the Youi-Lingam: in their temple architecture it became either a conoid or a perfect pyramid. Egypt denoted it by the obelisk, peculiar to that country; and the form appeared in different parts of the world – thus in England it was a mere upright stone, and in Ireland a round tower. This we might expect to see. D'Hanearville has successfully traced the worship itself, in its different modifications, to all people: the symbol would therefore be found everywhere. The old Arab minaret is a plain conoid or polygonal tower, without balcony or stages, widely different from the Turkish, Modern Egyptian, and Hejazi combinations of cylinder and prism, happily compared by a French traveller to 'une chandelle coiffée d'un eteignoir'. And finally the ancient minaret, made solid as all Gothic architecture is, and provided with a belfry, became the spire and pinnacle of our ancestors.

From time immemorial, in hot and rainy lands, a hypæthral court surrounded by a covered portico, either circular or square, was used for the double purpose of church and mart – a place where God and Mammon were worshipped turn by turn. In some places we find rings of stones, like the Persian Pyrætheia, in others, round concave buildings representing the vault of heaven, where fire, the divine symbol, was worshipped, and in Arabia, columnal aisles, which, surmounted by the splendid blue vault, resemble the palm-grove. The Greeks adopted this area in the fanes of Creator Bacchus; and at Puzzuoli, near Naples, it may be seen in the building vulgarly ealled the Temple of Scrapis. It was equally well known to the Celts: in some places the Temenos was circular, in others a quadrangle. And such to the present day is the Mosque of El-Islam.

Even the Riwak or porches surrounding the area in the Mosque are a revival of older forms. 'The range of square buildings which enclose the temple of Serapis are not, properly speaking, parts of the fane, but apartments of the priests, places for victims, and sacred utensils, and chapels dedicated to subordinate deities, introduced by a more complicated and corrupt, worship, and probably unknown to the founders of the original edifice'. The cloisters in the Mosque became cells, used as lecture rooms, and libraries for books, bequeathed to the college. They are unequal, because some are required to be of larger, others to be of smaller dimensions. The same reason causes difference of size when the distribution of the building is into four hyposteles which open upon the area: that in the direction of the Kaabah, where worshippers mostly congregate, demanding greater depth than the other three. The wings were not unfrequently made unequal, either from want of building materials, or because the same extent of accommodation was not required in both. The columns were of different substances; some of handsome marble, others of rough stone meanly plastered over with dissimilar capitals, vulgarly cut shafts of various sizes, here with a pediment, there without, now turned upside down, now joined together by halves in the centre, and almost invariably nescient of intercolumnar rule. This is the result of Byzantine syncretism, carelessly and ignorantly grafted upon Arab ideas of the natural and the sublime. Loving and admiring the great, or rather the huge in plan, they care little for the execution of mere details, and they have not the acumen to discern the effect which clumsy workmanship, crooked lines, and visible joints – parts apparently insignificant – exercise upon the whole of an edifice. Their use of colors was a false taste, commonly displayed by mankind in their religious houses, and statues of the gods. The Hindus paint their pagodas inside and outside; and rub vermilion, in token of honor, over their deities. The Persian Colossi of Kaiomars and his consort on the Balkh road, and the Sphinx of Egypt, as well as the temples of the Nile, still show traces of artificial complexion. The fanes in classic Greece, where we might expect a purer taste, have been dyed. In the Forum Romanum, one of the finest buildings still bears stains of the Tyrian purple. And to mention no other instances, in the churches and belfries of Modern Italy, we see alternate bands of white and black material so disposed as to give them the appearance of giant zebras. The origin of 'Arabesque' must be referred to one of the principles of El-Islam. The Moslem, forbidden by his law to decorate his Mosque with statuary and pictures, supplied their place with quotations from the Koran, and inscriptions, 'plastic metaphysics', of marvellous perplexity. His alphabet lent itself to the purpose, and hence probably arose that almost inconceivable variety of lace-like fretwork of incrustations, Arabesques, and geometric flowers, in which his eye delights to lose itself.

The Meccan mosque became a model to the World of El-Islam, and the nations that embraced the new faith copied the consecrated building, as religiously as Christendom produced imitations of the Holy Sepulchre. The Mosque of Omar at Jerusalem, of Amr at Babylon on the Nile, and Taylun at Cairo were erected with some trifling improvements, such as the arched cloisters and inscribed cornices, upon the plan of the Kaabah. From Egypt and Palestine the ichnography spread far and wide. It was modified, as might be expected, by national taste ; what in Arabia was simple and elegant became highly, ornate in Spain, florid in Turkey, and effeminate in India. Still divergence of detail had not, even after the lapse of twelve centuries, materially altered the fundamental form.

Perhaps no Eastern city affords more numerous or more accessible specimens of Mosque architecture than Cairo. Between 300 or 400 places of worship, some stately piles, others ruinous hovels, many new, more decaying and earthquake-shaken, with minarets that rival in obliquity the Pisan monster, are open to the traveller's inspection. And Europeans by following the advice of their hotelkeeper have penetrated, and can penetrate, into any one they please. If architecture be really what I believe it to be, the highest expression of a people's artistic feeling – highest because it includes all others – to compare the several styles of the different epochs, to observe how each monarch building his own Mosque, and calling it by his own name, identified the manner of the monument with himself, and to trace the gradual decadence of art through 1200 years, down to the present day, must be a work of no ordinary interest to orientalists. The limits of my plan, however, compel me to place only the heads of the argument before the reader. May I then be allowed to express a hope that it will induce some more learned traveller to investigate a subject in every way worthy his attention?

The Jami Taylun (9th century) is simple and massive, yet elegant, and in some of its details peculiar. One of the four colonnades still remains to show the original magnificence of the building; the other porches are walled up, and inhabited by paupers. In the centre of a quadrangle about 100 paces square is a domed building springing from a square which occupies the proper place of the Kaabah. This 'Jami' is interesting as a point of comparison. If it be an exact copy of the Meccan temple, as it stood in AD 879, it shows that the latter has greatly altered in this our modern days.

Next in date to the Taylun Mosque is that of the
Sultan El Hakim, third Caliph of the Fatimites, and
founder of the Drusian mysteries. The minarets are
remarkable in shape, as well as size: they are unprovided
with the usual outer gallery, are based upon a cube of
masonry, and pierced above with apertures apparently
meaningless. A learned Cairene informed me that
these spires were devised by the eccentric monarch to
disperse, like large censers, fragrant smoke over the city
during the hours of prayer. The Azhar and Hasanyn
Mosques are simple and artless piles, celebrated for
sanctity, but remarkable for nothing save ugliness. Few
buildings, however, are statelier in appearance, or give
a nobler idea of both founder and architect than that
which bears Sultan Hasan's name. The stranger stands
awe-struck before walls high towering without a single
break, a hypæthral court severe in masculine beauty, a
gateway that might suit the palace of the Titans, and
the massive grandeur of its lofty minaret. This Mosque,
with its fortress aspect, owns no more relationship
to the efforts of a later age than does Canterbury
Cathedral to an Anglo-Indian 'Gothic'. For dignified
elegance and refined taste, the mosque and tomb of
Kaid Bey and the other Mameluke kings are admirable.
Even in their present state beauty presides over decay,
and the traveller has seldom seen aught more striking
than the rich light of the stained glass pouring through
the first shades of evening upon the marble floor.

The modern Mosques must be visited, to see Egyptian
architecture in its decline and fall. That of Sittna
Zaynab (our Lady Zaynab), founded by Murad Bey,
the Mameluke, and interrupted by the French invasion,
shows, even in its completion, some lingering truces
of taste. But nothing can be more offensive than the
building which every tourist flogs donkey in his hurry

to see – old Mohammed Ali's 'Folly' in the citadel. Its Greek architect has toiled to caricature a Mosque, to emulate the glories of our English 'Oriental Pavilion'. Outside, 'The shining minarets, thin and high', tire so thin, so high above the lumpy domes, that they look like the spindles of crouching crones, and are placed in full sight of Sultan Hasan the Giant, so as to derive all the disadvantages of the contrast. Is the pointed arch forgotten by man, that this hapless building should be disgraced by large and small parallelograms of glass and wood, so placed and so formed as to give its exterior walls the appearance of a European theatre coiffé with oriental cupolas? Inside, money has been lavished upon alabaster full of flaws; round the bases of pillars run gilt bands; in places the walls are painted with streaks to mock marble, and the woodwork is overlaid with tinsel gold. After a glance at these abominations, one cannot be surprised to hear the old men of Egypt lament that, in spite of European education, and of prizes encouraging geometry and architecture, modern art offers a melancholy contrast to antiquity. It is said that H. H. Abbas Pacha proposed to erect for himself a mosque that should far surpass the boast of the last generation. I venture to hope that the future architects of Egypt will light the 'sacred fire' from Sultan Hasan's, not from Mohammed Ali's Turco-Grecian splendors. The former is like the genuine Osmanli of past ages, fierce, cold, with a stalwart frame, index of a strong mind – there was a sullen grandeur about the man. The latter is the pert and puny modern Turk in pantaloons, frock coat, and Fez, ill-dressed, and ill-bred, in body and soul.

We will now enter the El Azhar Mosque. At the dwarf wooden railing we take off our slippers, hold them in the left hand, sole to sole, that no dirt may fall from them, and cross the threshold with the right foot, ejaculating, Bismillah, etc. Next we repair to the Mayzaah, or large tank, for ablution, without which it is scarcely lawful to appear in the house of Allah. We then seek some proper place for devotion, place our slippers on some other object in front of us to warn the lounger, and perform a two-bow prayer in honor of the Mosque. This done, we may wander about, and consider the several objects of curiosity.

The moon shines splendidly upon a vast open court, paved with stones which are polished like glass by the feet of the Faithful. There is darkness in the body of the building, a large parallelogrammic hall, at least twice too long for its height, supported by a forest of pillars, thin, poor-looking, crooked marble columns, planted avenue-like, and lined with torn and dirty matting. A few oil lamps shed doubtfid light upon scanty groups, who are debating some point of grammar, or listening to the words of wisdom that fall from the mouth of a Waiz. Presently they will leave the hypostyle, and throw themselves upon the flags of the quadrangle, where they may enjoy the open air, and avoid some fleas. It is now 'long vacation', so the holy building has become a kind of caravanserai for travellers; perhaps a score of nations meet in it; there is a confusion of tongues, and the din at times is deafening. Around the court runs a tolerably well-built colonnade, whose entablature is garnished with crimson arabesques, and in the inner wall are pierced apartments, now closed with plank doors. Of the Riwaks, as they are called, the Azhar contains twenty-four, one for each recognised nation in El-Islam, and of these, fifteen are still open to students. Inside them we find nothing but matting, and a pile of large dingy wooden boxes, which once contained the college library, but are now, generally speaking, empty.

There is nothing worth seeing in the cluster of little dark chambers that form the remainder of the Azhar. Even the Zawiynt el Umyan (or the blind men's oratory), a place whence so many 'gown-rows' have emanated, is rendered interesting only by the fanaticism of its inmates, and the certainty that, if recognised in this sanctum, we shall run the gauntlet under the staves of its proprietors, the angry blind.

The Azhar is the grand collegiate Mosque of this city – the Christ Church, in fact, of Cairo – once celebrated throughout the world of El-Islam. It was built, I was told, originally in poor style by one Jauhar, the slave of a Moorish merchant, in consequence of a dream that ordered him to erect a place whence the light of science should shine upon El-Islam. It gradually increased by 'Wakf' of lands, money, and books; and pious rulers made a point of adding to its size and wealth. Of late years it has considerably declined, the result of sequestrations, and of the diminished esteem in which the purely religious sciences are now held in the land of Egypt. Yet it is calculated that between 2000 and 3000 students of all nations and ages receive instruction here gratis. Each one is provided with bread, in a quantity determined by the amount of endowment in the Riwak set apart for his nation, with some article of clothing on festival days, and with a few piastres once a year. The professors, who are about 150 in number, may not take fees from their pupils; some lecture on account of the religious merit of the action, others to gain the high title of 'Teacher in El Azhar'. Six officials receive stipends from the government – the Shaykh el Jami or dean, the Shaykh el Sakka, who regulates the provision of water for ablution, and others that may be called heads of departments.

The following is the course of study in the Azhar. The school-boy of four or five years' standing has been taught, by a liberal application of the maxim 'the green rod is of the trees of Paradise', to chaunt the Koran without understanding it, the elementary rules of arithmetic, and, if he is destined to be a learned man, the art of writing. He then registers his name in El Azhar, and applies himself to the branches of study most cultivated in El-Islam, namely Nahw (syntax), Fikh (the holy Law), Hadis (the traditions of the Prophet), and Tafsir, or exposition of the Koran.

The young Egyptian reads at the same time El Sarf, or Inflexion, and El Nahw. But as Arabic is his mother-tongue, he is not required to study the former so deeply as are the Turks, the Persians, and the Indians. If he desire, however, to be a proficient, he must carefully peruse five books in El Sarf, and six in El Nahw. Master of grammar, our student now applies himself to its proper end and purpose, Divinity. Of the four schools those of Abu Hanifah and El Shafei are most common in Cairo; the followers of Ibn Malik abound only in Southern Egypt and the Berberah country, and the Hanbali is almost unknown. The theologian begins with what is called a Mata or text, a short, dry, and often obscure treatise, a mere string of precepts; in fact, the skeleton of the subject. This he learns by repeated perusal, till he can quote almost every passage literally. He then passes to its 'Sharh', or commentary, generally the work of some other savant, who explains the difficulty of the text, amplifies its Laconicisms, enters into exceptional cases, and deals with principles and reasons, as well as with mere precept. A difficult work will sometimes require 'Hashiyah', or marginal notes; but this aid has a bad name.

'Who readeth with note,
But learneth by rote,'

says a popular doggrel. The reason is, that the student's reasoning powers being little exercised, he learns to depend upon the dixit of a master rather than to think for himself. It also leads to the neglect of another practice, highly advocated by the eastern pedagogue. 'The lecture is one. The dispute (upon the subject of the lecture) is one thousand.'

In order to become a Fakih, or divine of distinguished fame, the follower of Abu Hanifah must peruse about ten volumes, some of huge size, written in a diffuse style: the Shafei's reading is not quite so extensive.

Theology is much studied, because it leads directly to the gaining of daily bread, as priest or tutor; and other scientific pursuits are neglected for the opposite reason.

The theologian in Egypt, as in other parts of El- Islam, must have a superficial knowledge of the Prophet's traditions. Of these there are eight well known collections, but the three first only are those generally read.

School-boys are instructed, almost when in their infancy, to intone the Koran; at the university they are taught a more exact system of chaunting. The style called 'Hafs' is the most common in Egypt, as it is indeed throughout the Moslem world. And after learning to read the holy volume, some savans are ambitious enough to wish to understand it: under these circumstances they must dive into the II el Tafsir, or the exposition of the Koran.

Our student is now a perfect Fakih or Mulla. But the poor fellow has no scholarship or fellowship – no easy tutorship – no fat living to look forward to. After wasting seven years, or twice seven years, over his studies, and reading till his brain is dizzy, his digestion gone, and his eyes half blind, he must either starve upon college alms, or squat, like my old Shaykh Mohammed, in a druggist's shop, or become pedagogue and curate in some country place, on the pay of 8*l* per annum. With such prospects it is wonderful how the Azhar can present any attractions; but the southern man is essentially an idler, and many become Olema, like Capuchins, in order to do nothing. A favoured few rise to the degree of Mudarris (professors), and thence become Kazis and Muftis. This is another inducement to matriculate; every undergraduate having an eye upon the Kazi-ship, with as much chance of obtaining it as the country parocco has to become a cardinal. Others again devote themselves to laical pursuits, degenerate into Wakils (lawyers), or seek their fortunes as Katibs – public or private accountants.

To conclude this part of the subject, I cannot agree with Dr. Bowring when he harshly says, upon the subject of Moslem education: 'The instruction given by the Doctors of the Law in the religious schools, for the formation of the Mohammedan priesthood, is of the most worthless character'. His opinion is equally open to objection with that of those who depreciate the law itself because it deals rather in precepts than in principle, in ceremonies and ordinances rather than in ethics and aesthetics. Both are what Eastern faiths and Eastern training have ever been, both are eminently adapted for the child-like state of the Oriental mind. When the people learn to appreciate ethics, and to understand psychics and aesthetics, the demand will create a supply. Meanwhile they leave transcendentalism to their poets, and busy themselves with preparing for heaven by practising the only part of their faith now intelligible to them – the material.

It is not to be supposed that a people in this stage of civilisation could be so fervently devout as the

Egyptians are without the bad leaven of bigotry. The same tongue which is employed in blessing the Almighty, is, it is conceived, doing its work equally well in cursing his enemies. Wherefore the Kafir is denounced by every sex, age, class, and condition, by the man of the world as by the boy at the school, out of, as well as in, the mosque.

If you ask your friend who is the person with a black turban, he replies, 'A Christian. Allah make his countenance cold!' If you inquire of your servant, who are the people singing in the next house, it is ten to one that his answer will be, 'A Jew. May his lot be Jehannum!'

It appears unintelligible, still it is not less true, that Egyptians who have lived as servants under European roofs for years, retain the liveliest loathing for the manners and customs of their masters. Few Franks, save those who have mixed with the Egyptians in Oriental disguise, are aware of their repugnance to, and contempt for, Europeans – so well is the feeling veiled under the garb of innate politeness, and so great is their reserve, when conversing with those of strange religious. I had a good opportunity of ascertaining the truth when the first rumour of a Russian war arose. Almost every able-bodied man spoke of hastening to the Jihad, and the only thing that looked like apprehension was the too eager depreciation of their foes. All seemed delighted at the idea of French cooperation, for, somehow or other, the Frenchman is everywhere popular. When speaking of England, they were not equally easy: heads were rolled, pious sentences were ejaculated, and finally out came the old Eastern cry, 'Of a truth they are Shaitans, those English'. The Austrians are despised, because the East knows nothing of them since the days when Osmanli hosts threatened the gates of Vienna. The Greeks are hated as clever scoundrels, ever ready to do El-Islam a mischief. The Maltese, the greatest of cowards off their own ground, are regarded with a profound contempt: these are the protégés which bring the British nation into disrepute at Cairo. And Italians are known only as 'istruttori' and 'distruttori'– doctors, druggists, and pedagogues.

Yet Egyptian human nature is, like human nature everywhere, contradictory. Hating and despising Europeans, they still long for European rule. This people admire an iron-handed and lion-hearted despotism; they hate a timid and a grinding tyranny. Of all foreigners, they would prefer the French yoke – a circumstance which I attribute to the diplomatic skill and national dignity of our neighbours across the Channel. But whatever European nation secures Egypt will win a treasure. Moated on the north and south by seas, with a glacis of impassable deserts to the eastward and westward, capable of supporting an army of 180,000 men, of paying a heavy tribute, and yet able to show a considerable surplus of revenue, this country in western hands will command India, and by a ship-canal between Pelusium and Suez would open the whole of Eastern Africa.

There is no longer much to fear from the fanaticism of the people, and a little prudence would suffice to command the interests of the Mosque.

The chiefs of corporations, in the present state of popular feeling, would offer even less difficulty to an invader or a foreign ruler than the Olema. Briefly, Egypt is the most tempting prize which the East holds out to the ambition of Europe, not excepting even the Golden Horn.

CHAP. VI

Preparations To Quit Cairo

At length the slow 'month of blessings' passed away. We rejoiced like Romans finishing their Quaresima, when a salvo of artillery from the citadel announced the end of our Lenten woes. On the last day of Ramazan all gave alms to the poor, at the rate of a piastre and a half for each member of the household – slave, servant, and master. The next day, first of the three composing the festival, we arose before dawn, performed our ablutions, and repaired to the Mosque, to recite the peculiar prayer of the Eed, and to hear the sermon which bade us be 'merry and wise'. After which we ate and drank heartily, then with pipes and tobacco, pouches in hand, we sauntered on, to enjoy the contemplation of smiling faces and street scenery.

The favourite resort on this occasion is the large cemetery outside the Bab el Nasr – that stern, old, massive gateway which opens upon the Suez road. There we found a scene of jollity. Tents and ambulant coffee-houses were full of men equipped in their 'Sunday best', listening to singers and musicians, smoking, chatting, and looking at jugglers, buffoons, snake-charmers, Dervishes, ape-leaders, and dancing boys habited in women's attire. Eating stalls and lollipop-shops, booths full of playthings, and sheds for lemonade and syrups, lined the roads, and disputed with swings and merry-go-rounds the regards of the little Moslems and Moslemahs. The chief item of the crowd – fair Cairenes – carried in their hands huge palm branches, intending to ornament therewith the tombs of parents and friends. Yet, even on this solemn occasion, there is, they say, not a little flirtation and love-making; parties of policemen are posted, with orders to interrupt all such irregularities with a long cane; but their vigilance is notoriously unequal to the task. I could not help observing that frequent pairs – doubtless cousins or other relations – wandered to unusual distances among the sand-hills, and that sometimes the confusion of a distant bastinado struck the car. These trifles did not, however, by any means interfere with the general joy. Every one wore something new; most people were in the fresh suits of finery intended to last through the year, and so strong is personal vanity in the breasts of Orientals, men and women, young and old, that from Cairo to Calcutta it would be difficult to find a sad heart under a handsome coat. The men swaggered, the women minced their steps, rolled their eyes, and were eternally arranging, and coquetting with their head-veils. The little boys strutting about foully abused any one of their number who might have a richer suit than his neighbours. And the little girls ogled every one in the ecstacy of conceit, and glanced contemptuously at other little girls their rivals.

Weary of the country, the Haji and I wandered about the city, paying visits, which at this time are like new year calls in continental Europe. I can describe the operation in Egypt only as the discussion of pipes and coffee in one place, and of coffee and pipes in another. But on this occasion whenever we, meet a friend we throw ourselves upon each other's breast, placing right arms over left shoulders, and vice versâ, squeezing like wrestlers, with intermittent hugs, then laying cheeck to cheeck delicately, at the same time making the loud noise of many kisses in the air. The compliment of the season was, 'Kull'am Antum bil Khair' – 'Every year may you be well!' – in fact, our 'Many happy returns of the day to you!' After this came abundant good wishes, and kindly prophecies, and from a 'religious person' a blessing, and a short prayer. To complete the resemblance between a Moslem and a Christian festival, we had dishes of the day, fish, Shurayk, the cross-bun, and a peculiarly indigestible cake, called in Egypt Kahk, the plum-pudding of El-Islam.

This year's Eed was made gloomy, comparatively speaking, by the state of politics. Report of war with Russia, with France, with England, that was going to land 3 million men at Suez, and with Infideldom in general, rang through Egypt, and the city of Mars became unusually martial. The government armouries, arsenals, and manufactories, were crowded with kidnapped workmen. Those who purposed a pilgrimage feared forcible detention. Wherever men gathered together, in the Mosques, for instance, or the coffee-houses, the police closed the doors, and made forcible capture of the able-bodied. This proceeding, almost as barbarous as our impressment law, filled the main streets with detachments of squalid-looking wretches, marching with collars round their necks and handcuffed to be made soldiers. The dismal impression of the scene was deepened by crowds of women, who, habited in mourning, and scattering dust and mud upon their rent garments, followed their sons, brothers, and husbands, with cries and shrieks. The death-wail is a peculiar way of cheering on the patriot departing 'pro patriâ mori', and the origin of the custom is characteristic of the people.

The principal public amusements allowed to Oriental women are those that come under the general name of 'Fantasia' – birth-feasts, marriage festivals, and funerals. And the early campaigns of Mohammed Ali's family in Syria and El Hejaz having, in many cases, deprived the bereaved of their sex-right to keen for the dead, they have now determined not to waste the opportunity, but to revel in the luxury of woe at the live man's wake.

Another cloud hung over Cairo. Humors of conspiracy were afloat. The Jews and Christians – here as ready to take alarm as the English in Italy – trembled at the fancied preparations for insurrection, massacre, and plunder. And even the Moslems whispered that some hundred desperadoes had resolved to fire the city, beginning with the bankers' quarter, and to spoil the wealthy Egyptians. Of course H.H. Abbas Pasha was absent at the time, and, even had he been at Cairo, his presence would have been of little use: for the ruler can do nothing towards restoring confidence to a panic-stricken Oriental nation.

At the end of the Eed or Festival, as a counter-irritant to political excitement, the police magistrates began to bully the people. There is a standing order in the chief cities of Egypt, that all who stir abroad after dark without a lantern shall pass the night in the station-house. But at Cairo in certain quarters, the Ezbekiyeh for instance, a little laxity is usually allowed. Before I left the capital the licence was withdrawn, and the sudden strictness caused many ludicrous scenes.

If by chance you had sent on your lantern to a friend's house by your servant, and had leisurely followed it five minutes after the hour of eight, you were sure to be met, stopped, collared, questioned, and captured by the patrol. You probably punched three or four of them, but found the dozen too strong for you. Held tightly by the sleeves, skirts, and collar of your wide outer garment, you were hurried away on a plane of about nine inches above the ground, your feet mostly treading the air. You were dragged along with a rapidity which scarcely permitted you to answer strings of questions concerning your name, nation, dwelling, faith, profession, and self in general – especially concerning the present state of your finances. If you lent an ear to the voice of the charmer that began by asking a crown to release you, and gradually came down to two-pence half-penny, you fell into a simple trap; the butt-end of a musket applied à posteriori, immediately after the transfer of property, convicted you of wilful waste. But if, more sensibly, you pretended to have forgotten your purse, you were reviled, and dragged with increased violence of shaking to the Zabit's office. You were spun through the large archway leading to the court, every fellow in uniform giving you, as you passed, a Kafa, 'cuff', on the back of the neck. Despite your rage, you were forced up the stairs to a long gallery full of people in a predicament like your own. Again your name, nation – I suppose you to be masquerading – offence, and other particulars were asked, and carefully noted in a folio by a ferocious-looking clerk. If you knew no better, you were summarily thrust into the Hasil, or condemned cell, to pass the night with pickpockets and ruffians, pell-mell; but if an adept in such matters, you insisted upon being conducted before the 'Pacha of the night', and, the clerk fearing to refuse, you were hurried to the great man's office hoping for justice, and dealing out ideal vengeance to your captors – the patrol. Here you found the dignitary sitting with pen, ink, and paper before him, and pipe and coffee-cup in hand, upon a wide Divan of dingy chintz, in a large dimly-lit room, with two guards by his side, and a semicircle

of recent seizures vociferating before him. When your
turn came, you were carefully collared, and led up to
the presence, as if even at that awful moment you were
mutinously and murderously disposed. The Pacha,
looking at you with a vicious sneer, turned up his nose,
ejaculated 'Ajemi', and prescribed the bastinado. You
observed that the mere fact of being a Persian did not
give mankind a right to capture, imprison, and punish
you; you declared moreover that you were no Persian,
but an Indian under British protection. The Pacha, a
man accustomed to obedience, then stared at you, to
frighten you, and you, we will suppose, stared at him,
till, with an oath, he turned to the patrol, and asked
them your offence. They all simultaneously swore by
Allah, that you had been found without a lantern,
dead-drunk, beating respectable people, breaking into
houses, robbing and invading harems. You openly told
the Pacha, that they were eating abominations; upon
which he directed one of his guards to smell your
breath – the charge of drunkenness being tangible.
The fellow, a comrade of your capturers, advanced his
nose to your lips; as might be expected, cried, 'Kikh',
contorted his countenance, and answered, by the beard
of 'Effendina' that he perceived a pestilent odour of
distilled waters. This announcement probably elicited
a grim grin from the 'Pacha of the night', who loves
Cognac, and is not indifferent to the charms of Cognac.
Then by his favor (for you improved the occasion),
you were allowed to spend the hours of darkness on
a wooden bench, in the adjacent long gallery, together
with certain little parasites, for which polite language
has no name. In the morning the janissary of your
consulate was sent for; he came, and claimed you ;
you were led off criminally; again you gave your name
and address, and if your offence was merely sending

on your lantern, you were dismissed with advice to be more careful in future. And assuredly your first step was towards the bath.

But on the other hand, you had declared yourself a European, you would either have been dismissed at once, or sent to your consul, who is here judge, jury, and jailor. Egyptian authority has of late years lost half its prestige. When Mr. Lane first settled at Cairo, all Europeans accused of aggression against Moslems were, he tells us, surrendered to the Turkish magistrates. Now, the native powers have no jurisdiction over strangers, nor can the police enter their houses. If the West would raise the diameter of its Eastern co-religionists, it will be forced to push the system a point further, and to allow all Christians to register their names at the different consulates whose protection they might prefer. This is what Russia has so 'unwarrantably and outrageously' attempted. We confine ourselves to a lesser injustice, which deprives Eastern states of their right as independent Powers to arrest, and judge foreigners, who for interest or convenience settle in their dominions. But we still shudder at the right of arrogating any such claim over the born subjects of Oriental Powers. What, however, would be the result were Great Britain to authorise her sons resident at Paris, or Florence, to refuse attendance at a French or an Italian court of justice, and to demand that the police should never force the doors of an English subject? I commend this consideration to all those who 'stickle for abstract rights' when the interest and progress of others are concerned, and who become somewhat latitudinarian and concrete in cases where their own welfare and aggrandisement are at stake.

Besides patients I had made some pleasant acquaintances at Cairo. Anton Zananire, a young

Syrian of considerable attainments as a linguist, paid me the compliment of permitting me to see the fair face of his 'Hareem'. Mr. Hatchadoor Noory, an Armenian gentleman, well known in Bombay, amongst other acts of kindness, introduced me to one of his compatriots, Khwajah Yusuf, whose advice, as an old traveller, was most useful to me. He had wandered far and wide, picking up everywhere some scrap of strange knowledge, and his history was a romance. Expelled for a youthful peccadillo from Cairo, he started upon his travels, qualified himself for sanctity at Meccah and El Medinah, became a religious beggar at Bagdad, studied French at Paris, and finally settled down as a professor of languages, under an amnesty, at Cairo. In his house I saw an Armenian marriage. The occasion was memorable: after the gloom and sameness of Moslem society, nothing could be more gladdening than the unveiled face of a pretty woman. Some of the guests were undeniably charming brunettes, with the blackest possible locks, and the brightest conceivable eyes; only one pretty girl wore the national costume; yet they all smoked chibouques and sat upon the Divans, and, as they entered the room, kissed with a sweet simplicity the hands of the priest, and of the other old gentlemen present.

Among the number of my acquaintances was a Meccan boy, Mohammed El Basyuni, from whom I bought the pilgrim-garb called 'Elibram' and the Kafan or shroud, with which the Moslem usually starts upon such a journey as mine was. He, being in his way homewards after a visit to Constantinople, was most anxious to accompany me in the character of a 'companion'. But he had travelled too much to suit me ; he had visited India, seen Englishmen, and lived with the 'Nawab Baloo' of Surat. Moreover he showed signs of over-wisdom, he had been a regular visitor, till I cured one of his friends of an ophthalmia, after which he gave me his address at Meccah, and was seen no more, Haji Wali described him and his party to be 'Nas jarrar' (extractors), and certainly he had not misjudged them. But the sequel will prove how Providence disposes of what man proposes, and as the boy, Mohammed, eventually did become my companion throughout the pilgrimage, will place him before the reader as summarily as possible.

He is a beardless youth, of about eighteen, chocolate brown, with high features, and a bold profile; his bony and decided Meccan cast of face is lit up by the peculiar Egyptian eye, which seems to descend from generation to generation. His figure is short and broad, with a tendency to be obese, the result of a strong stomach and the power of sleeping at discretion. He can read a little, write his name, and is uncommonly clever at a bargain. Meccah had taught him to speak excellent Arabic, to understand the literal dialect, to be eloquent in abuse, and to be profound at prayer and pilgrimage. Constantinople had given him a taste for Anacreontic singing, and female society of the questionable kind, a love of strong waters – the hypocrite looked positively scandalised when I first suggested the subject – and an off-hand latitudinarian mode of dealing with serious subjects in general. I found him to be the youngest son of a widow, whose doting fondness had moulded his disposition; he was selfish and affectionate, as spoiled children usually are, volatile, easily offended and as easily pacified (the Oriental), coveting other men's goods, and profuse of his own (the Arab), with a matchless intrepidity of countenance (the traveller), brazen lunged, not more than half brave, exceedingly astute, with an acute sense of honor, especially where his relations were concerned (the individual). I have seen him in a fit of fury because some one cursed his father; and he and I nearly parted because on one occasion I applied to him an epithet which etymologically considered might be exceedingly insulting to a high-minded brother, but which in popular parlance signifies nothing. This 'point d'honneur' was the boy Mohammed's strong point.

During the Ramazan I laid in my stores for the journey. These consisted of tea, coffee, rice, loaf-sugar, dates, biscuit, oil, vinegar, tobacco, lanterns, and cooking utensils, a small bell-shaped tent, costing twelve shillings, and three water-skins for the desert. The provisions were placed in a 'Kafas' or hamper artistically made of palm sticks, and in a huge Sahharah, or wooden box, about three feet each way, covered with leather or skin, and provided with a small lid fitting into the top. The former, together with my green box containing medicines, and saddle-bags full of clothes, hung on one side of the camel, a counterpoise to the big Sahharah on the other flank, Bedouins always requiring a tolerably equal balance of weight. On the top of the load transversely was placed a Shibriyah or cot, in which Shaykh Nur squatted like a large crow. This worthy had strutted out into the streets armed with a pair of horse-pistols and a sword almost as long as himself. No sooner did the mischievous boys of Cairo – they are as bad as the gamins of Paris and London – catch sight of him than they began to scream with laughter at the sight of the 'Hindi (Indian) in arms', till like a vagrant owl pursued by a flight of larks he ran back into the caravanserai.

Having spent all my ready money at Cairo I was obliged to renew the supply. My native friends advised me to take at least eighty pounds, and considering the expense of outfit for desert travelling, the sum did not appear excessive. I should have found some difficulty in raising the money had it not been for the kindness of a friend at Alexandria and a compatriot at Cairo. My Indians scrutinised the diminutive square of paper – my letter of credit – as a raven may sometimes be seen peering, with head askance, into the interior of a suspected marrow-bone. 'Can this be a bonâ fide draft?' they mentally inquired. And finally they offered, most politely, to write to England for me to draw the money, and to forward it in a sealed bag directed 'El Medinah'. I need scarcely say that such a style of transmission would, in the case of precious metals, have left no possible chance of its safe arrival. When the difficulty was overcome, I bought fifty pounds' worth of German dollars (Maria Theresas), and invested the rest in English and Turkish sovereigns. The gold I myself carried; part of the silver I sewed up in Shaykh Nur's leather waistbelt, and part was packed in the boxes, for this reason – when Bedouins begin plundering a respectable man, if they find a certain amount of ready money in his baggage, they do not search his person. If they find none they proceed to a personal inspection, and if his waist-belt, be empty they are rather disposed to rip open his stomach, in the belief that he must have discovered some peculiarly ingenious way of secreting valuables.

Having got through this difficulty I immediately fell into another. My hardly-earned Alexandrian passport required a double visa, one at the Zabit's office, the other at the consul's. After returning to Egypt I found it was the practice of travellers who required any civility from the English official at Cairo to enter the presence furnished with an order from the Foreign Office. I had neglected the precaution, and had ample reason to regret having done so. Failing at the British consulate, and unwilling to leave Cairo without being 'en regle' – the Egyptians warned me that Suez was a place of obstacles to pilgrims. I was obliged to look elsewhere for protection. My friend Haji Wali was the first consulted: after a long discussion he offered to take me to his consul, the Persian, and to find out for what sum I could become a temporary subject of the Shah. We went to the sign of the 'Lion and the Sun', and found the dragoman, a subtle Syrian Christian, who, after a rigid inquiry into the state of my purse, (my country was no consideration at all) introduced me to the Great Man. I have described this personage once already, and truly he merits not a second notice. The interview was truly ludicrous. He treated us with exceeding hauteur, motioned me to sit almost out of hearing, and after rolling his head in profound silence for nearly a quarter of an hour, vouchsafed the information that though my father might he a Shirazi, and my mother an Afghan, he had not the honor of my acquaintance. His companion, a large old Persian with Polyphemean eyebrows and a mulberry beard, put some gruff and discouraging questions. I quoted the verses 'He is a man who benefits his fellow-men, Not he who says 'why' and 'wherefore' and 'how much?' upon which an imperious wave of the arm directed me to return to the dragoman, who had the effrontery to ask me four pounds sterling for a Persian passport. I offered one, he derided my offer, and I went away perplexed. On my return to Cairo some months afterwards, he sent to say that had he known me as an Englishman, I should have had the document gratis – a civility for which he was duly thanked.

At last my Shaykh Mohammed hit upon *the* plan. 'Thou art', said he, 'an Afghan; I will fetch hither the principal of the Afghan college at the Azhar, and he, if thou make it worth his while' (this in a whisper) 'will be thy friend'. The case was looking desperate; my preceptor was urged to lose no time.

Presently Shaykh Mohammed returned in company with the principal, a little, thin, ragged-bearded, one-eyed, hare-lipped divine, dressed in very dirty clothes, of nondescript cut. Born at Muscat of Afghan parents, and brought up at Meccah, he was a kind of cosmopolite, speaking five languages fluently, and full of reminiscences of toil and travel. He refused pipes and coffee, professing to be ascetically disposed : but he ate more than half my dinner, to reassure me I presume, should I have been fearful that abstinence might injure his health. We then chatted in sundry tongues. I offered certain presents of books, which were rejected (such articles being valueless), and the Shaykh Abd el Wahhab having expressed his satisfaction at my account of myself, told me to call for him at the Azhar Mosque next morning.

Accordingly at 6 p.m. Shaykh Mohammed and Abdullah Khan – the latter equipped in a gigantic sprigged-muslin turban, so as to pass for a student of theology – repaired to El Azhar. Passing through the open quadrangle we entered the large hall which forms the body of the Mosque. In the northern wall was a dwarf door, leading by breakneck stairs to a pigeon-hole, the study of the learned Afghan Shaykh. We found him ensconced behind piles of musty and greasy manuscripts, surrounded by scholars and scribes, with whom he was cheapening books. He had not much business to transact; but long before he was ready, the stifling atmosphere drove us out of the study, and we repaired to the hall. Presently the Shaykh joined us, and we all rode on away to the citadel, and waited in a mosque till the office hour struck. When the doors were opened we went into the 'Divan', and sat patiently till the Shaykh found an opportunity of putting in a word. The officials were two in number; one an old invalid, very thin and sickly-looking, dressed in the Tureo-European style, whose hand was being severely kissed by a troop of religious beggars, to whom he had done some small favors; the other was a stout young clerk, whose duty it was to engross, and not to have his hand kissed. My name and other essentials were required, and no objections were offered, for who holier than the Shaykh Abd el Wahhab ibn Yunus el Sulaymani? The clerk filled up a printed paper in the Turkish language, apparently borrowed from the European method for spoiling the traveller, certified me, upon the Shaykh's security, to be one Abdullah, the son of Yusuf, (Joseph) originally from Cabool, described my person, and in exchange for five piastres handed me the document. I received it with joy, and still keep it as a trophy.

With hows, and benedictions, and many wishes that Allah might make it the officials' fate to become pilgrims, we left the office, and returned towards El Azhar. When we had nearly reached the Mosque, Shaykh Mohammed lagged behind, and made the sign. I drew near the Afghan, and asked for his hand. He took the hint, and muttering 'It is no matter!' – 'It is not necessary!' – 'By Allah it is not required!' extended his fingers, and brought the musculus guineorum to hear upon three dollars. Poor man! I believe it was his necessity that consented to be paid for doing a common act of Moslem charity; he had a wife and children, and the calling of an Alim is no longer worth much in Egypt.

My departure from Cairo was hastened by an accident. I lost my reputation by a little misfortune that happened in this wise.

At Haji Wali's room in the caravanserai, I met a Yuz-bashi, or captain of Albanian Irregulars, who was in Egypt on leave from El Hejaz. He was a tall, bony, and broad-shouldered mountaineer, about forty years old, with the large 'bombé' brow, the fierce eyes, thin lips, lean jaws, and peaky chin of his race. His mustachios were enormously long and tapering, and the rest of his face, like his head, was close shaven. His 'Fustan' was none of the cleanest, nor was the red cap, which he wore rakishly pulled over his frowning forehead, quite free from stains. Not permitted to carry the favourite pistols, he contented himself with sticking his right hand in the empty belt, and stalking about the house with a most military mien. Yet he was as little of a bully as carpet knight, that same Ali Agha; his body showed many a grisly scar, and one of his shin bones had been broken by a Turkish bullet, when he was playing tricks on the Albanian hills – an accident inducing a limp, which he attempted to conceal by a heavy swagger. When he spoke, his voice was affectedly gruff; he had a sad knack of sneering, and I never saw him thoroughly sober.

Our acquaintance began with a kind of storm, which blew over, and left line weather. I was showing Haji Wali my pistols with Damascene barrels when Ali Agha entered the room. He sat down before me with a grin which said intelligibly enough, 'What business have you with weapons?' –snatched the arm out of my hand, and began to inspect it as a connoisseur. Not admiring this procedure, I wrenched it away from him, and, addressing myself to Haji Wali, proceeded quietly with my dissertation. The captain of Irregulars and I then looked at each other. He cocked his cap on one side, in token of excited pugnacity. I twirled my mustachios to display a kindred emotion. Had he been armed, and in El Hejaz, we should have fought it out at once, for the Arnaouts are 'terribili colla pistola', as the Italians say, meaning that upon the least provocation, they pull out a horse-pistol, and fire it in the face of friend or foe. Of course, the only way under these circumstances is to anticipate them; but even this desperate prevention seldom saves a stranger, as whenever there is danger, these men go about in pairs. I never met with a more reckless brood. Upon the line of march Albanian troops are not allowed ammunition; for otherwise there would be half a dozen duels a day. When they quarrel over their cups, it is the fashion for each man to draw a pistol, and to place it against his opponent's breast. The weapons being kept accurately clean seldom miss fire, and if one combatant draw trigger before the other, he would immediately be shot down by the bystanders. In Egypt these men – who are used as irregulars, and often quartered upon the hapless villagers, when unable or unwilling to pay up their taxes – were the terror of the population. On many occasions they have quarrelled with foreigners, and insulted European women. In El Hejaz their recklessness awes even the Bedouins. The townspeople say of them that 'tripe- sellers, and bath servants at Stamboul, they become Pharaohs in Arabia'. At Jeddah the Arnaouts have amused themselves with firing at the English consul (Mr Ogilvic) when he walked upon his terrace. And this man-shooting appears a favourite sport with them: at Cairo many stories illustrate the sang froid with which they used to knock over the camel-drivers, if any one dared to ride past their barracks. The Albanians vaunt their skill in using weapons, and their pretensions impose upon Arabs as well as Egyptians; yet I have never found them wonderful with any arm, (the pistol alone excepted) and our officers, who have visited their native hills, speak of them as tolerable, but by no means first-rate rifle shots.

The captain of Irregulars being unhappily debarred the pleasure of shooting me, after looking fierce for a time, rose, and walked majestically out of the room. A day or two afterwards, he called upon me civilly enough, sat down, drank a cup of coffee, smoked a pipe, and began to converse. But as he knew about a hundred Arabic words, and I as many Turkish, our conversation was carried on under difficulties. Presently he asked me in a whisper for 'Araki'. I replied that there was none in the house, which induced a sneer, and an ejaculation sounding like 'Himar' (ass) the slang synonym amongst fast Moslems for water-drinker. After rising to depart he seized me waggishly, with an eye to a trial of strength. Thinking that an Indian doctor and a temperance man would not be very dangerous, he exposed himself to what is professionally termed a 'cross-buttock', and had his head come in contact with the stone floor instead of my bed, he might not have drunk for many a day. The fall had a good effect upon his temper. He jumped up, patted my head, called for another pipe, and sat down to show me his wounds, and to boast of his exploits. I could not help remarking a ring of English gold, with a bezel of bloodstone, sitting strangely upon his coarse sun-stained hand. he declared that it had been snatched by him from a Konsul (a consul) at Jeddah, and volubly related, in a mixture of Albanian, Turkish, and Arabic, the history of his acquisition. He begged me to supply him with a little poison that 'would not lie', for the purpose of quieting a troublesome enemy, and he carefully stowed away in his pouch five grains of calomel, which I gave him for that laudable purpose. Before taking leave he pressed me strongly to go and drink with him: I refused to do so during the day, but, wishing to see how these men sacrifice to Bacchus, promised compliance that night.

About 9 o'clock, when the caravanserai was quiet, I took a pipe, and a tobacco-pouch, stuck my dagger in my belt, and slipped into Ali Agha's room. He was sitting on a bed spread upon the ground: in front of him stood four wax candles (all Orientals hate drinking in any but a bright light), and a tray containing a basin of stuff like soup maigre, a dish of cold stewed meat, and two bowls of Salatah and curds. The 'materials' peeped out of an iron pot filled with water; one was a long, thin, white-glass flask of Araki, the other a bottle of some strong perfume. Both were wrapped up in wet rag, the usual refrigerator.

Ali Agha welcomed me politely, and seeing me admire the preparations, bade me beware how I suspected an Albanian of not knowing how to drink; he made me sit by him on the bed, threw his dagger to a handy distance, signalled me to do the same, and prepared to begin the bout. Taking up a little tumbler, in shape like those from which French postilions used to drink 'la goutte', he inspected it narrowly, wiped out the interior with his forefinger, filled it to the brim, and offered it to his guest with a bow. I received it with a low salam, swallowed its contents at once, turned it upside down in proof of fair play, replaced it upon the floor, with a jaunty movement of the arm, somewhat like a 'British pugilis' delivering a 'rounder' bowed again, and requested him to help himself. The same ceremony followed on his part. Immediately after each glass – and rapidly the cup went about – we swallowed a draught of water, and ate a spoonful of the curds or the Salatah in order to cool our palates. Then we reapplied ourselves to our pipes, emitting huge puffs – a sign of being 'fast' men – and looked facetiously at each other – drinking being considered by Moslems a funny and pleasant manner of sin.

The Albanian captain was at least half seas over when we began the bout, yet he continued to fill and to drain without showing the least progress in ebriety.

I in vain for a time expected the 'bad-masti' (as the Persians call it), the horse play, and gross face facetiæ, which generally accompany southern and eastern tipsiness. Ali Agha, indeed, occasionally took up the bottle of perfume, filled the palm of his right hand, and dashed it in my face: I followed his example, but our pleasantries went no further.

Presently my companion started a grand project, namely, that I should entice the respectable Haji Wali into the room, where we might force him to drink. The idea was facetious: it was making a Bow-street magistrate polk at a casino. I started up to fetch the Haji: and when I returned with him Ali Agha was found in a new stage of 'freshness'. He had stuck a green-leaved twig upright in the floor, and had so turned over a goblet of water, that its contents trickled slowly, in a tiny stream under the verdure, and he was sitting before it mentally gazing, with an outward show of grim Quixotic tenderness, upon the shady trees and the cool rills of his fatherland. Possibly he had peopled the place with 'young barbarians at play'; for verily I thought that a tear 'which had no business ther' was glistening in his stony eye.

The appearance of Haji Wali suddenly changed the scene. Ali Agha jumped up, seized the visitor by the shoulder, compelled him to sit down, and, ecstasied by the good man's horror at the scene, filled a tumbler, and with the usual grotesque grimaces insisted upon his drinking it. Haji Wali stoutly refused; then Ali Agha put it to his own lips, and drained it with a hurt-feeling and reproachful aspect. We made our unconvivial friend smoke a few puffs, and then we returned to the charge. In vain the Haji protested that throughout life he had avoided the deadly sin; in vain he promised to drink with us tomorrow – in vain he quoted Koran, and alternately coaxed, and threatened us with the police. We were inexorable. At last the Haji started upon his feet, and rushed away, regardless of any thing but escape, leaving lits Tarbush, his slippers, and his pipe, in the hands of the enemy. The host did not dare to pursue his recreant guest beyond the door, but returning he carefully sprinkled the polluting liquid on the cap, pipe, and shoes, and called the Haji an ass in every tongue he knew.

Then we applied ourselves to supper, and dispatched the soup, the stew, and the Salatah. A few tumblers and pipes were exhausted to obviate indigestion, when Ali Agha arose majestically, and said that he required a troop of dancing girls to gladden his eyes with a ballet.

I represented that such persons are no longer admitted into caravanserais. He inquired, with calm ferocity, 'who hath forbidden it?' I replied 'the Pacha', upon which Ali Agha quietly removed his cap, brushed it with his fore-arm, fitted it on his forehead, raking forwards, twisted his mustachios to the sharp point of a single hair, shouldered his pipe, and moved towards the door, vowing, that he would make the Pacha himself come, and dance before us.

I foresaw a brawl, and felt thankful that my boon companion had forgotten his dagger. Prudence whispered me to return to my room, to bolt the door, and to go to bed, but conscience suggested that it would be unfair to abandon the Albanian in his present helpless state. I followed him into the outer gallery, pulling him, and begging him, as a despairing wife might urge a drunken husband, to return home. And he, like the British husband, being greatly irritated by the unjovial advice, instantly belaboured with his pipe-stick the first person he met in the gallery, and sent him flying down the stairs with fearful shouts of 'O Egyptians! O ye accursed! O genus of Pharoah! O race of dogs! O Egyptians!'

He then burst open a door with his shoulder, and reeled into a room where two aged dames were placidly reposing by the side of their spouses, who were basket-makers. They immediately awoke, seeing a stranger, and hearing his foul words, they retorted with a hot volley of vituperation.

Put to flight by the old women's tongues, Ali Agha, in spite of all my endeavours, reeled down the stairs, and fell upon the sleeping form of the night porter, whose blood he vowed to drink – the Oriental form of threatening 'spiflication'. Happily for the assaulted, the Agha's servant, a sturdy Albanian lad, was lying on a mat in the doorway cose by. Roused by the tumult he jumped up, and found the captain in a state of fury. Apparently the man was used to the master's mood. Without delay he told us all to assist, and we lending a helping hand, half dragged and half carried the Albanian to his room. Yet even in this ignoble plight, he shouted with all the force of his lungs the old war-cry, 'O Egyptians! O race of dogs! I have dishonored all Sikandariyah – all Kahirah – all Suways'. And in this vaunting frame of mind he was put to bed. No Welsh undergraduate at Oxford, under similar circumstances, ever gave more trouble.

'You had better start on your pilgrimage at once', said Haji Wali, meeting me the next morning with a 'goguenard' smile.

He was right. Throughout the caravanserai nothing was talked of for nearly a week but the wickedness of the captain of Albanian Irregulars, and the hypocrisy of the staid Indian doctor. Thus it was, gentle reader, that I lost my reputation of being a 'serious person' at Cairo. And all I have to show for it is the personal experience of an Albanian drinking bout.

I wasted but little time in taking leave of my friends, telling them by way of precaution, that my destination was Meccah via Jeddah, and firmly determining, if possible, to make El Medinah via Yambu. 'Conceal', says the Arabic proverb, 'thy tenets, thy treasure, and thy travelling'.

From Cairo To Suez

Shaykh Nassar, a Bedouin of Tur, (Mount Sinai), being on his way homewards, agreed to let me have two dromedaries for the sum of 60 piastres, or about ten shillings each. Being desirous to start with a certain display of respectability, I accepted these terms; a man of humbler pretensions would have travelled with a single animal, and a camel-man running behind him. But, besides ostentation, I wanted my attendant to be mounted, that we might make a forced march in order to ascertain how much a four years' life of European effeminacy had impaired my powers of endurance. The reader may believe the assertion that there are few better tests than an eighty-four mile ride in midsummer, on a bad wooden saddle, borne by a worse dromedary, across a desert. Even the Squire famed for being copper-sheeted might not have disdained a trial of the kind.

I started my Indian boy and heavy luggage for Suez two days before the end of the Eed – laden camels generally taking fifty-five or sixty hours to do the journey, and I spent the intermediate time with Haji Wali. He advised me to mount about 3 p.m., so that I might arrive at Suez on the evening of the next day, and assisted me in making due preparations of water, tobacco, and provisions. Early on the morning of departure the Afghan Shaykh came to the caravanserai, and breakfasted with us 'because Allah willed it'. After a copious meal he bestowed upon me a stately benediction, and would have embraced me, but I humbly bent over his hand: sad to relate, immediately that his back was turned, Haji Wali raised his forefinger to a right angle with the palm, and burst into a shout of irreverent laughter. At 3 o'clock Nassar, the Bedouin, came to announce that the dromedaries were saddled. I dressed myself, sticking a pistol in my belt, and passing the crimson silk cord of the Hamail or pocket Koran over my shoulder, in token of being a pilgrim – distributing a few trifling presents to friends and servants, and, accompanied by the Shaykh Mohammed, and Haji Wali, descended the stairs with an important gait. In the courtyard sat the camels (dromedaries they could not be called) and I found that a second driver was going to accompany us. I objected to this, as the extra Bedouin would, of course, expect to be fed by me; but Nassar swore the man was his brother, and, as you rarely gain by small disputes with these people, he was allowed to have his own way.

Then came the preparatory leave-takings. Haji Wali embraced me heartily, and so did my poor old Shaykh, who, despite his decrepitude and my objections, insisted upon accompanying me to the city gate. I mounted the camel, crossed my legs before the pommel – stirrups are not used in Egypt – and, preceding my friend, descended the street leading towards the desert. As we emerged from the huge gateway of the caravanserai all the bystanders, except only the porter, who believed me to be a Persian, and had seen me with the drunken captain, exclaimed, 'Allah bless thee, Y'al Hajj, and restore thee to thy country and thy friends!' And passing through the Bab el Nasr, where I addressed the salutation of peace to the sentry, and to the officer commanding the guard, both gave me God-speed with great cordiality – the pilgrim's blessing in Asia, like the old woman's in Europe, being supposed to possess peculiar efficacy. Outside the gate my friends took a final leave of me, and I will not deny having felt a tightening of heart as their honest faces and forms faded in the distance.

But Shaykh Nassar switches his camel's shoulder, and appears inclined to take the lead. This is a trial of manliness. There is no time for emotion. Not a moment can be spared, even for a retrospect. I kick my dromedary, who steps out into a jog trot. The Bedouins with a loud ringing laugh attempt to give me the go-by. I resist, and we continue like children till the camels are at their speed, though we have eighty-four miles before us, and above an atmosphere like a furnace blast. The road is deserted at this hour, otherwise grave Moslem travellers would have believed the police to be nearer than convenient to us.

Presently we drew rein, and exchanged our pace for one more seasonable, whilst the sun began to tell on man and beast. High raised as we were above the ground, the reflected heat struck us sensibly, and the glare of a macadamised road added a few extra degrees of caloric. The Bedouins, to refresh themselves, prepare to smoke. They fill my chibouque, light it with a flint and steel, and cotton dipped in a solution of gunpowder, and pass it over to me. After a few pulls I return it to them, and they smoke it turn by turn. Then they begin to while away the tedium of the road by asking questions, which passe-temps is not easily exhausted; for they are never satisfied till they know as much of you as you do of yourself. They next resort to talking about victuals; for with this hungry race of Bedouins, food, as a topic of conversation, takes the place of money in more civilised lands. And lastly, even this engrossing subject being exhausted for the moment, they take refuge in singing: and, monotonous and droning as it is, their song has yet an artless plaintiveness, which admirably suits the singer and the scenery. If you listen to the words, you will surely hear allusions to bright verdure, cool shades, bubbling rills, or something which hereabouts man hath not, and yet which his soul desires.

And now while Nassar and his brother are chaunting a duet – the refrain being,

"W'al arz mablul bi matar,"
"And the earth was wet with rain,"

I must crave leave to say a few words, despite the triteness of the subject, about the modern Sinaitic race of Arabs.

Besides the tribes occupying the northern parts of the peninsula, five chief clans are enumerated by Burckhardt. Nassar, and other authorities at Suez, divided them into six, namely:

1. Karashi (in the plural Kararishah), who, like the Gara in Eastern Arabia, claim an apocryphal origin from the great Koraysh tribe.
2. Salihi (*pl*. Sawalihah), the principal family of the Sinaitic Bedouins.
3. Arimi (*pl*. Awarimah): according to Burckhardt this clan is merely a sub-family of the Sawalihahs.
4. Saidi. Burckhardt. calls them Welad Said, and derives them also from the Sawalihahs.
5. Aliki (*pl*. Alaykah, erroneously written Elegat, and Aleykah), and lastly, the
6. Muzaynah, generally pronounced M'zaynah. This class is an off-shoot from the great Jehaymah tribe inhabiting the deserts about Yambu. According to oral tradition five persons, the ancestors of the present Muzaynah race, were forced by a blood-feud to fly their native country. They landed at the Shurum, and have now spread themselves over the eastern parts of the peninsula. In El Hejaz the

Muzaynah is an old and noble tribe. It produced Kaab el Ahbar, the celebrated poet, to whom Mohammed gave the cloak which the Ottomans believe to have been taken by Sultan Selim from Egypt, and, under the name of Khirkah Sherif, to have been converted into the national Oriflamme.

There are some interesting ethnographical points about these Sinaitic clans – interesting at least to those who would trace the genealogy of the great Arabian family. Anyone who knows the Bedouins can see that the Muzaynah are pure blood. Their brows are broad, their faces narrow, their features regular, and their eyes of a moderate size: whereas the other Tawarah clans are as palpably Egyptian. They have preserved that roundness of face which may still be seen in the Sphinx as in the modern Copt, and their eyes have that peculiar size, shape, and look which the old Egyptian painters attempted to express by giving to the profile eye the form of the full organ. Upon this feature, so characteristic of the Nilotic race, I would lay great stress. No traveller familiar with the true Egyptian eye, long, almond-shaped, deeply fringed, slightly raised at the outer corner and dipping in front like the Chinese, can ever mistake it. It is to be seen in half-castes, and, as I have before remarked, families originally from the banks of the Nile, but settled in El Hejaz for generations, retain the peculiarity in all its integrity.

I therefore believe the Turi Bedouin to be an impure race, Egypto-Arab, whereas his neighbour the Hejazi is the pure Syrian or Mesopotamian.

A wonderful change has taken place in the Tawarah tribes, whilome portrayed by Sir John Mandeville as 'folke fulle of alle evylle condiciouns'. Niebuhr notes the trouble they gave him, and their perpetual hankering for both murder and pillage. Even in the late Mohammed Ali's early reign, no governor of Suez dared to flog, or to lay hands upon a Turi, whatever offence he might have committed within the walls of the town. Now the wild man's sword is taken from him, before he is allowed to enter the gates, and my old acquaintance, Giaffar Bey, would think no more of belabouring a Bedouin than of flogging a Fellah. Such is the result of Mohammed Ali's rigorous policy, and such the effects of even semi-civilisation, when its influence is brought to bear direct upon barbarism.

To conclude this subject, the Tawarah still retain many characteristics of the Bedouin race. The most good-humoured and sociable of men, they delight in a jest, and may readily be managed by kindness and courtesy. Yet they are passionate, nice upon points of honor, revengeful and easily offended where their peculiar prejudices are misunderstood. I have always found them pleasant companions, and deserving of respect, for their hearts are good, and their courage is beyond a doubt. Those travellers who complain of their insolence and extortion may have been either ignorant of their language or offensive to them by assumption of superiority – in the Desert man meets man – or physically unfitted to acquire their esteem.

We journeyed on till near sunset through the wilderness without ennui. It is strange how the mind can be amused amid scenery that presents so few objects to occupy it. But in such a country every slight modification of form or color rivets observation: the senses are sharpened, and the perceptive faculties, prone to sleep over a confused shifting of scenery, act vigorously when excited by the capability of embracing each detail. Moreover desert views are eminently suggestive; they appeal to the Future, not to the Past; they arouse because they are by no means memorial.

To the solitary wayfarer there is an interest in the wilderness unknown to Cape seas and Alpine glaciers, and even to the rolling Prairie – the effect of continued excitement on the mind, stimulating its powers to their pitch. Above, through a sky terrible in its stainless beauty, and the splendors of a pitiless blinding glare, the Simoom caresses you like a lion with flaming breath. Around lie drifted sand heaps, upon which each puff of wind leaves its trace in solid waves, flayed rocks, the very skeletons of mountains, and hard unbroken plains, over which he who rides is spurred by the idea that the bursting of a water-skin, or the pricking of a earners hoof would be a certain death of torture – a haggard land infested with wild beasts, and wilder men – a region whose very fountains murmur the warning words 'Drink and away!' What can be more exciting? what more sublime? Man's heart bounds in his breast at the thought of measuring his puny force with Nature's might, and of emerging triumphant from the trial. This explains the Arab's proverb, 'Voyaging is a Victory'. In the Desert even more than upon the ocean, there is present death: hardship is there, and piracies, and shipwreck solitary, not in crowds, where, as the Persians say, 'Death is a Festival,' – and this sense of danger, never absent, invests the scene of travel with an interest not its own.

Let the traveller who suspects exaggeration leave the Suez road for an hour or two, and gallop northwards over the sands: in the drear silence, the solitude, and the fantastic desolation of the place, he will feel what the Desert may be. And then the Oases, and little lines of fertility – how soft and how beautiful!–even though the Wady El Ward (the Vale of Flowers) be the name of some stern flat upon which a handful of wild shrubs blossom while struggling through a cold season's ephemeral existence.

In such circumstances the mind is influenced through the body. Though your mouth glows, and your skin is parched, yet you feel no languor, the effect of humid heat; your lungs are lightened, your sight brightens, your memory recovers its tone, and your spirits become exuberant; your fancy and imagination are powerfully aroused, and the wildness and sublimity of the scenes around you stir up all the energies of your soul – whether for exertion, danger, or strife. Your morale improves: you become frank and cordial, hospitable and single-minded: the hypocritical politeness and the slavery of civilisation are left behind you in the city. Your senses are quickened: they require no stimulants but air and exercise – in the Desert spirituous liquors excite only disgust. There is a keen enjoyment in mere animal existence. The sharp appetite disposes of the most indigestible food, the sand is softer than a bed of down, and the purity of the air suddenly puts to flight a dire cohort of diseases. Hence it is that both sexes, and every age, the most material as well as the most imaginative of minds, the tamest citizen, the most peaceful student, the spoiled child of civilisation, all feel their hearts dilate, and their pulses beat strong, as they look down from their dromedaries upon the glorious Desert. Where do we hear of a traveller being disappointed by it? It is another illustration of the ancient truth that Nature returns to man, however unworthily he has treated her. And believe me, gentle reader, that when once your tastes have conformed to the tranquillity of such travel, you will suffer real pain in returning to the turmoil of civilisation. You will anticipate the bustle and the confusion of artificial life, its luxury and its false pleasures, with repugnance. Depressed in spirits, you will for a time after your return feel incapable of mental or bodily exertion. The air of cities will suffocate you, and the care-worn and cadaverous countenances of citizens will haunt you like a vision of judgment.

As the black shadow mounted in the East, I turned off the road, and was suddenly saluted by a figure rising from a little hollow with an 'As' Salmo Alaykum' of truly Arab sound. I looked at the speaker for a moment without recognising him. He then advanced with voluble expressions of joy, invited me to sup, seized my camel's halter without waiting for an answer, 'nakh'd' him, led me hurriedly to a carpet spread in a sandy hollow, pulled off my slippers, gave me cold water for ablution, told me that he had mistaken me at a distance for a 'Sherif' of the Arabs, but was delighted to find himself in error, and urged me to hurry over ablution, otherwise that night would come on before we could say our prayers. It was Mohammed el Basyuni, the Meccan boy of whom I had bought my pilgrim-garb at Cairo. There I had refused his companionship, but here for reasons of his own – one of them was an utter want of money – he would take no excuse. When he prayed he stood behind me, thereby proving pliancy of conscience, for he suspected me from the first of being at least a heretic.

After prayer he lighted a pipe, and immediately placed the snake-like tube in my hand ; this is an argument which the tired traveller can rarely resist. he then began to rummage my saddle-bags; drew forth stores of provisions, rolls, watermelons, boiled eggs, and dates, and whilst lighting the fire, and boiling the coffee, managed to distribute his own stock, which was neither plentiful nor first-rate, to the camel-men. Shaykh Nassar and his brother looked aghast at this movement, but the boy was inexorable. They tried a few rough hints, which he noticed by singing a Hindustani couplet that asserts the impropriety of anointing rats' heads with jasmine oil. They suspected abuse, and waxed cross; he acknowledged this by deriding them. 'I have heard of Nasrs and Nasirs, and Mansúrs, but may Allah spare me the mortification of a Nassár!' said the boy, relying upon my support. And I urged him on, wanting to see how the city Arab treats the countryman. He then took my tobacco-pouch from the angry Bedouins, and in a stage-whisper reproved me for entrusting it to such thieves; insisting, at the same time, upon drinking all the coffee, so that the poor guides had to prepare some for themselves. He improved every opportunity of making mischief. 'We have eaten watermelon!' cried Nassar, patting its receptacle in token of repletion. 'Dost thou hear, my lord, how they grumble? – the impudent ruffians!' remarked Mohammed – 'We have eaten watermelon! that is to say, we ought to have eaten meat!' The Bedouins, completely out of temper, told him not to trust himself among their hills. He seized a sword, and began capering about after the fashion of the Indian school of arms, and boasted that he would attack single-handed the whole clan, which elicited an ironical ''Allah! Allah!' from the hearers.

After an hour most amusingly spent, in this way I arose, much to the dissatisfaction of my guides, who wished to sleep there, and insisted upon mounting. Shaykh Nassar and his brother had reckoned upon living gratis, for at least three days, judging it improbable that a soft Effendi would hurry himself. When they saw the fair vision dissolve, they began to finesse: they induced the camel-man, who ran by the side of Mohammed's dromedary, to precede the animal – a favourite manoeuvre to prevent overspeed. Ordered to fall back, the man pleaded fatigue, and inability to walk. The boy Mohammed immediately asked if I had any objection to dismount one of my guides, and to let his weary attendant ride for an hour or so. I at once assented, and the Bedouins obeyed me with ominous grumblings. When we resumed our march the melancholy Arabs had no song left in them, whereas Mohammed chanted vociferously, and quoted bad Hindostani and worse Persian till silence was forcibly imposed upon him. The camel-men lagged behind, in order to prevent my dromedary advancing too fast, and the boy's guide, after dismounting, would stride along in front of us, under pretext of showing the way. And so we jogged on, now walking, then trotting, till the dromedaries begun to grunt with fatigue, and the Arabs clamoured for a halt.

At midnight we reached the centre station, and lay down under its walls to take a little rest. The dews fell heavily, wetting the sheets that covered us; but who cares for such trifes in the Desert? The moon shone bright; the breeze blew coolly, and the jackal sang a lullaby which lost no time in inducing the soundest sleep. As the wolf's tail appeared in the heavens we arose. Grey mists floating over the hills northwards gave the Dar el Baida the look of some old feudal castle. There was a haze in the atmosphere, which beautified even the face of Desolation. The swift-flying Kata rose in noisy coveys from the road, and a stray gazelle paced daintily over the stony plain. As we passed by the Pilgrims' tree, I added another rag to its coat of tatters. We then invoked the aid of the holy saint El Dakruri from his cream-colored abode, mounted our camels, and resumed the march in real earnest. The dawn passed away in its delicious coolness, and sultry morning came on. Then day arose in its fierceness, and the noontide sun made the plain glow with terrible heat. Still we pressed onwards.

At 3 p.m. we turned off the road into a dry watercourse, which is not far from No. 13 station. The sand was dotted with the dried-up leaves of the Datura, and strongly perfumed by a kind of Absinthe, the sweetest herb of the desert. A Mimosa was there, and although its shade at this season is little better than a cocoa tree's, the Bedouins would not neglect it. We lay down upon the sand, to rest among a party of Maghrabi pilgrims travelling to Suez. These wretches, who were about a dozen in number, appeared to be of the lowest class; their garments consisted of a Burnoos and a pair of sandals, their sole weapon a long knife, and their only stock a bag of dry provisions. Each had his large wooden bowl, but none carried water with him. It was impossible to help pitying their state, nor could I eat, seeing them hungry, thirsty, and wayworn. Nassar served out about a pint of water and a little bread to each man. Then they asked for more. None was to be had, so they cried out that money would do as well. I had determined upon being generous to the extent of a few pence. Custom, as well as inclination, was in favor of the act; but when the alms became a demand, and the demand was backed by fierce looks and a derisive sneer, and a kind of reference to their knives, gentle Charity took the alarm and fled. My pistols kept them at bay, for they were only making an attempt to intimidate, and, though I took the precaution of sitting apart from them, there was no real danger. The Suez road, by the wise regulations of Mohammed Ali, has become as safe to European travellers as that between Hampstead and Highgate, and even Easterns have little to fear but what their cowardice creates. My Indian servant was full of the dangers he had run, but I did not believe in them. I afterwards heard that the place where the Maghrabis attempted to frighten what they thought a timid Effendi once notorious for plunder and murder. Here the spurs of two opposite hills almost meet upon the plain, a favorable ground for Bedouin ambuscade. Of the Maghrabis I shall have more to say when relating my voyage in the Pilgrim Ship: they were the only travellers from whom we experienced the least annoyance. Numerous parties of Turks, Arabs, and Afghans, and a few Indians were on the same errand as ourselves. All, as we passed them, welcomed us with the friendly salutation that so becomes men engaged in a labor of religion.

About half an hour before sunset, I turned off the road leftwards, and, under pretext of watering the dromedaries, rode up to inspect the El Ajrudi fort. It is a quadrangle with round towers at the gateway and at the corners, newly built of stone and mortar; the material is already full of crevices, and would not stand before a twelve- pounder. Without guns or gunners, it is occupied by about a dozen Fellahs, who act as hereditary 'Ghafirs' (guardians); they were expecting at that time to be reinforced by a party of Bashi Buzuks – irregulars from Cairo. The people of the country were determined that an English fleet would soon appear in the Red Sea, and this fort is by them ridiculously considered the key of Suez. As usual in these Vauban-backing lands, the well supplying the stronghold is in a detached and distant building, which can be approached by an enemy with the greatest security. Over the gateway was on ancient inscription reversed; the water was brackish, and of bad quality.

We resumed our way: Suez was now near. In the blue distance rose the castellated peaks and the wide sand-tracts over which lies the land route to El Hejaz. Before us the sight ever dear to English eyes – a strip of sea gloriously azure, with a gallant steamer walking the waters. On the right-hand side lay the broad slopes of Jebel Mukattem, a range of hills which flanks the road all the way from Cairo. It was at this hour a spectacle not easily to be forgotten. The near range of chalk and sandstone wore a russet suit, gilt where the last rays of the sun seamed it with light, and the deep folds were shaded with the richest purple; whilst the background of the higher hill, Abu Deraj (the Father of Steps), was sky-blue streaked with the lightest plum color. We drew up at a small building called Bir Suways (well of Suez), and under pretext of watering the cattle, I sat for half an hour admiring the charms of the Desert. The eye never tires of such loveliness of hue, and the memory of the hideousness of this range, when a sun in front exposed each barren and deformed feature, supplied the evening view with another element of attraction.

It was already night when we passed through the tumbling gateway of Suez; and there still remained the task of finding my servant and effects. After wandering in and out of every Wakaleh in the village, during which peregrination the boy Mohammed proved himself so useful that I determined to make him my companion at all risks, we accidentally heard that an Indian had taken lodgings at a hostelry bearing the name of Jirjis. On arriving there our satisfaction was diminished by the intelligence that the same Indian, after locking the door, had gone out with his friends to a ship in the harbour; in fact, that he had made all preparations for running away. I dismounted, and tried to persuade the porter to break open the wooden bolt, but he absolutely refused, and threatened the police. Meanwhile Mohammed had found a party of friends, men of El Medinah, returning to the pilgrimage after a begging tour through Egypt and Turkey. The meeting was characterised by vociferous inquiries, loud guffaws, and warm embraces. I was invited to share their supper, and their dormitory – an uncovered platform projecting from the gallery over the square court below – but I had neither appetite nor spirits to be sociable. The porter, after persuasion, showed me an empty room, in which I spread my carpet. That night was a sad one. My eighty-four mile ride had made; every bone ache; I had lost much epidermis, and the sun had seared every portion of skin exposed to it. So, lamenting my degeneracy and the ill effects of four years' domicile in Europe, and equally disquieted in mind about the fate of my goods and chattels, I fell into an uncomfortable sleep.

CHAP. VIII

Suez

Early on the morning after my arrival, I arose, and consulted my new acquaintances about what steps should be taken towards recovering the missing property. They unanimously advised a visit to the governor, whom, however, they described to he a 'Kalb ibn kalb' (dog, son of a dog,) who never returned Moslems' salutations, and thought all men dirt to be trodden under foot by the Turks. The boy Mohammed showed his savoir faire by extracting from his huge box a fine embroidered cap, and a grand peach-coloured coat, with which I was instantly invested; he dressed himself with similar magnificence, and we then set out to the 'palace'.

Giaffar Bey – he has since been deposed – then occupied the position of judge, officer commanding, collector of customs, and magistrate of Suez. He was a Mirliwa, or brigadier-general, and had some reputation as a soldier, together with a slight tincture of European science and language. The large old Turk received me most superciliously, disdained all return of salaam, and fixing upon me two little eyes like gimlets, demanded my business. I stated that one Shaykh Nur, my Indian servant, had played me false; therefore I required permission to break into the room supposed to contain my effects.

He asked my profession. I replied the medical. This led him to inquire if I had any medicine for the eyes, and being answered in the affirmative, he sent a messenger with me to enforce obedience on the part of the porter. The obnoxious measure was, however, unnecessary. As we entered the caravanserai, there appeared at the door the black face of Shaykh Nur, looking, though accompanied by sundry fellow countrymen, uncommonly as if he merited and expected the bamboo. He had, by his own account, been seduced into the festivities of a coal-hulk, manned by Indian Lascars, and the vehemence of his self-accusation saved him from the chastisement which I had determined to administer.

I must now briefly describe the party into which fate threw me: the names of these men will so frequently appear in the following pages, that a few words about their natures will not be misplaced.

First of all comes Umar Effendi – so called in honor – a Daghistani or Circassian, the grandson of a Hanafi Mufti at El Medinah, and the son of a Shayk Rakb, an officer whose duty it is to lead dromedary-caravans. He sits upon his cot, a small, short, plump body, of yellow complexion and bilious temperament, grey-eyed, soft-featured, and utterly beardless – which affects his feelings – he looks fifteen, and owns to twenty-eight. His manners are those of a student; he dresses respectably, prays regularly, hates the fair sex, like an Arab, whose affections and aversions are always in extremes, is serious, has a mild demeanour, an humble gait, and a soft slow voice. When roused he becomes furious as a bengal tiger. His parents have urged him to marry, and he, like Camaralzaman, has informed his father that he is a person of great age, but little sense. Urged moreover by a melancholy turn of mind, and the want of leisure for study at El Medinah, he fled the paternal domicile, and entered himself a pauper Talib ilm (student) in the Azhar Mosque. His disconsolate friends and afflicted relations sent a confidential man to fetch him home by force, should it be necessary; he has yielded, and is now awaiting the first opportunity of travelling, if possible, gratis to El Medinah.

That confidential man is a negro-servant, called Saad, notorious in his native city as El Jinni, the devil. Born and bred a slave in Umar Effendi's family, he obtained manumission, became a soldier in El Hejaz, was dissatisfied with pay perpetually in arrears, turned merchant, and wandered far and wide, to Russia, to Gibraltar, and to Baghdad. He is the pure African, noisily merry at one moment, at another silently sulky, affectionate and abusive, brave and boastful, reckless and crafty, exceedingly quarrelsome, and unscrupulous to the last degree. The bright side of his character is his love for, and respect to, the young master Umar Effendi; yet even him he will scold in a paroxysm of fury, and steal from him whatever he can lay his hands on. He is generous with his goods, but is ever borrowing and never paying money; he dresses like a beggar, with the dirtiest Tarbush upon his tufty poll, and only a cotton shirt over his sooty skin, whilst his two boxes are full of handsome apparel for himself and the three ladies his wives at El Medinah. He knows no fear but for those boxes. Frequently during our search for a vessel he forced himself into Giaffar Bey's presence, and demeaned himself so impudently, that we expected to see him lamed by the bastinado; his forwardness, however, only amused the dignitary, he wanders all day about the bazar, talking about freight and passage, for he has resolved, cost what it will, to travel gratis, and, with doggedness like his, he must succeed.

Shaykh Hamid el Samman derives his cognomen, the 'clarified butter-seller', from a celebrated saint and Sufi of the Kadiriyah order, who left a long line of holy desendants at El Medinah. This Shaykh squats upon a box full of presents for the daughter of his paternal uncle, a perfect specimen of the town Arab. His head is crowned with a rough Shushah or tuft of hair on the poll; his face is of a dirty brown, his little goat's beard untrimmed; his feet are bare, and his only garment is an exceedingly unclean, ochre-colored blouse, tucked at the waist into a leathern girdle beneath it. He will not pray, because he is unwilling to take pure clothes out of his box; but he smokes when he can get other people's tobacco, and groans between the whiffs, conjugating the verb all day, for he is of active mind. He can pick out his letters, and he keeps in his bosom a little dog's-eared MS. full of serious romances and silly prayers, old and exceedingly ill written: this he will draw forth at times, peep into for a moment, devoutly kiss, and restore to its proper place with all the veneration of the vulgar for a book. He can sing all manner of songs, slaughter a sheep with dexterity, deliver a grand call to prayer, shave, cook, fight, and he excels in the science of vituperation: like Saad, he never performs his devotions, except when necessary to 'keep up appearances', and though he has sworn to perish before he forgets his vow to the 'daughter of his uncle' I shrewdly suspect he is no better than he should be. His brow crumples at the word wine, but there is quite another expression about the region of the mouth; and Stamboul, where he has lived some months, without learning ten words of Turkish, is a notable place for displacing prejudice. And finally, he has not more than a piastre or two in his pocket, for he has squandered the large presents given to him at

Cairo and Constantinople by noble ladies, to whom he acted as master of the ceremonies, at the tomb of the Prophet.

Stretched on a carpet, smoking a Persian Kalioon all day, lies Salih Shakkar, a Turk on the father's, and an Arab on the mother's side, born at El Medinah. This lanky youth may be 16 years old, but he has the ideas of forty; he is thoroughly greedy, selfish, and ungenerous, coldly supercilious as a Turk, and energetically avaricious as an Arab. He prays more often, and dresses more respectably, than the descendant of the clarified-butter seller; he affects the Constantinople style of toilette, and his light yellow complexion makes people consider him a 'superior person'. We were intimate enough on the road, when he borrowed from me a little money. But at El Medinah he cut me piteously, as a 'town man' does a continental acquaintance accidentally met in Hyde Park, and of course he tried, though in vain, to evade repaying his debt. He had a tincture of letters, and appeared to have studied critically the subject of 'largesse'. 'The generous is Allah's friend, ay, though he be a sinner, and the miser is Allah's foe, ay, though he be a saint', was a venerable saying always in his mouth, he also informed me that Pharaoh, although the quintessence of impiety, is mentioned by name in the Koran, by reason of his liberality, whereas Nimrod, another monster of iniquity, is only alluded to, because he was a stingy tyrant. It is almost needless to declare that Salih Shakkar was, as the Indians say, a very 'fly-sucker'. There were two other men of El Medinah in the Wakalat Girgis; but I omit description, as we left them, they being penniless, at Suez. One of them, Mohammed Shiklibha, I afterwards met at Meccah, and seldom have I seen a more honest and warm-hearted fellow. When we were embarking at Suez, he fell upon

Hamid's bosom, and both of them wept bitterly, at the prospect of parting even for a few days.

All the individuals above mentioned lost no time in opening the question of a loan. It was a lesson in oriental metaphysics to see their condition. They hail a twelve days' voyage, and a four days' journey, before them; boxes to carry, custom-houses to face, and stomachs to fill; yet the whole party could scarcely, I believe, muster two dollars of ready money. Their boxes were full of valuables, arms, clothes, pipes, slippers, sweet meats, and other 'notions', but nothing short of starvation would have induced them to pledge the smallest article.

I foresaw that their company would be an advantage, and therefore I hearkened favourably to the honeyed request for a few crowns. The boy Mohammed obtained six dollars; Hamid about five pounds – I intended to make his house at El Medinah my home; Umar Effendi three dollars; Saad the Devil, two – I gave the money to him at Yambu – and Salih Shakkar fifty piastres. But since in these lands, as a rule, no one ever lends coins, or borrowing ever returns them, I took care to exact service from the first, to take two rich coats from the second, a handsome pipe from the third, a 'bala' or yataghan from the fourth, and from the fifth an imitation Cashmere shawl. After which, we sat down and drew out the agreement. It was favorable to me: I lent them Egyptian money, and bargained for repayment in the currency of El Hejaz, thereby gaining the exchange, which is sometimes 16 per cent. This was done, not so much for the sake of profit, as with the view of becoming a Hatim, by a 'never mind' on settling day. My companions having received these small sums, became affectionate, and eloquent in my praise: they asked me to make one of their number for the future at meals, overwhelmed me with questions, insisted upon a present of sweetmeats, detected in me a great man under a cloud, – perhaps my claims to being a Dervish assisted them to this discovery – and declared that I should perforce be their guest at Meccah and El Medinah. On all occasions precedence was forced upon me; my opinion was the first consulted, and no project was settled without my concurrence: briefly, Abdullah the Dervish suddenly found himself a person of consequence. This sudden elevation led me into an imprudence which might have cost me dear, and aroused the only suspicion about me ever expressed during the summer's trip. My friends had looked at my clothes, overhauled my medicine-chest, and criticised my pistols; they sneered at my copper-cased watch, and remembered having seen a compass at Constantinople. Therefore I imagined they would think little about a sextant. This was a mistake. The boy Mohammed I afterwards learned waited only my leaving the room to declare that the would-be Haji was one of the infidels from India, and a council sat to discuss the case. Fortunately for me Umar Effendi had looked over a letter which I had written to Haji Wali that morning, and he had at various times received categorical replies to certain questions in high theology. He felt himself justified in declaring, ex cathedrâ, the boy Mohammed's position perfectly untenable. And Shaykh Hamid, who looked forward to being my host, guide, and debtor in general, and probably cared scantily for catechism or creed, swore that the light of El-Islam was upon my countenance, and consequently that the boy Mohammed was a pauper, a 'fakir', an owl, a cut-off-one, a stranger, and a Wahhabi, for daring to impugn the faith of a brother believer. The scene ended with a general abuse of the acute youth, who was told on all sides that he had no shame, and was directed to fear Allah. I was struck with the expression of my friends' countenances when they saw the sextant, and, determining with a sigh to leave it behind, I prayed five times a day for nearly a week.

We all agreed not to lose an hour in securing places on board some vessel bound to Yambu, and my companions, hearing that my passport as a British Indian was scarcely 'en règle', earnestly advised me to have it signed by the governor without delay, whilst they occupied themselves about the harbour. They warned me that if I displayed the Turkish Tezkireh given to me at the citadel of Cairo, I should infallibly be ordered to await the caravan, and lose their society and friendship. Pilgrims arriving at Alexandria, be it known to the reader, are divided into bodies, and distributed by means of Tezkirehs to the three great roads, namely Suez, Cosseir, and the Hajj route by land round the Gulf of Akabah. After the division has once been made, government turns a deaf ear to the representations of individuals. The Bey of Suez has an order to obstruct pilgrims as much its possible till the end of the season, when they are hurried down that way, lest they should arrive at Meccah too late. As most of the Egyptian high officials have boats, which sail up the Nile laden with pilgrims and return freighted with corn, the government naturally does its utmost to force the delays and discomforts of this line upon strangers. And as those who travel by the Hajj route must spend money in the Egyptian territories, at least fifteen days longer than they would if allowed to embark at once for Suez, the Pacha very properly assists them in the former, and obstructs them in the latter case. Knowing these facts, I felt that a difficulty was at hand. The first thing was to take Shaykh Nur's passport, which was 'en règle', and my own which was not, to the Bey for signature. He turned the papers over and over, as if unable to read them, and raised false hopes high by referring me to his clerk. The under official at once saw the irregularity of the document, asked me why it had not been visé at Cairo, swore that under such circumstances nothing would induce the Bey to let me proceed, and when I tried persuasion, waxed insolent. I feared that it would be necessary to travel via Cosseir, for which there was scarcely time, or to transfer myself on camel back to the harbour of Tur, and there to await the chance of finding a place in some half-filled vessel to El Hejaz – which would have been relying upon an accident. My last hope at Suez was to obtain assistance from Mr. George West, H. B. M.'s vice-consul. I therefore took the boy Mohammed with me, choosing him on purpose, and excusing the step to my companions by concocting an artful fable about my having been, in some part of Afghanistan, a benefactor to the British nation. We proceeded to the consulate. Mr. West, who had been told by an imprudent friend to expect me, saw through the disguise, despite jargon assumed to satisfy official scruples, and nothing could be kinder than the part he took. His clerk was directed to place himself in communication with the Bey's factotum, and when objections to signing the Alexandrian Tezkireh were offered, the vice-consul said that he would, at his own risk, give me a fresh passport as a British subject from Suez to Arabia. His firmness prevailed, and on the second day, the documents were returned to me in a satisfactory state. I take a pleasure in owning this obligation to Mr. West: in the course of my wanderings, I have often received from him hospitality and the most friendly attentions.

Whilst these passport difficulties were being solved, the rest of the party was as busy in settling about passage and passage-money. The peculiar rules of the port of Suez require a few words of explanation.

'About thirty-five years ago, the ship-owners proposed to the then government, with the view of keeping up freight, a Farzeh, or system of rotation. It might be supposed that the Pacha, whose object notoriously was to retain all monopolies in his own hands, would have refused his sanction to such a measure. But it so happened in those days that all the court had ships at Suez. Ibrahim Pacha alone owned four or five. Consequently they expected to share profits with the merchants, and thus to be compensated for the want of port dues. From that time forward all the vessels in the harbour were registered, and ordered to sail in rotation. This arrangement benefits the owner of the craft 'en départ', giving him in his turn a temporary monopoly, with the advantage of a full market; and freight is so high that a single trip often clears off the expense of building and the risk of losing the ship – a sensible succedaneum for insurance companies. On the contrary, the public must always be a loser by the 'Farzeh.' Two of a trade do not agree elsewhere; but at Suez even the Christian and the Moslem ship-owner are bound by a fraternal tie, in the shape of this rotation system, it injures the general merchant, and the Red Sea trader, not only by perpetuating high freight, but also by causing at one period of the year a break in the routine of sales and in the supplies of goods for the Jeddah market. At this moment (Nov. 1853), the vessel to which the turn belongs happens to be a large one; there is a deficiency of export to El Hejaz – her owner will of course wait any length of time for a full cargo; consequently no vessel with merchandise has left Suez for the last seventy-two days. Those who have bought goods for the Jeddah market at three months' credit will therefore have to meet their acceptances for merchandise still warehoused at the Egyptian port. This strange contrast to 'free-trade' principle is another proof that protection benefits only one party, the protected, while it is detrimental to the interests of the other party, the public'. [this information was kindly supplied to me by Henry Levick, Esq.]

To these remarks of Mr. Levick's, I have only to add that the government supports the Farzeh with all the energy of protectionists. A letter from Mr. Drummond Hay was insufficient to induce the Bey of Suez to break through the rule of rotation in favour of certain princes from Morocco. The recommendations of Lord Stratford de Redcliffe met with no better fate; and all Mr. West's good will could not procure me a vessel out of her turn. We were forced to rely upon our own exertions, and the activity of Saad the Devil. This worthy, after sundry delays and differences, mostly caused by his own determination to travel gratis, and to make us pay too much, finally closed with the owner of the Golden Thread. He took places for us upon the poop – the most eligible part of the vessel at this season of the year; he premised that we should not be very comfortable, as we were to be crowded with Maghrabi pilgrims, but that 'Allah makes all things easy!' Though not penetrated with the conviction that this would happen in our case, I paid for two deck passages eighteen Riyals, my companions seven each, whilst Saad secretly entered himself as an able seaman. Mohammed Shiklibha we were obliged to leave behind, as he could, or would, not afford the expense, and none of us would afford it for him. Had I known him to be the honest, true-hearted fellow he was – his kindness at Mccoah quite won my heart – I should not have grudged the small charity.

Nothing more comfortless than our days and nights in the 'George' Inn. The ragged walls of our rooms were clammy with dirt, the smoky rafters foul with cobwebs, and the floor, bestrewed with kit, in terrible confusion, was black with hosts of ants and flies. Pigeons nestled on the shelf, cooing amatory ditties the live-long day, and cats like tigers crawled through a hole in the door, making night hideous with their cat-a-waulings. Now a curious goat, then an inquisitive jackass, would walk stealthily into the room, remark that it was tenanted, and retreat with dignified demeanour, and the mosquitoes sang Io Pæns over our prostrate forms throughout the twenty-four hours. I spare the reader the enumeration of the other Egyptian plagues that infested the place. After the first day's trial, we determined to spend the hours of light in the passages, lying upon our boxes or rugs, smoking, wrangling, and inspecting one another's chests. The latter occupation was a fertile source of disputes, for nothing was more common than for a friend to seize an article belonging to another, and to swear by the Prophet's beard that he admired it, and, therefore, would not return it. The boy Mohammed and Shaykh Nur, who had been intimates the first day, differed in opinion on the second, and on the third, came to pushing each other against the wall. Sometimes we went into the bazar, a shady street flanked with poor little shops, or we sat in the coffee-house, drinking hot salt water tinged with burnt bean, or we prayed in one of the three tumble-down old Mosques, or we squatted upon the pier, lamenting the want of Hammams, and bathing in the tepid sea. I presently came to the conclusion that Suez as a 'watering place' is duller even than Dover. The only society we found – excepting an occasional visitor – was that of a party of Egyptian women, who with their husbands and families occupied some rooms adjoining ours. At first they were fierce, and used bad language, when the boy Mohammed and I, whilst Umar Effendi was engaged in prayer, and the rest were wandering about the town, ventured to linger in the cool passage, where they congregated, or to address a facetious phrase to them. But hearing that I was a Hakim-bashi – for fame had promoted me to the rank of a 'Physician General' at Suez – all had some ailments; they began prudently with requesting me to display the effects of my drugs by dosing myself, but they ended submissively by swallowing nauseous compounds in a body. To this succeeded a primitive form of flirtation, which mainly consisted of the demand direct; the most charming of the party was one Fattumah, a plump-personed dame fast verging upon her thirtieth year, fond of a little flattery, and possessed, like all her people, of a most voluble tongue. The refrain of every conversation was 'Marry me, O Fattumah! O daughter! O female pilgrim!' In vain the lady would reply, with a coquettish movement of the sides, and toss of the head, and a flirting manipulation of her head-veil, 'I am mated, O young man!' – it was agreed that she, being a person of polyandrous propensities, could support the weight of at least three matrimonial engagements. Sometimes the entrance of the male Fellahs interrupted these little discussions, but people of our respectability and nation were not to be imposed upon by such husbands In their presence we only varied the style of conversation – inquiring the amount of 'Mahr', or marriage settlement, deriding the cheapness of womanhood in Egypt, and requiring to be furnished on the spot with brides at the rate of ten shillings a head. More often the amiable Fattumah – the fair sex in this country, though passing frail, have the best tempers in the world – would laugh at our impertinences. Sometimes vexed by our imitating her Egyptian accent, mimicking her gestures, and depreciating her country-women, she would wax wroth, and order us to be gone, and stretch out her forefinger – a sign that she wished to put out our eyes, or adjure Allah to cut the hearts out of our bosoms. Then the 'Marry me, O Fattumah, O daughter, O female pilgrim!' would give way to Y'al-ago-o-oz! (O old woman and decrepit!) 'O daughter of sixty sires, and only fit to carry wood to market!' – whereupon would burst a storm of wrath, at the tail of which all of us, like children, starting upon our feet, rushed out of one another's way. But – 'qui se dispute, s'adore' – when we again met all would be forgotten, and the old tale be told over de novo. This was the amusement of the day. At night we, men, assembling upon the little terrace, drank tea, recited stories, read books, talked of our travels, and indulged in various pleasantries. The great joke was the boy Mohammed's abusing all his companions to their faces in Hindostanee, which none but Shaykh Nur and I could understand; the others, however, guessed his intention, and revenged themselves by retorts of the style uncourteous in the purest Hejazi. I proceed to offer a few more extracts from Mr. Levick's letter about Suez and the Suezians.

'It appears that the number of pilgrims who pass through Suez to Meccah has of late been steadily on the decrease. When I first came here (in 1838) the pilgrims who annually embarked at this port amounted to between 10,000 and 12,000, the shipping was more numerous, and the merchants were more affluent.

'I have ascertained from a special register kept in the government archives that in the Moslem year 1268 (from 1851 to 1852) the exact number that passed through was

4893. In 1269 A.H. it had shrunk to 3136. The natives assign various causes to the falling off, which I attribute chiefly to the indirect effect of European civilisation upon the Moslem powers immediately in contact with it. The heterogeneous mass of pilgrims is composed of people of all classes, colors, and costumes. One sees among them, not only the natives of countries contiguous to Egypt, but also a large proportion of central Asians from Bokhara, Persia, Circassia, Turkey and the Crimea, who prefer this route by way of Constantinople to the difficult, expensive, and dangerous caravan line through the desert from Damascus and Baghdad. The West sends us Moors, Algerines, and Tunisians, and Inner Africa a mass of sable Takrouri, and others from Bornou, the Sudan, Ghedamah near the Niger, and Jabarti from the Habash.

The Suez ship-builders are an influential body of men, originally Candiots and Alexandrians. When Mohammed Ali fitted out his fleet for the Hejaz war, he transported a number of Greeks to Suez, and the children now exercise their fathers' craft. There are at present three great builders at this place. Their principal difficulty is the want of material. Teak comes from India via Jeddah, and Venetian boards, owing to the expense of camel-transport, are a hundred percent dearer here than at Alexandria. Trieste and Turkey supply spars, and Jeddah, canvass: the sail-makers are Suez men, and the crews a mongrel mixture of Arabs and Egyptians; the Rais, or captain, being almost invariably, if the vessel be a large one, a Yambu man. There are two kinds of craft, distinguished from each other by tonnage, not by build. The Baghlah is a vessel above 50 tons burden, the Sambuk from 15 to 50. The ship-owner bribes the Amir el Bahr, or port-captain, and the Nazir el Safain, or the captain commanding the government vessels, to rate his ship as high as possible – if he pay the price, he will be allowed 9 ardebbs to the ton. The number of ships belonging to the port of Suez amounts to 92; they vary from 25 to 250 tons. The departures in A.H. 1269 (1852 and 1853) were 38, so that each vessel, after returning from a trip, is laid up for about two years. Throughout the passage of the pilgrims, that is to say, during four months, the departures average twice a week ; during the remainder of the year from six to ten vessels may leave the port. The homeward trade is carried on principally in Jeddah bottoms, which are allowed to convey goods to Suez, but not to take in return cargo there: they must not interfere with, nor may they partake in any way of the benefits of the rotation system.

During the present year the imports were contained in 41,395 packages, the exports in 15,988. Specie makes up in some manner for this preponderance of imports: a sum of from 30,000*l.* to 40,000*l,* in crown, or Maria Theresa, dollars annually leaves Egypt for Arabia, Abyssinia, and other parts of Africa. I value the imports at about 350,000*l*; the export trade to Jeddah at 300,000*l* per annum. The former consists principally of coffee and gum Arabic; of these there were respectively 17,460 and 15,132 bales, the aggregate value of each article being from 75,000*l.* to 80,000*l.*, and the total amount 160,000*l.* In the previous year the imports were contained in 36,840 packages, the exports in 13,498: of the staple articles – coffee and gum Arabic – they were respectively 15,499 and 14,129 bales, each bale being valued at about 5*l.* Next in importance comes wax from Yemen and the Hejaz, mother-of-pearl from the Red Sea, sent to England in rough, pepper from Malabar, cloves brought by Moslem pilgrims from Java, Borneo, and Singapore, cherry pipe-sticks from Persia and Bussora, and Persian or Surat 'Timbak' (tobacco). These I value at 20,000*l.* per annum. There were also (A.D. 1853) of cloves 708 packages and of Malabar pepper 948: the cost of these two might be 7000*l.* Minor articles of exportation are general spiceries (ginger, cardamoms, etc.), Eastern perfumes, such as aloes wood, ottar of rose, ottar of pink and others, tamarinds from India and Yemen, Banca tin, hides supplied by the nomade Bedouins, senna leaves from Yemen and the Hejaz, and blue chequered cotton Melayahs (women's mantillas) manufactured in southern Arabia. The total value of these smaller imports may be 20,000*l.* per annum.

The exports chiefly consist of English and native 'grey domestics,' bleached Madipilams, Paisley lappets, and muslins for turbans; the remainder being Manchester prints, antimony, Syrian soap, iron in bars, and common ironmongery, Venetian or Trieste beads, used as ornaments in Arabia and Abyssinia, writing paper, Tarbooshes, Papooshes (slippers), and other minor articles of dress and ornament.

The average annual temperature of the year at Suez is 67° Fahrenheit. The extremes of heat and cold are found in January and August; during the former month the thermometer ranges from a minimum of 38° to a maximum of 68°; during the latter the variation extends from 68° to 102°, or even to 104°, when the heat becomes oppressive. Departures from these extremes are rare. I never remember to have seen the thermometer rise above 108° during the severest Khamsin, or to have sunk below 34° in the rawest wintry wind. Violent storms come up from the south in March. Rain is very variable: sometimes three years have passed without a shower, whereas in 1841 torrents poured for nine successive days, deluging the town, and causing many buildings to fall.

The population of Suez now numbers about 4800. As usual in Mohammedan countries no census is taken here. Some therefore estimate the population at 6000. Sixteen years ago it was supposed to be under 3000. After that time it rapidly increased till 1850, when a fatal attack of cholera reduced it to about half its previous number. The average mortality is about twelve a month. The endemic diseases are fevers of typhoid and intermittent types in spring, when strong northerly winds cause the waters of the bay to recede, and leave a miasma-breeding swamp exposed to the rays of the sun. In the month of October and November febrile attacks are violent ; ophthalmia more so. The eye-disease is not so general here as at Cairo, but the symptoms are more acute; in some years it becomes a virulent epidemic, which ends either in total blindness or in a partial opacity of the cornea, inducing dimness of vision, and a permanent weakness of the eye. In one month three of my acquaintances lost their sight. Dysenteries are also common, and so are bad boils, or rather ulcers. The cold season is not unwholesome, and at this period the pure air of the Desert restores and invigorates the heat-wasted frame.

The walls, gates, and defences of Suez are in a ruinous state, being no longer wanted to keep out the Sinaitic Bedouins. The houses are about 500 in number, but many of the natives prefer occupying the upper stories of the Wakálehs, the rooms on the ground floor serving for stores to certain merchandise, wood, dates, cotton, etc.

The Suezians live well, and their bazar is abundantly stocked with meat and clarified butter brought from Sinai, and fowls, corn, and vegetables from the Sharkiyah province; fruit is supplied by Cairo as well as by the Sharkiyah, and wheat conveyed down the Nile in flood to the capital is carried on camel-back across the Desert. At sunrise they eat the Fatur, or breakfast, which in summer consists of a 'fatireh', a kind of muffin, or of bread and treacle. In winter it is more substantial, being generally a mixture of lentils and rice, with clarified butter poured over it, and a 'kitchen ' of pickled lime or stewed onions. At this season they greatly enjoy the 'Ful mudammas' (boiled horsebeans), eaten with an abundance of linseed oil, into which they steep bits of bread. The beans form a highly nutritive diet, which, if the stomach can digest it – the pulse is never shelled – gives great strength. About the middle of the day comes 'El Ghada,' a light dinner of wheaten bread, with dates, onions or cheese: in the hot season melons and cooling fruits are preferred, especially by those who have to face the sun. 'El Asha,' or supper, is served about half an hour after sunset; at this meal all but the poorest classes eat meat. Their favourite flesh, as usual in this part of the world, is mutton; beef and goal are little prized.'

The people of Suez are a finer and a fairer race than the Cairenes. The former have more the appearance of Arabs: their dress is more picturesque, their eyes are carefully darkened with Kohl, and they wear sandals, not slippers. They are, according to all accounts, a turbulent and somewhat fanatic set, fond of quarrels, and slightly addicted to 'pronunciamentos'. The general programme of one of these latter diversions is said to be as follows. The boys will first be sent by their fathers about the town in a disorderly mob, and ordered to cry out 'Long live the Sultan!' with its usual sequel, 'Death to the infidels!' The infidels, Christians or others, must hear and may happen to resent this; or possibly the governor, foreseeing a disturbance, orders an ingenuous youth or two to be imprisoned, or to be caned by the police. Whereupon some person, rendered influential by wealth or religious reputation, publicly complains that the Christians are all in all, and that in these evil days El Islam is going to destruction. On this occasion the speaker conducts himself with such insolence, that the governor must perforce consign him to confinement, which exasperates the populace still more. Secret meetings are now convened, and in them the chiefs of corporations assume a prominent position. If the disturbance be intended by its main spring to subside quietly, the conspirators are allowed to take their own way; they will drink copiously, become lions about midnight, and recover their hare-hearts before noon next day. But if mischief be intended, a case of bloodshed is brought about, and then nothing can arrest the torrent of popular rage. The Egyptian, with all his good humour, merriment, and nonchalance, is notorious for doggedness, when, as the popular phrase is, his 'blood is up'. And this, indeed, is his chief merit as a soldier. He has a certain mechanical dexterity in the use of arms, and an Egyptian regiment will fire a volley as correctly as a battalion at Chobham. But when the head, and not the hands, is required, he notably fails, as all

Orientals do. The reason of his superiority in the field is his peculiar stubbornness, and this, together with his powers of digestion and of enduring hardship on the line of march, is the quality that make him terrible to his old conqueror, the Turk.

The Pilgrim Ship

The larger craft anchor some three or four miles from the Suez pier, so that it is necessary to drop down in a skiff or shore-boat.

Immense was the confusion on the eventful day of our departure. Suppose us standing upon the beach, on the morning of a fiery July day, carefully watching our hurriedly-packed goods and chattels, surrounded by a mob of idlers, who are not too proud to pick up waifs and strays, whilst pilgrims rush about apparently mad, and friends are keeping, acquaintances vociferating adieux, boatmen demanding fees, shopmen claiming debts, women shrieking and talking with inconceivable power children crying – in short, for an hour or so we are in the thick of a human storm. To confound confusion, the boatmen have moored their skiff half a dozen yards away from the shore, lest the porters should be unable to make more than double their fare from the Hajis. Again the Turkish women raise a hideous howl, as they are carried off struggling vainly in brawny arms; the children howl because their mothers howl; and the men scold and swear, because in such scenes none may be silent. The moment we had embarked, each individual found that he or she had missed something of vital importance – a pipe, a child, a box, or a watermelon; and naturally all the servants were in the bazars, when they should have been in the boat. Briefly, despite the rage of the sailors, who feared being too late for a second trip, we stood for some time on the beach before putting off.

From the beach we poled to the little pier, where sat the Bey in person to perform a final examination of our passports. Several were detected without the necessary document. Some were bastinadoed, others peremptorily ordered back to Cairo, and the rest were allowed to proceed. At about 10 a.m. we hoisted sail, and ran down the channel leading to the roadstead. On our way we had a specimen of what we might expect from our fellow passengers, the Maghrabi. A boat crowded with these ruffians caught us up, ran alongside of us, and, before we could organise a defence, about a score of them poured into our vessel. They carried things too with a high hand, laughed at us, and seemed quite ready to fight. My Indian boy, who happened to slip the word 'Muarras', narrowly escaped a blow with a palm-stick, which would have felled a camel. They outnumbered us, and were armed; so that, on this occasion, we were obliged to put up with their insolence, and not murmur.

Our Pilgrim Ship, the Silk el Zahab, or the 'Golden Wire', was a Sambuk of about fifty tons, with narrow wedge-like bows, a clean water line, a sharp keel, undecked, except upon the poop, which was high enough to act as a sail in a gale of wind. She carried two masts, imminently raking forward, the main considerably larger than the mizen; the former was provided with a huge triangular latine, very deep in the tack, but the second sail was unaccountably wanting. She had no means of reefing, no compass, no log, no sounding lines, nor even the suspicion of a chart; and in her box-like cabin and ribbed bold there was something which savoured of close connexion between her model and that of the Indian Toni. Such, probably, were the craft which carried old Sesostris across the Red Sea to Dire; such the cruisers which once every three years left Ezion-Geber for Tarshish; such the transports of which 130 were required to convey Ælius Gallos, with his 10,000 men; and – the East moves slowly – such most probably in A.D. 1900 will be the 'Golden Wire', which shall convey future pilgrims from Suez to El-Hejaz. 'Bakhshish' was the last as well as the first odious sound I heard in Egypt. The owner of the shore-boat would not allow us to climb the sides of our vessel before paying him his fare, and when we did so, he asked for Bakhshish. If Easterns would only imitate the example of Europeans – I never yet saw an Englishman give Bakhshish to a soul – the nuisance would soon be done away with. But on this occasion all my companions complied with the request, and at times it is unpleasant to be singular.

The first look at the interior of our vessel showed a hopeless sight; for Ali Murad, the greedy owner, had promised to take sixty passengers in the hold, but had stretched the number to ninety-seven. Piles of boxes and luggage in every shape and form filled the ship from stem to stern, and a torrent of Hajis were pouring over the sides like ants into the Indian sugar-basin. The poop, too, where we had taken our places, was covered with goods, and a number of pilgrims had established themselves there by might, not by right.

Presently, to our satisfaction, appeared Saad the Devil, equipped as an able seaman, and looking most unlike the proprietor of two large boxes full of valuable merchandise. This energetic individual instantly prepared for action. With our little party to back him, he speedily cleared the poop of intruders and their stuff by the simple process of pushing or rather throwing them off it into the pit below. We then settled down as comfortably as we could; three Syrians, a married Turk with his wife and family, the rais or captain of the vessel, with a portion of his crew, and our seven selves, composing a total of eighteen human beings, upon a space certainly not exceeding 10 feet by 8. The cabin – a miserable box about the size of the poop, and three feet high – was stuffed, like the hold of a slave ship, with fifteen wretches, children and women, and the other ninety-seven were disposed upon the luggage, or squatted on the bulwarks. Having some experience in such matters, and being favoured by fortune, I found a spare bed-frame slung to the ship's side; and giving a dollar to its owner, a sailor – who flattered himself that, because it was his, he would sleep upon it – I instantly appropriated it, preferring any hardship outside to the condition of a packed herring inside the place of torment.

Our Maghrabis were fine-looking animals from the deserts about Tripoli and Tunis; so savage that, but a few weeks ago, they had gazed at the cock-boat, and wondered how long it would be growing to the size of the ship that was to take them to Alexandria. Most of them were sturdy young fellows, round-headed, broad-shouldered, tall and large-limbed, with frowning eyes, and voices in a perpetual roar. Their manners were rude, and their faces full of fierce contempt or insolent familiarity. A few old men were there, with countenances expressive of intense ferocity; women as savage and full of fight as men; and handsome boys with shrill voices, and hands always upon their daggers. The women were mere bundles of dirty white ras. The males were clad in Burnooses – brown or striped woollen cloaks with hoods; they had neither turban nor Tarbush, trusting to their thick curly hair or to the prodigious hardness of their scalps as a defence against the sun; and there was not a slipper nor a shoe amongst the party. Of course all were armed; but, fortunately for us, none had anything more formidable than a cut-and-thrust dagger about ten inches long. These Maghrabis travel in hordes under a leader who obtains the temporary title of 'Maula' – the master. He has generally performed a pilgrimage or two, and has collected a stock of superficial information which secures for him the respect of his followers, and the profound contempt of the heaven-made Ciceroni of Meccah and El Medinah. No people endure greater hardships when upon the pilgrimage than these Africans, who trust almost entirely to alms and to other such dispensations of Providence. It is not therefore to be wondered at that they rob whenever an opportunity presents itself. Several cases of theft occurred on board the 'Golden Wire' and as such plunderers seldom allow themselves to be baulked by insufficient defence, they are perhaps deservedly accused of having committed some revolting murders.

The first thing to be done after gaining standing-room was to fight for greater comfort; and never a Holyhead packet in the olden time showed a finer scene of pugnacity than did our pilgrim ship. A few Turks, rugged old men from Anatolia and Caramania, were mixed up with the Maghrabis, and the former began the war by contemptuously elbowing and scolding their wild neighbours. The Maghrabis under their leader, 'Maula Ali', a burly savage, in whom I detected a ridiculous resemblance to an old and well-remembered schoolmaster, retorted so willingly that in a few minutes nothing was to be seen but a confused mass of humanity, each item indiscriminately punching and pulling, scratching and biting, butting and trampling whatever was obnoxious to such operations, with cries of rage, and all the accompaniments of a proper fray. One of our party on the poop, a Syrian, somewhat incautiously leapt down to aid his countrymen by restoring order. He sank immediately below the surface of the living mass; and when we fished him out, his forehead was cut open, half his beard had disappeared, and a fine sharp set of teeth belonging to some Maghrabi had left their mark in the calf of his leg. The enemy showed no love of fair play, and never appeared contented unless five or six of them were setting upon a single man. This made matters worse. The weaker of course drew their daggers, and a few bad wounds were soon given and received. In a few minutes five men were completely disabled, and the victors began to dread the consequences of their victory.

Then the fighting stopped, and, as many could not find places, it was agreed that a deputation should wait upon Ali Murad, the owner, to inform him of the crowded state of the vessel. After keeping us in expectation at least three hours, he appeared in a row-boat, preserving a respectful distance, and informed us that any one who pleased might leave the ship and take back his fare. This left the case exactly as it was before; none would abandon his party to go on shore: so Ali Murad was rowed off towards Suez, giving us a parting injunction to be good, and not fight; to trust in Allah, and that Allah would make all things easy to us. His departure was the signal for a second fray, which in its accidents differed a little from the first. During the previous disturbance we kept our places with weapons in our hands. This time we were summoned by the Maghrabis to relieve their difficulties, by taking about half a dozen of them on the poop. Saad the Devil at once rose with an oath, and threw amongst us a bundle of 'Nebut' – goodly ashen staves six feet long, thick as a man's wrist, well greased, and tried in many a rough bout. He shouted to us, 'Defend yourselves if you don't wish to be the meat of the Maghrabis!' and to the enemy, 'Dogs and sons of dogs! now shall you see what the children of the Arab are'–'I am Umar of Daghistan!' 'I am Abdullah the son of Joseph!' 'I am Saad the Devil!' we exclaimed, 'renowning it' by this display of name and patronymic. To do the enemy justice, they showed no sign of flinching; they swarmed towards the poop like angry hornets, and encouraged each other with loud cries of 'Allah akbar!' But we had a vantage ground about four feet above them, and their palm-sticks and short daggers could do nothing against our terrible quarter-staves. In vain the 'Jacquerie' tried to scale the poop and to overpower us by numbers; their courage only secured them more broken heads.

At first I began to lay on load with main morte, really fearing to kill some one with such a weapon; but it soon became evident that the Maghrabis' heads and shoulders could bear and did require the utmost exertion of strength. Presently a thought struck me. A large earthen jar full of drinking water – in its heavy frame of wood the weight might have been 100lbs. – stood upon the edge of the poop, and the thick of the fray took place beneath. Seeing an opportunity I crept up to the jar, and, without attracting attention, by a smart push with the shoulder rolled it down upon the swarm of assailants. The fall caused a shriller shriek to rise above the ordinary din, for heads, limbs, and bodies were sorely bruised by the weight, scratched by the broken potsherds, and wetted by the sudden discharge. A fear that something worse might be coming made the Maghrabis shrink off towards the end of the vessel. After a few minutes, we, sitting in grave silence, received a deputation of individuals in whity-brown Burnooses, spotted and striped with what Mephistopheles calls a 'curious juice'. They solicited peace, which we granted upon the condition that they would bind themselves to keep it. Our heads, shoulders, and hands were penitentially kissed, and presently the fellows returned to bind up their hurts in dirty rags. We owed this victory entirely to our own exertions, and the meek Umar was by far the fiercest of the party. Our Rais, as we afterwards learned, was an old fool who could do nothing but call for the Fatihah, claim Bakhshish at every place where we moored for the night, and spend his leisure hours in the 'Caccia del Mediterraneo'. Our crew consisted of half a dozen Egyptian lads, who, not being able to defend themselves, were periodically chastised by the Maghrabi, especially when any attempt was made to cook, to fetch water, or to prepare a pipe.

At length, about 3 a.m. on the 6th July, 1854, we shook out the sail, and, as it bellied in the favourable wind, we recited the Fatihah with upraised hands which we afterwards drew down our faces. As the 'Golden Wire' started from her place, I could not help casting one wistful look upon the British flag proudly floating over the Consulate. But the momentary regret was stifled by the heart-bounding which prospects of an adventure excite, and by the real pleasure of leaving Egypt. I had lived there a stranger in the land, and a hapless life it had been: in the streets every man's face, as he looked upon the Persian, was the face of a foe. Whenever I came in contact with the native officials, insolence marked the event; and the circumstance of living within hail of my fellow countrymen, and yet in an impossibility of enjoying their society, still throws a gloom over the memory of my first sojourn in Egypt.

The ships of the Red Sea – infamous region of rocks, reefs, and shoals – cruise along the coast by day, and for the night lay to in the first cove they can find; they do not sail when it blows hard, and as in winter time the weather is often stormy and the light of day does not last long, the voyage is intolerably slow. At sunset we stayed our adventurous course, and still, within sight of Suez, comfortably anchored under the lee of Jebel Atakah, the 'Mountain of Deliverance'. We were now on classic waters. The Eastern shore was dotted with the little grove of palm-trees which clusters around the Uyun Musa, or Moses' Wells; and on the west, between two towering ridges, lay the mouth of the valley down which, according to Father Sicard, the Israelites fled to the Sea of Sedge. The view was by no means deficient in a sort of barbarous splendour. Verdure there was none, but under the violet and orange tints of the sky the chalky rocks became heaps of topazes, and the black ridges masses of amethyst. The rising mists, here silvery white, there deeply rosy, and the bright blue of the waves, lining long strips of golden sand, compensated for the want of softness by a semblance of savage gorgeousness.

Next morning, before the cerulean hue had vanished from the hills, we set sail. It was not long before we came to a proper sense of our position. The box containing my store of provisions, and, worse still, my opium, was at the bottom of the hold, perfectly unapproachable; we had, therefore, the pleasure of breaking our fast on 'Mare's skin', and a species of biscuit, hard as a stone and quite as tasteless. During the day, whilst unsufferable splendor reigned above, a dashing of the waters below kept my nest in a state of perpetual drench. At night rose a cold bright moon, with dews falling so thick and clammy that the skin felt as though it would never be dry again. It is, also, by no means pleasant to sleep upon a cot about four feet long by two broad, with the certainty that a false movement would throw you overboard, and a conviction that if you do fall from a Sambuk under sail, no mortal power can save you. And as under all circumstances in the East, dozing is one's chief occupation, the reader will understand that the want of it left me in utter idleness.

The gale was light that day, and the sunbeams were fire; our crew preferred crouching in the shade of the sail to taking advantage of what wind there was. In spite of our impatience we made but little way: near evening time we anchored on a tongue of sand, about two miles distant from the well-known heights called by the Arabs Hammam Faram, which 'like giants stand, To sentinel enchanted land.'

The strip of coarse quartz and sandstone gravel is obviously the offspring of some mountain torrent; it stretches southwards, being probably disposed in that direction by the currents of the sea, as they receive the deposit. The distance of the Bluffs prevented my visiting them, which circumstance I regretted the less as they have been described by pens equal to the task.

That evening we enjoyed ourselves upon clean sand, whose surface, drifted by the wind into small yellow waves, by a little digging and heaping up, was easily converted into the coolest and most comfortable of couches. Indeed, after the canescent heat of the day, and the tossing of our ill-conditioned vessel, we should have been contented with lodgings far less luxurious. Fuel was readily collected, and while some bathed, the others erected a hearth – three large stones and a hole open to leeward – lit the fire, and put the pot on to boil. Shaykh Nur had fortunately brought a line with him; we had been successful in fishing; a little rice also bad been bought; with this boiled and rock cod broiled upon the charcoal, we made a dinner that caused every one to forget the breakfast of mare's skin and hard biscuit. A few Maghrabis had ventured on shore – the Rais having terrified the others by threatening them with those 'bogles', the Bedouins – they offered us Kus-kusu in exchange for a little fish. As evening came we determined before sleeping, to work upon their morale as effectually as we had attacked their physique. Shaykh Hamid stood up and indulged them with the Azan, or call to prayers, pronounced after the fashion of El Medinah. They performed their devotions in lines ranged behind us as a token of respect, and when worship was over we were questioned about the Holy City till we grew tired of answering. Again our heads and shoulders, our hands and knees}, were kissed, but this time in devotion, not in penitence. My companions could scarcely understand half the rugged words which the Maghrabis used, as this dialect was fresh from the distant desert, still we succeeded in making ourselves intelligible to them, vaunting our dignity as the Sons of the Prophet, and the sanctity of our land which should protect its children from every description of fraud and violence. We benignantly promised to be their guides at El Medinah, and the boy Mohammed would conduct their devotions at Meccah, always provided that they repented their past misdeeds, avoided any repetition of the same, and promised to perform the duties of good and faithful pilgrims. Presently the Rais joined our party, and the usual story-telling began. The old man knew the name of each bill, and had a legend for every nook and corner in sight. He dwelt at length upon the life of

Abu Zulaymah, the patron saint of these seas, whose little tomb stands at no great distance from our bivouac place, and told us how he sits watching over the safety of pious mariners in a cave among the neighbouring rocks, and sipping his coffee, which is brought in a raw state from Meccah by green birds, and prepared in the usual way by the hands of ministering angels. He showed us the spot where the tenable king of Egypt, when close upon the heels of the children of Israel, was whelmed in the 'hell of waters', and he warned us that next day our way would be through breakers, and reefs, and dangerous currents, over whose troubled depths, since that awful day, the Ifrit of the storm has never ceased to flap his sable wing. The wincing of the hearers proved that the shaft of the old man's words was sharp; but as night was advancing, we unrolled our rugs, and fell asleep upon the sand, all of us happy, for we had eaten and drunk, and – the homo sapiens is a hopeful animal – expecting on the morrow that the Ifrit would be merciful, and allow us to eat fresh dates at the harbour of Tur.

Fair visions of dates doomed to the Limbo of things which should have been! The grey dawn looked down upou us in difficulties. The water is deep near this coast; we had anchored at high tide close to the shore, and the ebb had left us high and dry. When this fact became apparent, a storm was upon the point of breaking. The Maghrabis, but for our interference, would have bastinadoed the Rais, who, they said with some reason, ought to have known better. When this phase of feeling passed away, they applied themselves to physical efforts. All except the women and children, who stood on the shore encouraging their relatives with shrill quaverings, threw themselves into the water; some pushed, others applied their shoulders to the vessel's side, and all used their lungs with might and main. But the 'Golden Wire' was firmly fixed, and their exertions were too irregular. Physical force failed, upon which they changed their tactics. At the suggestion of their 'Maula', they prepared to burn incense in honor of the Shaykh Abu Zulaymah. The material not being forthcoming, they used coffee, which perhaps accounts for the short-comings of that holy man. After this the Rais remembered that their previous exertions had not begun under the auspices of the Fatihah. Therefore they prayed, and then re-applied themselves to work. Still they failed. Finally, each man called aloud upon his own particular saint or spiritual guide, and rushed forward as if he alone sufficed for the exploit. Shaykh Hamid unwisely quoted the name, and begged the assistance of his great ancestor, the 'clarified-butter-seller'; the obdurate 'Golden Wire' was not moved, and Hamid retired in momentary confusion.

It was now about 9 a.m., and the water had risen considerably. My morning had been passed in watching the influx of the tide, and the grotesque efforts of the Maghrabis. When the vessel showed some symptoms of unsteadiness, I arose, walked gravely up to her, ranged the pilgrims around her with their shoulders to the sides, and told them to heave with might when they should hear me invoke the revered name of the Indian saint. I raised my hands and voice; 'Ya Piran Pir!' Ya Abd el Kader Jilani was the signal. Each Maghrabi worked like an Atlas, the 'Golden Wire' canted half over, and, sliding heavily through the sand, once more floated off into deep water. This was generally voted a minor miacle, and the Effendi was greatly respected – for a day or two.

The wind was fair, but we had all to re-embark, an operation which went on till noon. After starting, I remarked the natural cause which gives this Birkat

Farann – 'Pharaoh's Bay' – a bad name. Here the gulf narrows, and the winds, which rush down the clefts and valleys of the lolly mountains on the Eastern and Western shores, meeting tides and counter-currents, cause a perpetual commotion. That day the foam-tipped waves repeatedly washed over my cot, by no means diminishing its discomforts. In the evening, or rather late in the afternoon, we anchored, to our infinite disgust, under a ridge of rocks, behind which lies the plain of Tur. The Rais deterred all from going on shore by terrible stories about the Bedouins that haunt the place, besides which there was no sand to sleep upon. We remained, therefore, on board that night, and, making sail early the next morning, threaded through reefs and sand-banks into the intricate and dangerous entrance of Tur about noon.

Nothing can be meaner than the present appearance of the old Phænician colony, although its position as a harbour, and its plentiful supply of fruit and fresh water, make it one of the most frequented places on the coast. The only remains of any antiquity – except the wells – are the fortifications which the Portuguese erected to keep out the Bedouins. The little town lies upon a plain that stretches with a gradual rise from the sea to the lofty mountains, which form the axis of the Sinaitic group. The country around reminded me strongly of maritime Sindh – a flat of clay and sand, clothed with sparse tufts of Salsolæ, and bearing strong signs of a (geologically speaking) recent origin. The town is inhabited principally by Greek and other Christians, who live by selling water and provisions to ships. A fleecy cloud hung lightly over the majestic head of Jebel Tur, about eventide, and the outlines of the giant hills stood 'picked out' from the clear blue sky. Our Rais, weather-wise man, warned us that these were indications of a gale, and that, in case of rough weather, he did not intend to leave Tur. I was not sorry to hear this. We had passed a pleasant day, drinking sweet water, and eating the dates, grapes, and pomegranates, which the people of the place carry down to the beach for the benefit of hungry pilgrims. Besides which, there were various sights to see, and with these we might profitably spend the morrow. We therefore pitched the tent upon the sand, and busied ourselves with extricating a box of provisions – a labor rendered lighter by the absence of the Maghrabis – some of whom were wandering about the beach, whilst others had gone off to fill their bags with fresh water. We found their surliness insufferable; even when we were passing from poop to forecastle, landing or boarding, they grumbled forth their dissatisfaction.

Our Rais was not mistaken in his prediction. When morning broke, we found the wind strong, and the sea white with foam. Most of us thought lightly of these terrors, but our valorous captain swore that he dared not for his life cross the mouth of ill-omened Akabah in such a storm. We breakfasted, therefore, and afterwards set out to visit Moses' hot baths, mounted on wretched donkeys with pack-saddles, ignorant of stirrups, and without tails, whilst we ourselves suffered generally from boils, which, as usual upon a journey, make their appearance in localities the most inconvenient. Our road lay northward across the plain towards a long narrow strip of date ground, surrounded by a ruinous mud well. After a ride of two or three miles, we entered the gardens, and came suddenly upon the Hammam. It is a prim little bungalow, built by the present Pacha of Egypt for his own accommodation, glaringly whitewashed, and garnished with divans and calico curtains of a gorgeous hue. The guardian had been warned of our visit, and was present to supply us with bathing-cloths and other necessaries. One by one, we entered the cistern, which is now in an inner room. The water is about four feet deep, warm in winter, cool in summer, of a saltish and bitter taste, but celebrated for its invigorating qualities, when applied externally. On one side of the calcareous rock, near the ground, is the hole opened for the spring by Moses' rod, which must have been like the 'mast of some tall Ammiral', and near it are the marks of Moses' nails – deep indentations in the stone, which were probably left there by some extinct Saurian. Our cicerone informed us that formerly the finger-marks existed, and that they were long enough for a man to lie in. The same functionary attributed the sanitary properties of the spring to the blessings of the Prophet, and, when asked why Moses had not made sweet water to flow, informed us that the great lawgiver had intended the spring for bathing, not for drinking. We sat with him, eating the small yellow dates of Tur, which are delicious, melting like honey in the mouth, and leaving a surpassing arrière goût. After finishing sundry pipes and cups of coffee, we gave the man a few piastres, and, mounting our donkeys, started eastward for the Bir Musa, which we reached in half an hour. It is a fine old well, built round and domed over with roughly squared stones, very like what may be seen in some rustic parts of Southern England. The sides of the pit were so rugged that a man could climb down them, and at the bottom was a pool of water, sweet and abundant. We had intended to stay there, and to dine al fresco, but the hated faces of our companions, the Maghrabis, meeting us at the entrance, nipped that project in the bud. Accordingly we retired from the burning sun to a neighbouring coffeehouse – a shed of palm-leaves kept by a Tur man, and there, seated on mats, we demolished the contents of our basket. Whilst we were eating, some Bedouins came in and joined us, when invited so to do. They were poorly dressed, and all armed with knives and cheap sabres, hanging to leathern bandoleers: in language and demeanour they showed few remains of their old ferocity. As late as Mohammed Ali's time these people were noted wreckers, and formerly they were dreaded pirates – now they are lions with their fangs and claws drawn.

In the even, when we returned to our tent, a Syrian, one of our party on the poop, came out to meet us with the information that several large vessels had arrived from Suez, comparatively speaking, empty, and that the captain of one of them would land us at Yambu for three dollars a head. The proposal was tempting. But, presently it became apparent that my companions were unwilling to shift their precious boxes, and moreover, that I should have to pay for those who could not or would not pay for themselves – that is to say, for the whole party. As such a display of wealth would have been unadvisable, I dismissed the idea with a sigh. Amongst the large vessels was one freighted with Persian pilgrims, a most disagreeable race of men on a journey or a voyage. They would not land at first, because they feared the Bedouins. They would not take water from the town people, because some of these were Christians. Moreover, they insisted upon making their own call to prayer, which heretical proceeding – it admits live extra words – our party, orthodox Moslems, would rather have died than permitted. When their crier, a small wizwn-faced man, began the Azan with a voice '... in quel tenore, Che fa il cappon quando talvolta canta'.

We received it with a shout of derision, and some, hastily snatching up their weapons, offered him an opportunity of martyrdom. The Maghrabis, too, hearing that the Persians were Rafaz (heretics) crowded fiercely round to do a little Jihad, or fighting for the faith. The long-bearded men took the alarm. They were twice the number of our small party, and therefore had been in the habit of strutting about with nonchalance, and looking at us fixedly, and otherwise demeaning themselves in an indecorous way. But when it came to the point, they showed the white feather. These Persians accompanied us to the end of our voyage. As they approached the Holy Land, visions of the 'Nebut' caused a change for the better in their manners. At Mahar they meekly endured a variety of insults, and at Yambu they cringed to us like dogs.

CHAP. X

To Yambu

On the 11th July, about dawn, we left Tur, with the unpleasant certainty of not touching ground for thirty-six hours. I passed the time in steadfast contemplation of the web of my umbrella, and in making the following meteorological remarks.

Morning. The air is mild and balmy as that of an Italian spring; thick mists roll down the valleys along the sea, and a haze like mother-o'-pearl crowns the headlands. The distant rocks show Titanic walls, lofty donjons, huge projecting bastions, and moats full of deep shade. At their base runs a sea of amethyst, and as earth receives the first touches of light, their summits, almost transparent, mingle with the jasper tints of the sky. Nothing can be more delicious than this hour. But, as '... Les plus belles choses, Out le pire destin ...' so morning soon fades. The sun bursts up from behind the main, a fierce enemy, a foe that will compel every one to crouch before him. He dyes the sky orange, and the sea incarnadine, where its violet surface is stained by his rays, and mercilessly puts to flight the mists and haze and the little agate-coloured masses of cloud that were before floating in the firmament: the atmosphere is so clear that now and then a planet is visible. For the two hours following sunrise the rays are endurable; after that they become a fiery ordeal. The morning beams oppress you with a feeling of sickness; their steady glow, reflected by the glaring waters, blinds your eyes, blisters your skin, and parches your mouth: you now become a monomaniac; you do nothing but count the slow hours that must 'minute by' before you can be relieved.

Noon. The wind, reverberated by the glowing hills, is like the blast of a lime-kiln. All color melts away with the canescence from above. The sky is a dead milk-white, and the mirror-like sea so reflects the tint that you can scarcely distinguish the line of the horizon. After noon the wind sleeps upon the recking shore; there is a deep stillness; the only sound heard is the melancholy flapping of the sail. Men are not so much sleeping as half senseless; they feel as if a few more degrees of heat would be death.

Sunset. The enemy sinks behind the deep cerulean sea, under a canopy of gigantic rainbow which covers half the face of heaven. Nearest to the horizon is an arch of tawny orange; above it another of the brightest gold, and based upon thesis a semicircle of tender sea green blends with a score of delicate gradations into the sapphire sky. Across the rainbow the sun throws its rays in the form of giant wheel-spokes tinged with a beautiful pink. The Eastern sky is mantled with a purple flush that picks out the forms of the desert and the hills. Language is a thing too cold, too poor, to express the harmony and the majesty of this hour, which is evanescent, however, as it is lovely. Night falls rapidly, when suddenly the appearance of the zodiacal light restores the scene to what it was. Again the grey hills and the grim rocks become rosy or golden, the palms green, the sands saffron, and the sea wears a lilac surface of dimpling waves. But after a quarter of an hour all fades once more; the cliffs are naked and ghastly under the moon, whose light (ailing upon this wilderness of white crags and pinnacles is most strange – most mysterious.

Night. The horizon is all darkness, and the sea reflects the white visage of the moon as in a mirror of steel. In the air we see giant columns of pallid light, distinct, based upon the indigo-coloured waves, and standing with their heads lost in endless space. The stars glitter with exceeding brilliance. At this hour

> '–River and hill and wood,
> With all the numberless goings on of life,
> Inaudible as dreams–'

the planets look down upon you with the faces of smiling friends. You feel the 'sweet influence of the Pleiades'. You are bound by the 'bond of Orion'. Hesperus bears with him a thousand things. In communion with them your hours pass swiftly by, till the heavy dews warn you to cover up your face and sleep. And with one look at a certain little star in the north, under which lies all that makes life worth living through – surely it is a venial superstition to sleep with your face towards that Kiblah! – you fall into oblivion.

Those thirty-six hours were a trial even to the hard-headed Bedouins. The Syrian and his two friends were ill. Umar Effendi, it is true, had the courage to say his sunset prayers, but the exertion so altered him that he looked another man. Salih Shakkar in despair ate dates till threatened with a dysentery. Saad the Devil had rigged out for himself a cot three feet long, which, arched over with bent bamboo and covered with cloaks, he had slung on the larboard side; but the loud grumbling which proceeded from his nest proved that his precaution had not been a remedy. Even the boy Mohammed forgot to chatter, to scold, to smoke, and to make himself generally disagreeable. The Turkish baby appeared dying, and was not strong enough to wail. How the poor mother stood her trials so well, made everyone wonder. The most pleasant trait in my companions' characters was the consideration they showed to her, and their attention to her children. Whenever one of the party drew forth a little delicacy – a few dates or a pomegranate – they gave away a share of it to the children, and most of them took their turns to nurse the baby. This was genuine politeness – kindness of heart. It would be well for those who sweepingly accuse Easterns of want of gallantry to contrast this trait of character with the savage scenes of civilisation that take place among the 'Overlands' at Cairo and Suez. No foreigner could be present for the first time without bearing away the lasting impression that the sons of Great Britain are model barbarians. On board the 'Golden Wire' Salih Shakkar was the sole base exception to the general gallantry of my companions.

As the sun starts towards the west, falling harmlessly upon our heads, we arise, still faint and dizzy, calling for water, which before we had not the strength to drink, and pipes, and coffee, and similar luxuries. Onr primitive kitchen is a square wooden box, lined with clay, and filled with sand, upon which three or four large stones are placed to form a hearth. Preparations are now made for the evening meal, which is of the simplest description. A little rice, a few dates, or an onion, will keep a man alive in our position; a single 'good dinner' would justify long odds against his seeing the next evening. Moreover, it is impossible in such cases to have an appetite – fortunately, as our store of provisions is a scanty one. Arabs consider it desirable on a journey to eat hot food once in the twenty-four hours; so we determined to cook, despite all difficulties. The operation, however, is by no means satisfactory;

twenty expectants surround the single fire, and there is sure to be a quarrel amongst them every five minutes.

As the breeze, cooled by the dew, begins to fan our parched faces, we recover our spirits amazingly. Songs are sung, and stories are told, and rough jests are bandied about, till not unfrequently Oriental sensitiveness is sorely touched. Or, if we see the prospect of storm or calm, we draw forth, and piously peruse, a 'Hizb el Bahr'. As this prayer is supposed to make all sale upon the ocean wave, I will not selfishly withhold it from the British reader. To draw forth all its virtues, the reciter should receive it from the hands of his Murshid or spiritual guide, and study it during the Chillah, or forty days of fast, of which, I venture to observe, few Britons are capable.

> 'O Allah, O Exalted, O Almighty, O All-pitiful, O All-powerful, thou art my God, and sufficeth to me the knowledge of it! Glorified be the Lord my Lord, and glorified be the Faith my Faith! Thou givest victory to whom thou pleasest, and thou are the Glorious, the Merciful! We pray thee for safety in our goings forth and our standings still, in our words and our designs, in our dangers of temptation and doubts, and the secret designs of our hearts. Subject unto us this sea, even as thou didst subject the deep to Musa (Moses), and as thou didst subject the fire to Ibrahim (Abraham), and as thou didst subject the iron to Daud (David), and as thou didst subject the wind and the devils and genii and mankind to Sulayman (Solomon), and as thou didst subject the moon and El Burak to Mohammed, upon whom be Allah's mercy and his blessing! And subject unto us all the seas in earth and heaven, in the visible and in thine invisible worlds, the sea of this life, and the sea of futurity. O thou who reignest over everything, and unto whom all things return, Khyas! Khyas! Khyas!'

And lastly, we lie down upon our cribs, wrapped up in thickly padded cotton coverlets, and forget the troubles of the past day, and the discomforts of that to come.

Late on the evening of the 11th of July we passed in sight of the narrow mouth of Akabah, whose famosi rupes are a terror to the voyagers of these latitudes. Like the Gulf of Cambay, here a tempest is said to be always brewing, and men raise their hands to pray as they cross it. We had no storm from without that day, but a fierce one was about to burst within our ship. The essence of Oriental discipline is personal respect, based upon fear. Therefore it often happens, that the commanding officer, if a mild old gentleman, is the last person whose command is obeyed – his only privilege being that of sitting apart from his inferiors. And such was the case with our Rais. On the present occasion, irritated by the refusal of the Maghrabis to standout of the steerman's way, and excited by the prospect of losing sight of shore for a whole day, he threatened one of the fellows with his slipper. It required all our exertions, even to a display of the dreaded quarter-staves, to calm the consequent excitement. After passing Akabah, we saw nothing but sea and sky, and we spent a weary night and day tossing upon the waters – our only exercise: every face brightened as, about sunset on the 12th, we suddenly glided into the mooring-place.

Marsa Damghah – 'Damghah Anchorage' – is scarcely visible from the sea. An islet of limestone rock defends the entrance, leaving a narrow passage on each side. It is not before he enters that the mariner discovers the extent and the depth of this creek, which indents far into the land, and offers 20 feet of fine clear anchorage which no swell can reach. Inside it looks more like a lake, and at night its colour is gloriously blue as Geneva itself. I could not help calling to mind, after dinner, the old school lines,

'Est in secessu longo locus. Fasula portum.
Efficit objecta laterum, quibus omnis ab alto
Frangitur inque sinus seidit sese unda reductos'

Nothing was wanted but the 'atrum nemus'. Where, however, shall we find such luxuries in arid Arabia?

The Rais, as usual, attempted to deter us from landing, by romancing about the 'Bedoynes and Ascopards', representing them to be 'folke ryghte felonouse and foule and of cursed kynde'. To which we replied by shouldering our Nebuts and scrambling into the cock boat. On shore we found a few wretched looking beings, Jahaynahs seated upon heaps of dried wood, which they sold to travellers, and three boat-loads of Syrian pilgrims who had preceded us. We often envied them their small swift craft, with their double latine sails disposed in 'hare-ears' – which, about evening time in the far distance, looked like white gulls alighting upon the purple wave; and they justified our envy by arriving at Yambu two days before us. The pilgrims had bivouacked upon the beach, and were engaged in drinking their after dinner coffee. They received us with all the rights of hospitality, as natives of the Medinah should everywhere be received; we sat an hour with them, ate a little fruit, satisfied our thirst, smoked their pipes, and when taking leave blessed them. Then returning to the vessel we fed, and lost no time in falling asleep.

The dawn of the next day saw our sail flapping in the idle air. And it was not without difficulty that in the course of the forenoon we entered Wijh Harbour, distant from Damghah but very few miles. Wijh is also a natural anchorage, in no way differing from that where we passed the night, except in being smaller and shallower. The town is a collection of huts meanly built of round stones, and clustering upon a piece of elevated rock on the northern side of the creek. It is distant about five miles from the inland fort of the same name, which receives the Egyptian caravan, and thrives, like its port, by selling water and provisions to pilgrims. The little bazar, which the sea almost washes every high tide, provided us with mutton, rice, baked bread, and the other necessaries of life, at a moderate rate. Luxuries also were to be found: a druggist sold me an ounce of opium at a Chinese price.

With reeling limbs we landed at Wijh, and finding a large coffee-house above and over the beach, we installed ourselves there. But the Persians who preceded us had occupied all the shady places outside; we were forced to content ourselves with the interior. It was a building of artless construction, consisting of little but a roof supported by wooden posts, roughly hewn from date trees, and round the tamped earthen floor ran a raised bench of unbaked brick forming a Divan for mats and sleeping-rugs. In the centre a huge square Mastabah, or platform, answered a similar purpose. Here and there appeared attempts at long and side walls, but these superfluities had been allowed to admit daylight through large gaps. In one corner stood the apparatus of the 'Kahwahji', an altar-like elevation, also of earthen work, containing a hole for a charcoal fire, upon which were three huge coffee-pots dirtily tinned. Near it were ranged the Shishas, or Egyptian hookahs, old, exceedingly unclean, and worn by age and hard work. A wooden framework, pierced with circular apertures, supported a number of porous earthenware gullehs full of cold sweet water; the charge for these was, as usual in El Hejaz, five paras apiece. Such was the furniture of the cafe, and the only relief to the barrenness of the view was a fine mellowing atmosphere composed of smoke, steam, flies, and gnats, in about equal proportions. I have been diffuse in my description of this coffee-house, as it was a type of its class: from Alexandria to Aden the traveller will everywhere meet with buildings of the same kind.

Our happiness in this Paradise – for such it was to us after the 'Golden Wire' – was nearly sacrificed by Saad the Devil, whose abominable temper led him at once into a quarrel with the master of the coffee-house. And the latter, an ill-looking, squint-eyed, low-browed, broad-shouldered fellow, showed himself no wise unwilling to meet the Devil half way. The two worthies, after a brief bandying of bad words, seized each other's throats leisurely, so as to give the spectators time and encouragement to interfere. But when friends and acquaintances were hanging on to both heroes so firmly that they could not move hand or arm, their wrath, as usual, rose, till it was terrible to see. The little village resounded with the war, and many a sturdy knave rushed in, sword or cudgel in hand, so as not to lose the sport. During the heat of the fray, a pistol which was in Umar Effendi's hand went off – accidentally of course – and the ball passed so close to the tins containing the black and muddy mocha, that it drew the attention of all parties. As if by magic, the storm was lulled. A friend recognised Saad the Devil, and swore that he was no black slave, but a soldier at El Medinah – 'no waiter, but a Knight Templar' – this caused him to be looked upon as rather a superior person, which he proved by insisting that his late enemy should dine with him, and when the other decorously hung back, by dragging him to dinner with loud cries.

My character that day was severely tried. Besides the Persian pilgrims, a number of nondescripts who came in the same vessel were hanging about the coffee-house, lying down, smoking, drinking water, bathing, and correcting their teeth with their daggers. One inquisitive man was always at my side. He called himself a Pathan; he could speak five or six languages, knew a number of people everywhere, and had travelled far and wide over central Asia. These men are always good detectors of an incognito. I avoided answering his question about my native place, and after telling him that I had no longer name or nation, being a Dervish, asked him, when he insisted upon my having been born somewhere, to guess for himself. To my joy he claimed me for a brother Pathan, and in course of conversation he declared himself to be the nephew of an Afghan merchant, a gallant old man who had been civil to me at Cairo. We then sat smoking together with 'effusion'. Becoming confidential, he complained that he, a Sunni or orthodox Moslem, had been abused, maltreated, and beaten by his fellow-travellers, the heretical pilgrims. I naturally offered to arm my party, to take up our cudgels, and to revenge my compatriot. This thoroughly Afghan style of doing business could not fail to make him sure of his man. He declined, however, wisely remembering that he had nearly a fortnight of the Persians' society still to endure. But he promised himself the gratification, when he reached Meccah, of sheathing his Charay – the terrible Afghan knife – in the chief offender's heart.

At 8 a.m. next morning we left Wijh, after passing a night tolerably comfortable, by contrast, in the coffee-house. We took with us the stores necessary, for though our Rais had promised to anchor under Jebel Hasan that evening, no one believed him. We sailed among ledges of rock, golden sands, green weeds, and in some places through yellow lines of what appeared to me at a distance foam after a storm. All day a sailor sat upon the mast-head, looking at the water, which was transparent as blue glass, and shouting out the direction. This precaution was somewhat stultified by the roar of voices, which never failed to mingle with the warning, but we wore every half hour, and did not run aground. About mid-day we passed by Shaykh Hasan el Marabit's tomb. It is the usual domed and whitewashed building, surrounded by the hovels of its guardians, standing upon a low flat island of yellow rock, vividly reminding me of certain scenes in Sindh. Its dreary position attracts to it the attention of passing travellers; the dead saint has a prayer and a Fatihah for the good of his soul, and the live sinner wends his way with religious refreshment.

Near sunset the wind came on to blow freshly, and we cast anchor together with the Persian pilgrims upon a rock. This was one of the celebrated coral reefs of the Red Sea, and the sight justified Forskal's emphatic description – luxus lususque naturæ. It was a huge ledge or platform rising but little above the level of the deep; the water-side was perpendicular as the wall of a fort, and whilst a frigate might have floated within a yard of it, every ripple dashed over the reef, replenishing the little basins and hollows in the surface. The colour of the waves near it was a vivid amethyst. In the distance the eye rested upon what appeared to be meadows of brilliant flowers resembling those of earth, only brighter far and more lovely. Nor was this land of the sea wholly desolate. Gulls and terns here swain the tide, there, seated upon the coral, devoured their prey. In the air, troops of birds contended noisily for a dead flying fish, and in the deep water they chased a shoal, which, in their fright and hurry to escape the pursuers, veiled the surface with spray and foam. And as night came on the scene shifted, displaying fresh beauties. Shadows clothed the background, whose features, dimly revealed, allowed full scope to the imagination. In the forepart of the picture lay the sea, shining under the rays of the moon with a metallic lustre, while its border, where the wavelets dashed upon the reef, was lit by what the Arabs call the 'jewels of the deep' – brilliant flashes of phosphoric light giving an idea of splendour which art would strive in vain to imitate. Altogether it was a bit of fairy-land, a spot for nymphs and sea-gods to disport upon: you might have heard, without astonishment, old Proteus calling his flocks with the writhed horn; and Aphrodite seated in her conch would have been only a fit and proper climax of its loveliness.

But – as philosophically remarked by Sir Cauline the Knyghte – 'Every whyte must have its black, And every sweete its soure'.

This charming coral reef was nearly being the scene of an ugly accident. The breeze from seaward slowly but steadily drove us towards the reef, a fact of which we soon became conscious. Our anchor was not dragging; it had not rope enough to touch the bottom, and vainly we sought for more. In fact the 'Golden Wire' was as disgracefully deficient in all the appliances of safety, as any English merchantman in the nineteenth century – a circumstance which accounts for the shipwrecks and the terrible loss of life perpetually occurring about the pilgrimage season in these seas. Had she struck upon the razor-like edges of the coral-reef, she would have melted away like a sugar-plum in the ripple, for the tide was rising at the time. Having nothing better to do, we began to make as much noise as possible. Fortunately for us, the Rais commanding the Persian's boat was an Arab from Jeddah, and more than once we had treated him with great civility. Guessing the cause of our distress, he sent two sailors overboard with a rope; they swam gallantly up to us; and in a few minutes we were safely moored to the stern of our useful neighbour. Which done, we applied ourselves to the grateful task of beating our Rais, and richly had he deserved it. Before noon, when the wind was shifting, he had not given himself the trouble to wear once; and when the breeze fell he preferred dozing to taking advantage of what little wind remained: with energy we might have been moored that night comfortably under the side of Mount Hasan, instead of floating about on an unquiet sea with a lee-shore of coral reef within a few yards of our counter.

At dawn next day we started; we made Jebel Hasan about noon, and an hour or so before sunset we glided into Marsa Mahar. Our resting-place resembled Marsa Damghah at an humble distance; the sides of the cove, however, were bolder and more precipitous. The limestone rocks presented a peculiar appearance; in some places the base and walls had crumbled away, leaving a coping to project like a canopy; in others the wind and rain had cut deep holes, and pierced the friable material with caverns that looked like the work of art. There was a pretty opening of back wood at the bottom of the cove, and palm trees in the blue distance gladdened our eyes, which pined for the sight of something green. The Rais, as usual, would have terrified us with a description of the Hutaymi tribe that holds these parts, and I knew from Welsted and Moresby that it is a troublesome race. But forty-eight hours of cramps on board-ship would make a man think lightly of a much more imminent danger.

Wading on shore we cut our feet with the sharp rocks. I remember to have felt the acute pain of something running into my toe; but after looking at the place and extracting what appeared to be a bit of thorn, I dismissed the subject, little guessing the trouble it was to give me. Having scaled the rocky side of the cove, we found some half-naked Arabs lying in the shade; they were unarmed, and had nothing about them except their villanous countenances wherewith to terrify the most timid. These men still live in caves, like the Thamud tribe of tradition; they are still Ichthyophagi, existing without any other subsistence but what the sea affords. They were unable to provide us with dates or milk, but they sold us a kind of fish called Bui, which, broiled upon the embers, proved delicious.

After we had eaten and drunk and smoked, we began to make merry; and the Persians, who, fearing to come on shore, had kept to their conveyance, appeared proper butts for the wit of some of our party: one of whom stood up and pronounced the orthodox call to prayer, after which the rest joined in a polemical hymn, exalting the virtues and dignity of the three first Caliphs. Then, as general on such occasions, the matter was made personal by informing the Persians in a kind of rhyme sung by the Meccan gamins, that they were the 'slippers of Ali and the dogs of Omar'. But as they were too frightened to reply, my companions gathered up their cooking utensils, and returned to the 'Golden Wire', melancholy, like disappointed candidates for the honors of Donnybrook.

Our next day was silent and weary, for we were all heartily sick of being on board-ship. We should have made Yambu in the evening but for the laziness of the Rais. Having duly beaten him, we anchored on the open coast, insufficiently protected by a reef, and almost in sight of our destination. In the distance rose Jebel Radhwah or Radhwa, one of the 'Mountains

of Paradise' in which honored Arabia abounds. It is
celebrated by poetry as well as by piety. 'Were Radwah
to strive to support my woes, Radwah itself would
lie crushed by the weight' says Antar. It supplies El
Medinah with hones. I heard much of its valleys and
fruits and bubbling springs, but afterwards learned to
rank these tales with the superstitious legends which
are attached to it. Gazing at its hare and ghastly
heights, one of our party, whose wit was soured by
the want of fresh bread, surlily remarked that such
a heap of ugliness deserved ejection from heaven –
an irreverence which was too public to escape general
denunciation. We waded on shore, cooked there and
passed the night; we were short of fresh water, which,
combined with other grievances, made us as surly as
bears. Saad the Devil was especially vicious; his eyes
gazed fixedly on the ground, his lips protruded till
you might have held his face by them, his mouth was
garnished with bad wrinkles, and he never opened it
but he grumbled out a wicked word. He solaced himself
that evening by crawling slowly on all fours over the
boy Mohammed, taking scrupulous care to place one
knee upon the sleeper's face. The youth awoke in a fiery
rage; we all roared with laughter, and the sulky Negro,
alter savouring the suceess of his spite, grimly, as but
half satisfied, rolled himself into a ball like a hedgehog,
and, resolving to be offensive even in his forgetfulness,
snored violently all night.

We slept upon the sands and arose before dawn,
determined to make the Rais start in time that day.
A slip of land separated us from our haven, but the
wind was foul, and by reason of rocks and shoals, we
had to make a considerable détour.

It was about noon on the 12th day after our
departure from Suez, when, after slowly beating up the

narrow creek leading to Yambu harbour, we sprang into a shore boat and felt new life, when bidding an eternal adieu to the 'Golden Wire'.

I might have escaped much of this hardship and suffering by hiring a vessel to myself. There would then have been a cabin to retire into at night, and shade from the sun; moreover the voyage would have lasted five, not twelve days. But I wished to witness the scenes on board a pilgrim ship – scenes so much talked of by the Moslem palmer home returned. Moreover the hire was exorbitant, ranging from 40*l* to 50*l*, and it would have led to a greater expenditure, as the man who can afford to take a boat must pay in proportion during his land journey. In these countries you perforce go on as you begin: to 'break one's expenditure', that is to say, to retrench expenses, is considered all but impossible; the prudent traveller therefore will begin as he intends to go on.

The Halt At Yambu

The heat of the sun, the heavy dews, and the frequent washings of the waves, had so affected my foot, that on landing at Yambu, I could scarcely place it upon the ground. But traveller's duty was to be done; so, leaning upon my 'slave's' shoulder, I started at once to see the town, whilst Shaykh Hamid and the others of our party proceeded to the custom-house.

Yanbua el Bahir, Yambu of the sea, identified, by Abyssinian Bruce, with the Iambia village of Ptolemy, is a place of considerable importance, and shares with others the title of 'Gate of the Holy City'. It is the third quarter of the caravan road from Cairo to Meccah; and here, as well as at El Bedr, pilgrims frequently leave behind them in hired warehouses goods too heavy to be transported in haste, or too valuable to risk in dangerous times. Yambu being the port of El Medinah, as Jeddah is of Meccah, is supported by a considerable transport trade and extensive imports from the harbour on the western coasts of the Bed Sea. Here the Sultan's dominion is supposed to begin, whilst the authority of the Pacha of Egypt ceases; there is no Nizam, however, in the town, and the governor is a Sherif or Arab chief. I met him in the great bazar; he is a fine young man of light complexion and the usual high profile, handsomely dressed, with a Cashmere turban, armed to the extent of sword and dagger, and followed by two large fierce-looking Negro slaves leaning upon enormous Nebuts.

The town itself is in no wise remarkable. Built on the edge of a barren plain that extends between the mountains and the sea, it fronts the northern extremity of a narrow winding creek. Viewed from the harbour, it is a long line of buildings, whose painful whiteness is set of by a sky like cobalt and a sea like indigo; behind it lies the flat, here of a bistre-brown, there of a lively tawny; whilst the background is formed by dismal Radhwah, 'Barren and bare, unsightly, unadorned'.

Outside the walls are a few little domes and tombs, which by no means merit attention. Inside, the streets are wide, and each habitation is placed at an unsociable distance from its neighbour, except near the port and the bazars, where ground is valuable. The houses are roughly built of limestone and coralline, and their walls full of fossils crumble like almond cake; they have huge hanging windows, and look mean after those in the Moslem quarters of Cairo. There is a 'Suk' or market-place, in the usual form, a long narrow lane darkened by a covering of palm leaves, with little shops let into the walls of the houses on both sides. The cafes, which abound here, have already been described in the last chapter; they are rendered dirty in the extreme by travellers, and it is impossible to sit in them without a fan to drive away the flies. The customhouse fronts the landing-place upon the harbour; it is managed by Turkish officials – men dressed in Tarbushes, who repose the live-long day upon the Divans near the windows. In the case of us travellers they had a very simple way of doing business, charging each person of the party three piastres for each large box, but by no means troubling themselves to meddle with the contents. Yambu also boasts of a Hammam or hot bath, a mere date-leaf shed, tenanted by an old Turk, who, with his surly Albanian assistant, lives by 'cleaning' pilgrims and travellers. Some whitewashed mosques and minarets of exceedingly simple form, a Wakalch or two for the reception of merchants, and a saint's tomb, complete the list of public buildings.

In one point Yambu claims superiority over most other towns in this part of El Hejaz. Those who can afford the luxury drink sweet rain water, collected amongst the hills in tanks and cisterns, and brought on camel-back to the town. Two sources are especially praised, the Ayn el Berkat, and the Ayn Ali, which suffice to supply the whole population: the brackish water of the wells is confined to coarser purposes. Some of the old people here, as at Suez, are said to prefer the drink to which years of habit have accustomed them, and it is a standing joke that, arrived at Cairo, they salt the water of the Nile to make it palatable.

The population of Yambu – one of the most bigoted and quarrelsome races in El Hejaz – strikes the eye after arriving from Egypt, as decidedly a new feature. The Shaykh or gentleman of Yambu is over-armed and over-dressed as Fashion, the tyrant of the Desert as well as of the court, dictates to a person of his consequence. The civilised traveller from El Medinah sticks in his waist-shawl a loaded pistol, garnished with crimson silk cord, but he partially conceals the butt end under the Hap of his jacket. The irregular soldier struts down the street a small armoury of weapons: one look at the mail's countenance suffices to tell you what he is. Here and there stalk grim Bedouins, wild as their native wastes, and in all the dignity of pride and dirt; they also are armed to the teeth, and even the presence of

161

the policeman's quarter-staff cannot keep their swords in their scab hards: what we should call the peaceful part of the population never leave the house without a 'nebut' over the right shoulder, and the larger, the longer, and the heavier the weapon is, the more gallantry does the bearer claim. The people of Yambu practise the use of this implement diligently ; they become expert in delivering a head blow so violent as to break through any guard, and with it they always decide their trivial quarrels. The dress of the women differs but little from that of the Egyptians, except in the face veil, which is generally white. There is an independent bearing about the people, strange in the East; they are proud without insolence, and look manly without blustering. Their walk partakes somewhat of the nature of a strut, owing, perhaps, to the shape of the sandals, not a little assisted by the self-esteem of the wearer, but there is nothing offensive in it; moreover, the population has a healthy appearance, and, fresh from Egypt, I could not help noticing their freedom from ophthalmic disease. The children, too, appear vigorous, nor are they here kept in that state of filth to which fear of the Evil Eye devotes them in the Valley of the Nile.

My companions found me in a coffee-house, where I had sat down to rest from the fatigue of halting on my wounded foot through the town. They had passed their boxes through the custom-house, and were now inquiring 'Where's the Effendi?' in all directions. After sitting for half an hour, we rose to depart, when an old Arab merchant whom I had met at Suez, politely insisted upon paying for my coffee, still a mark of attention in Arabia as it was whilome in France. We then went to a Wakaleh, near the bazar, in which my companions had secured an airy upper room on the terrace opposite the sea, and tolerably free from Yambu's plague, the flies. It had been tenanted by a party of travellers, who were introduced to me as Umar Effendi's brothers; he had by accident met them in the streets the day before their start for Constantinople, where they were travelling to receive the Ikram. The family was, as I have said before, from Daghistan (Circassia), and the male members still showed unequivocal signs of a northern origin, in light yellowish skins, grey eyes fringed with dark lashes, red lips, and a very scant beard. They were broad-shouldered, large-limbed men, distinguished in look only by a peculiar surliness of countenance; perhaps their expression was the result of their suspecting me; for I observed them watching every movement narrowly during Wuzu and prayers. There was a good opportunity for displaying the perfect nonchalance of a true believer, and my efforts were, I believe, successful, for afterwards they seemed to treat me as a mere stranger, from whom they could expect nothing, and who therefore was hardly worth their notice.

On the afternoon of the day of our arrival we sent for a Mukharrij, and began to treat for camels. One Amm Jemal, a respectable native of El Medinah who was on his way home, undertook to be the spokesman: after a long palaver (for the Shaykh of the camels and his attendant Bedouins were men that fought for farthings, and we were not far inferior to them) a bargain was struck. We agreed to pay three dollars for each camel, half in ready money, the other half after reaching our destination, and to start on the evening of the next day with a grain-caravan, guarded by an escort of irregular cavalry. I hired two animals, one for my luggage and servant, the other for the boy Mohammed and myself, expressly stipulating, that we were to ride the better beast, and that if it broke down on the road, its place should be supplied by another as good. My friends could not dissemble their uneasiness, when informed by the Mukharrij, that the Hazimi tribe was 'out', and that travellers had to fight every day. The Daghistanis also contributed to their alarm. 'We met', said they, 'between 200 and 300 devils on a Razzia near El Medinah; we gave them the Salam, but they would not reply, although we were all on dromedaries. Then they asked us if we were men of El Medinah, and we replied "Yes", and lastly, they wanted to know the end of our journey; so we said Bir Abbas.' The Bedouins who had accompanied the Daghistanis belonged to some tribe unconnected with the Hazimi: the spokesman rolled his head, as much as to say, 'Allah has preserved us!' And a young Indian of the party – I shrewdly suspect him of having stolen my pen-knife that night – displayed the cowardice of a 'Miyan', by looking aghast at the memory of his imminent and deadly risk. 'Sir', said Shaykh Nur to me, 'we must wait till all this is over'. I told him to hold his tongue, and sharply reproved the boy Mohammed, upon whose manner the effect of finding himself suddenly in a fresh country had wrought a change for the worse. 'Why, ye were lions at Cairo – and here, at Yambu, you are cats – hens!' It was not long, however, before the youth's impudence returned upon him with increased violence.

We sat through the afternoon in the little room on the terrace, whose reflected heat, together with the fiery winds from the wilderness, seemed to incommode even my companions. After sunset we dined in the open air, a body of twenty: master, servants, children and strangers. All the procurable rugs and pillows had been seized to make a Divan, and we all squatted round a large cauldron of boiled rice, containing square masses of mutton, the whole covered with clarified butter. Saad the Devil was now in his glory. With what anecdotes the occasion supplied him! His tongue seemed to wag with a perpetual motion, for each man he had a boisterous greeting, and to judge from his whisperings he must have been in everyone's privacy and confidence. Conversation over pipes and coffee was prolonged to 10 p.m., a late hour in these lands; then we prayed the Isha, and, spreading our mats upon the terrace, slept in the open air.

The forenoon of the next day was occupied in making sundry small purchases. We laid in seven days' provisions for the journey, repacked our boxes, polished and loaded our arms, and attired ourselves appropriately for the road. By the advice of Amm Jemal I dressed as an Arab, in order to avoid paying the Jizyat, a capitation tax, which upon this road the settled tribes extort from stranger travellers; and he warned me not to speak any language but Arabic, even to my slave, in the vicinity of a village. I bought for my own conveyance a Shugduf or litter for which I paid two dollars. It is a vehicle appropriated to women and children, fathers of families, married men, 'Shelebis', Exquisites, and generally to those who are too effeminate to ride. My reason for choosing it was that notes are more easily taken in it than on a dromedary's back; the excuse of lameness prevented it detracting from my manhood, and I was careful when entering any populous place to borrow or hire a saddled beast.

Our party dined early that day, for the camels had been sitting at the gate since noon. We had the usual trouble in loading them: the owners of the animals vociferating about the unconscionable weight, the owners of the goods swearing that such weight a child could carry, while the beasts, taking part with their proprietors, moaned piteously, roared, made vicious attempts to bite, and started up with an agility that threw the half secured boxes or sacks headlong to the ground. About 3 p.m. all was ready – the camels formed into Indian file, and were placed standing in the streets – but, as usual with Oriental travellers, all the men dispersed about the town, so we did not mount before it was late in the afternoon.

I must now take the liberty of presenting to the reader an Arab Shaykh fully equipped for travelling. Nothing can be more picturesque than the costume, and it is with regret that we see it exchanged in the towns and more civilised parts for any other. The long locks or the shaven scalps are surmounted by a white cotton skull-cap, over which is a Kufiyah – a large square kerchief of silk and cotton mixed, and generally of a dull red color with a bright yellow border, from which depend crimson silk twists ending in little tassels that reach the wearers waist. Doubled into a triangle, and bound with an Aakal or fillet of rope, a skein of yarn or a twist of wool, the kerchief fits the head close behind: it projects over the forehead, shading the eyes, and giving a fierce look to the countenance. On certain occasions one end is brought round the lower part of the face, and is fastened behind the head. This veiling the features is technically called Lisam: the chiefs generally fight so, and it is the usual disguise when a man fears the avenger of blood, or a woman starts to take her Sar. In hot weather it is supposed to keep the Simoon, in cold weather the catarrh, from the lungs.

The body dress is simply a Kamis or cotton shirt; tight sleeved, opening in front, and adorned round the waist and collar, and down the breast, with embroidery like network, it extends from neck to foot. Some wear wide trousers, but the Bedouins consider such things effeminate, and they have not yet fallen into the folly of socks and stockings. Over the Kamis is thrown a long skirted and short-sleeved cloak of camel's hair, called an Aba. It is made in many patterns, and of all materials from pure silk to coarse sheep's wool; some prefer it brown, others white, others striped: in El Hejaz the favourite Aba is white, embroidered with gold, tinsel, or yellow thread in two large triangles, capped with broad bands and other figures running down the shoulders and sides of the back. It is lined inside the shoulders and breast with handsome stuffs of silk and cotton mixed, and is tied in front by elaborate strings, and tassels or acorns of silk and gold. A sash confines the Kamis at the waist, and supports the silver-hilled Jambiyah or crooked dagger, and the picturesque Arab sandal, complete the costume. Finally, the Shaykh's arms are a matchlock slung behind his back, and a sword; in his right band he carries a light crooked stick about two feet and a half long, called a Mashab, used for guiding camels, or a short javelin.

The poorer clans of Arabs twist round their waist, next to the skin, a long plait of greasy leather, to support the back, and they gird the shirt at the middle merely with a cord, or with a coarse sash. The dagger is stuck in this scarf, and a bandoleer slung over the shoulders carries their cartridge-case, powder-flask, flint and steel, priming-horn, and other necessaries. With the traveller, the waist is an elaborate affair. Below all is worn the money-pouch, concealed by the Kamis; the latter is girt with a waist shawl, over which is strapped a leathern belt. The latter article should always be well garnished with a pair of long-barrelled and silver-mounted flint pistols, a large and a small dagger, and an iron ramrod with pincers inside; a little leathern pouch fastened to the waist-strap on the right side contains cartridge, wadding, and priming powder.

The sword hangs over the shoulder with crimson silk cords and huge tassels: well-dressed men apply the same showy ornaments to their pistols. In the hand may be carried a bell-mouthed blunderbuss, or, better still, a long single-barrel gun with an ounce bore. All these weapons must shine like silver, if you wish to be respected; for the knightly care of arms is here a sign of manliness.

Pilgrims, especially those from Turkey, carry a 'Ha-mail', to denote their holy errand. This is a pocket Koran, in a handsome gold-embroidered crimson velvet or red morocco case, slung by red silk cords over the left shoulder. It must hang down by the right side, and should never depend below the waist-belt. For this I substituted a most useful article. To all appearance a 'Hamail', it had inside three compartments, one for my watch and compass, the second for ready money, and the third contained penknife, pencils, and slips of paper, which I could hold concealed in the hollow of my hand. These were for writing and drawing: opportunities of making a 'fair copy' into the diary-book, are never wanting to the acute traveller. He must, however, beware of sketching before the Bedouins, who would certainly proceed to extreme measures, suspecting him to be a spy or a sorcerer. Nothing so effectually puzzles these people as our habit of putting everything on paper; their imaginations are set at work, and then the worst may be expected from them. The only safe way of writing in presence of a Bedouin would be when drawing out a horoscope or preparing a charm; he also objects not, if you can warm his heart upon the subject, to seeing you take notes in a book of genealogies. You might begin with, 'And you, men of Harb, on what origin do you pride yourselves?' And while the listeners became fluent upon the, to them, all interesting theme, you could put down whatever you please upon the margin. The towns-people are more liberal, and years ago the holy shrines have been drawn, surveyed, and even lithographed, by Eastern artists: still, if you wish to avoid all suspicion, you must rarely be seen with pen or with pencil in hand.

At 6 p.m. descending the stairs of our Wakaleh, we found the camels standing loaded in the street and shifting their ground in token of impatience. My Shugduf, perched upon the back of a tall strong animal, nodded and swayed about with his every motion, impressing me with the idea that the first step would throw it over the shoulders or the crupper. The camel-men told me I must climb up the animal's neck, and so creep into the vehicle. But my foot disabling me from such exertion, I insisted upon their bringing the beast to squat, which they did grumblingly. We took leave of Umar Effendi's brothers and their dependents, who insisted upon paying us the compliment of accompanying us to the gate. Then we mounted and started, which was a signal for all our party to disperse once more. Some heard the report of a vessel having arrived from Suez, with Mahommod Shilibha and other friends on board; these hurried down to the harbour for a parting word. Others, declaring they had forgotten some necessaries for the way, ran off to the bazar to spend one last hour in gossip at the coffee-house. Then the sun set, and prayers must be said. The brief twilight had almost faded away before all had mounted. With loud cries of 'Wassit, ya hu!' and "Jannib, y'al Jammal!' we threaded our way through long, dusty, narrow streets, flanked with white-washed habitations at considerable intervals, and large heaps of rubbish, sometimes higher than the houses. We were stopped at the gate to ascertain if we were strangers, in which case, the guard would have done his best to extract a few piastres before allowing our luggage to pass; but he soon perceived by my companions' accent, that they were sons of the Holy City, consequently, that the case was hopeless. While standing here, Shaykh Hamid vaunted the strong walls and turrets of Yambu, which he said were superior to those of Jeddah: they kept Saud, the Wahhabi, at bay in A.D. 1802, but would scarcely, I should say, resist a field battery in A.D. 1853. The moon rose fair and clear, dazzling us with light as we emerged from the shadowy streets, and when we launched into tho Desert the sweet air delightfully contrasted with the close offensive atmosphere of the town. My companions, as Arabs will do on such occasions, began to sing.

CHAP. XII

From Yambu To Bir Abbas

On the 18th July, about 7 p.m., we passed through the gate of Yambu, and took a due easterly course. Our route lay over the plain between the mountains of Radhwah on the left, and the sea on the right hand; the land was desert, that is to say, a hard level plain, strewed with rounded lumps of granite and greenstone schist, with here and there a dwarf Acacia, and a tuft of rank camel grass. By the light of a glorious moon, nearly at the full, I was able to see the country tolerably well.

Our little party consisted of twelve camels, and we travelled in Indian file, head tied to tail, with but one out-rider, Umar Effendi, whose rank required him to mount a dromedary with showy trappings. Immediately in front of me was Amm Jemal, whom I had to reprove for asking the boy Mahommed 'Where have you picked up that Hindi (Indian)?' 'Are we, the Afghans, the Indian-slayers, become Indians?' I vociferated with indignation, and brought the thing home to his feelings, by asking him how he, an Arab, would like to be called an Egyptian – a Fellah? The rest of the party was behind, sitting or dozing upon the rough platforms made by the lids of the two huge boxes slung to the sides of their camels. Only one old woman, El Sitt Maryam (the lady Mary), returning to

El Medinah, her adopted country, after a visit to a sister at Cairo, allowed herself the luxury of a half dollar Shibriyah or cot, fastened crosswise over the animal's load. Moreover, all the party, except Umar Effendi, in token of poverty, were dressed in the coarsest and dirtiest of clothes – the general suit consisting of a shirt torn in divers places and a bit of rag wrapped round the head. They carried short chibouques without mouth-pieces, and tobacco-pouches of greasy leather. Though the country hereabouts is perfectly safe, all had their arms in readiness, and the unusual silence that succeeded to the singing (even Saad the Devil held his tongue) was sufficient to show how much they feared for themselves and their property. After a slow march of two hours facing the moon, we turned somewhat towards the N.E., and began to pass over undulating ground, in which a steady rise was perceptible. We arrived at the halting-place at three in the morning after a short march of about eight hours, during which we could not have passed over more than sixteen miles. The camels were 'nakh'd'; the boxes were taken off and piled together as a precaution against invisible robbers; my little tent, the only one in the party, was pitched; we then spread our rugs upon the ground and lay down to sleep.

We arose at about 9 a.m., and after congratulating one another upon being once more in the 'dear Desert', we proceeded in exhilarated mood to light the fire for pipes and breakfast. The meal – a biscuit, a little rice, and a cup of milkless tea – was soon despatched, after which I proceeded to inspect our position.

About a mile to the westward lay the little village of Musahhal, a group of miserable mud hovels. On the south was a strip of bright blue sea, and all around, an iron plain producing naught but stones and grass-hoppers, bounded northward by a grisly wall of blackish rock. Here and there a shrub fit only for fuel, or a tuft of coarse grass, crisp with heat, met the eye. All was sun-parched ; the furious heat from above was drying up the sap and juice of the land, as the shivering and quivering atmosphere showed; moreover the heavy dews of these regions, forming in large drops upon the plants and stones, concentrate the morning rays upon them like a system of burning-glasses. After making these few observations I followed the example of my companions, and went to sleep.

At 2 p.m. we were roused to a dinner as simple as the breakfast had been. Boiled rice with an abundance of clarified butter, in which Easterns delight, some fragments of Kahk, and stale bread and a handful of stoned and pressed date-paste, called Ajwah, formed the menu. Our potations began before dinner with a vile-tasted but wholesome drink called Akit; at the meal we drank leather-flavoured water, and ended with a large cupful of scalding tea. Enormous quantities of liquid were consumed, for the sun seemed to have got into our throats, and the perspiration trickled from us as after a shower of rain. Whilst we were eating, a Bedouin woman passed close by the tent, leading a flock of sheep and goats, seeing which I expressed a desire to drink milk. My companions sent by one of the camel-men a bit of bread, and asked in exchange for a cupful of 'laban'. Thus I learned that the Arabs, even in this corrupt region, still adhere to the meaningless custom of their ancestors, who chose to make the term 'Labban' (milk-seller) an opprobrium and a disgrace. Possibly the origin of the prejudice might be the recognising of a traveller's guest-right to call for milk gratis. However this may be, no one will in the present day sell this article of consumption, even at civilised

Meccah, except Egyptians, a people supposed to be utterly without honor. As a general rule in the Hejaz, milk abounds in the spring, but at all other times of the year it is difficult to be procured. The Bedouin woman managed, however, to send me back a cupful.

At 3 p.m. we were ready to start, and all saw, with unspeakable gratification, a huge black nimbus rise from the shoulder of Mount Radhwah, and range itself, like a good Genius, between us and our terrible foe, the sun. We hoped that it contained rain, but presently a blast of hot wind, like the breath of a volcano, blew over the plain, and the air was filled with particles of sand. This is the 'dry storm' of Arabia; it appears to depend upon some electrical phenomena which it would be desirable to investigate. When we had loaded and mounted, my coachmen, two in number, came up to the Shugduf and demanded 'Bakhshish', which, it appears, they are now in the habit of doing each time the traveller starts. I was at first surprised to find the word here, but after a few days of Bedouin society, my wonder diminished. The men were Beni-Harb of the great Hejazi tribe, which has kept its blood pure for the last thirteen centuries – how much more we know not – but they had been corrupted by intercourse with pilgrims, retaining none of their ancestral qualities but greed of gain, revengefulness, pugnacity, and a frantic kind of bravery, displayed on rare occasions. Their nobility, however, did not prevent my quoting the Prophet's saying, 'Of a truth, the worst names among the Arabs are the Beni-Kalb and the Beni-Harb', whilst I taunted them severely with their resemblance to the Fellahs of Egypt. They would have resented this with asperity, had it proceeded from their own people, but the Turkish pilgrim – the character in which they knew me, despite my Arab dress – is a privileged person.

Their outer man was contemptible; small chocolate-colored beings, stunted and thin, with mops of coarse bushy hair burned brown by the sun, straggling beards, vicious eyes, frowning brows, screaming voices, and well-made, but attenuated, limbs. On their heads were Kufiyahs (kerchiefs) in the last stage of wear; a tattered shirt, indigo-dyed, and girt with a bit of common rope, composed their clothing; and their feet were protected from the stones by soles of thick leather, kept in place by narrow thongs tied to the ancle. Both were armed, one with a matchlock, and a Shintiyan in a leathern scabbard, slung over the shoulder, the other with a Nebut, and both showed at the waist the Arab's invariable companion, the Jambiyah (dagger). These ragged fellows, however, had their pride. They would eat with me, and not disdain, like certain self-styled Caballeros, to ask for more, but of work they would do none. No promise of 'Bakhshish', potent as the spell of that word is, would induce them to assist in pitching my tent; they even expected Shaykh Nur to cook for them, and I had almost to use violence, for even the just excuse of a sore foot was insufficient to procure the privilege of mounting my Shugduf while the camel was sitting. It was, they said, the custom of the country from time immemorial to use a ladder when legs would not act. I agreed with them, but objected that I had no ladder. At last, wearied with their thick-headedness, I snatched the camel's string, and by main force made him kneel.

Our party was now strong enough. We had about 200 camels carrying grain, attended by their proprietors, truculent looking as the contrabandistas of the Pyrenees. The escort was composed of seven Irregular Turkish cavalry, tolerably mounted, and supplied each with an armoury in epitome. They were privily derided by our party, who, being Arabs, had a sneaking fondness for the Bedouins, however loth they might be to see them amongst the boxes.

For three hours we travelled in a south-easterly direction upon a hard plain and a sandy flat, on which several waters from the highlands find a passage to the sea west-ward. Gradually we were siding towards the mountains, and at sunset I observed that we had sensibly neared them. We dismounted for a short halt, and, strangers being present, my companions before sitting down to smoke said their prayers – a pious exercise in which they did not engage for three days afterwards, when they met certain acquaintances at El Hamra. As evening came on, we emerged from a scrub of Acacias and tamarisk and turned due east, traversing an open country with a perceptible rise. Scarcely was it dark before the cry of 'Harami' (thieves) rose loud in the rear, causing such confusion as one may see in a boat in the Bay of Naples when suddenly neared by a water-spout. All the camel-men brandished their huge staves, and rushed back vociferating in the direction of the robbers. They were followed by the horsemen, and truly, had the thieves possessed the usual acuteness of the profession, they might have driven off the camels in our van with safety and convenience. But these contemptible beings were only half a dozen in number, and they had lighted their match-locks, which drew a bullet or two in their direction, whereupon they ran away. This incident aroused no inconsiderable excitement, for it seemed ominous of worse things about to happen to us when entangled in the hills, and the faces of my companions, perfect barometers of fair and foul tidings, fell to zero. For nine hours we journeyed through a brilliant moonlight, and as the first grey streak appeared in the Eastern sky we entered a scanty 'Misyal', or Fiumara, strewed with pebbles and rounded stones, about half a mile in breadth, and flanked by almost perpendicular hills of primitive formation. I began by asking the names of peaks and other remarkable spots, when I found that a folio volume would not contain a three months' collection: every hill and dale, flat, valley, and water-course here has its proper name or rather names. The ingenuity shown by the Bedouins in distinguishing between localities the most similar, is the result of a high organisation of the perceptive faculties, perfected by the practice of observing a recurrence of landscape features few in number and varying but little amongst themselves. After travelling two hours up this torrent bed, winding in an easterly direction, and crossing some 'Harrah', or ridges of rook, and 'Ria', steep descents, we found ourselves at 8 a.m., after a march of about thirty-four miles, at Bir Said (Said's well), our destination.

I had been led to expect a pastoral scene, wild flowers, flocks and flowing waters at the 'well'; so I looked with a jaundiced eye upon a deep hole full of slightly brackish water dug in a tamped hollow – a kind of punch-bowl with granite walls, upon whose grim surface a few thorns of exceeding hardihood braved the sun for a season. Not a house was in sight – it was as barren and desolate a spot as the sun ever 'viewed in his wide career'. But this is what the Arabian traveller must expect. He is to traverse, for instance, a Yale of Flowers. He indulges in sweet recollections of Indian lakes beautiful with the lotus, and Persian plains upon which Narcissus is the meanest of grasses. He sees a plain like tamp-work, where knobs of granite act daisies, and at every fifty yards some hapless bud or blossom dying of inanition among the stones.

The sun scorched our feet as we planted the tent, and, after drinking our breakfast, we passed the usual day of perspiration and semi-lethargy. In discomfort man naturally hails a change, even though it be one from bad to worse. When our enemy began slanting towards the west, we felt ready enough to proceed on our journey. The camels were laden shortly after 3 p.m., and we started with water jars in our hands through a storm of Simoom.

We travelled five hours in a north-easterly course up a diagonal valley, through a country fantastic in its desolation – a mass of huge hills, barren plains, and desert vales. Even the sturdy Acacias here failed, and in some places the camel grass could not find earth enough to take root in. The road wound among mountains, rocks and hills of granite, over broken ground, flanked by huge blocks and boulders, piled up as if man's art had aided Nature to disfigure herself. Vast clefts seamed like scars the hideous face of earth; here they widened into dark caves, there they were choked up with glistening drift sand. Not a bird or a beast was to be seen or heard; their presence would have argued the vicinity of water, and though my companions opined that Bedouins were lurking among the rocks, I decided that these Bedouins were the creatures of their fears. Above, a sky like polished blue steel with a tremendous blaze of yellow light glared upon us without the thinnest veil of mist cloud. The distant prospect, indeed, was more attractive than the near view, because it borrowed a bright azure tinge from the intervening atmosphere; but the jagged peaks and the perpendicular streaks of shadow down the flanks of the mountainous background showed that, no change for the better was yet in store for us.

Between 10 and 11 p.m., we reached human habitations – a phenomenon unseen since we left

Musahhal – in the long straggling village called El Hamra, from the redness of the sands near which it is built, or El Wasitah, the 'half-way' village, because it. is the middle station between Yambu and El Medinah. It is therefore considerably out of place in Burckhardt's map, and those who copy from him make it about half-way nearer the seaport than it really is. We wandered about nearly an hour in search of an encamping place, for the surly villagers ordered us off every flatter bit of ground, without, however, deigning to show us where the jaded beasts might rest. At last, after much wrangling, we found the usual spot; the camels were unloaded, the boxes and baggage were disposed in a circle for greater security against the petty pilferers in which this part of the road abounds, and my companions spread their rugs so as to sleep upon their valuables. I was invited to follow the general example, but I absolutely declined the vicinity of so many steaming and snoring fellow-travellers. Some wonder was excited by the Afghan Haji's obstinacy and recklessness; but resistance to these people is sometimes bien placé, and a man from Cabool is allowed to say and to do strange things. In answer to their warnings of nightly peril I placed a drawn sword by my side and a cocked pistol under my pillow; the saddle-bag, a carpet spread upon the cool loose sand, formed by no means an uncomfortable couch, and upon it I enjoyed a sound sleep till day-break.

Rising at dawn, I proceeded to visit the village. It is built upon a narrow shelf at the top of a precipitous hill to the North, and on the South runs a sandy Fiumara about half a mile broad. On all sides are rocks and mountains rough and stony; so you find yourself in another of those punch-bowls which the Arabs seem to consider choice sites for settlements. The Fiumara, which hereabouts is very winding, threads the high grounds all the way down from the plateau of El Medinah, and during the rainy season it becomes a raging torrent, carrying westwards to the Red Sea the drainage of a hundred hills. Water of good quality is readily found in it by digging a few feet below the surface at the angles where the stream as it runs forms the deepest hollows, and in some places the stony sides give out bubbling springs.

El Hamra itself is a collection of stunted houses or rather hovels, made of unbaked brick and mud, roofed over with palm leaves, and pierced with air-holes, which occasionally boast a bit of plank for a shutter. It appears thickly populated in the parts where the walls are standing, but, like all settlements in El Hejaz, it abounds in ruins, it is well supplied with provisions, which are here cheaper than at El Medinah – a circumstance that induced Saad the Devil to overload his hapless camel with a sack of wheat. In the village are a few shops where grain, huge plantains, ready-made bread, rice, clarified butter, and other edibles are to be purchased. Palm orchards of considerable extent supply it with dates. The bazar is, like the generality of such places in the Eastern villages, a long lane, here covered with matting, there open to the sun, and the streets – if they may be so called – though narrow are full of dust and glare. Near the encamping ground of caravans is a fort for the officer commanding a troop of Albanian cavalry, whose duty it is to defend the village, to hold the country, and to escort merchant travellers. The building consists of an outer wall of hewn stone, loopholed for musketry, and surmounted by 'Shararif' – 'remparts coquets' – about as useful against artillery as the sugar gallery round a twelfth-cake. Nothing would be easier than to take the place: a false attack would draw off the attention of the defenders, who in these latitudes know nothing of sentry-duty, whilst scaling-ladders or a bag full of powder would command a ready entrance into the other side. Around the El Hamra fort are clusters of palm-leaf huts, where the soldiery lounge and smoke, and near it the usual coffee-house, a shed kept by an Albanian. These places are frequented probably on account of the intense heat inside the fort.

We passed a comfortless day at the 'Red Village'. Large flocks of sheep and goats were being driven in and out of the place, but their surly shepherds would give no milk, even in exchange for bread and meat. The morning was spent in watching certain Bedouins, who, matchlock in hand, had climbed the hills in pursuit of a troop of cranes: not one bird was hit of the many fired at – a circumstance which did not say much for their vaunted marksmanship. Before breakfast I bought a moderately sized sheep for a dollar. Shaykh Hamid 'halaled' it, according to rule, and my companions soon prepared a feast of boiled mutton. But that sheep proved a 'bone of contention'. The boy Mohammed had, in a fit of economy, sold its head to a Bedouin for three piastres, and the others, disappointed in their anticipations of haggis, lost temper. With the Devil's voluble tongue, and impudent countenance in the van, they opened such a volley of raillery and sarcasm upon the young 'tripe-seller', that he in his turn became excited – furious. I had some difficulty to keep the peace, for it did not suit my interests that they should quarrel. But to do the Arabs justice, nothing is easier for a man who knows them than to work upon their good feelings. 'He is a stranger in your country – a guest!' acted as a charm; they listened patiently to Mohammed's gross abuse, only promising to answer him when in his land, that is to say, near Meccah.

But what especially soured our day was the report that Saad, the great robber-chief, and his brother were in the field; consequently that our march would be delayed for some time: every half-hour some fresh tattle from the camp or the coffee-house added fuel to the fire of our impatience.

A few particulars about this Schinderhans of El Hejaz may not be unacceptable. He is the chief of the Sumaydah and the Mahamid, two influential sub-families of the Hamidah, the principal family of the Beni-Harb tribe of Bedouins, He therefore aspired to rule all the Hamidah, and through them the Beni-Harb, in which ease he would have been, de facto, monarch of the Holy Land. But the Sherif of Meccah, and Ahmed Pacha, the Turkish governor of the chief city, for some political reason degraded him, and raised up a rival in the person of Shaykh Fahd, another ruffian of a similar stamp, who calls himself chief of the Beni-Amr, the third sub-family of the Hamidah family. Hence all kinds of confusion. Saad's people, who number it is said 5,000, resent, with Arab asperity, the insult offered to their chief, and beat Fahd's, who do not amount to 800. Fahd, supported by the government, cuts off Saad's supplies. Both are equally wild and reckless, and – nowhere doth the glorious goddess, Liberty, show a more brazen face than in this Eastern 'Inviolate land of the brave and the free'. Both seize the opportunity of shooting troopers, of plundering travellers, and of closing the roads. This state of things continued till I left the Hejaz, when the Sherif of Meccah proposed, it was said, to take the field in person against the arch-robber. And, as will afterwards be seen in these pages, Saad, because the Pachas of El Medinah and of the Damascus caravan would not guarantee his restitution to his former dignity, had the audacity to turn back the

Sultan's Mahmal – the ensign of Imperial power – and to shut the road against its cortege. That such vermin is allowed to exist proves the imbecility of the Turkish government. The Sultan pays pensions in corn and cloth to the very chiefs who arm their varlets against him, and the Pachas, after purloining all they can, hand over to their enemies the means of resistance. It is more than probable, that Abdul Mejid has never heart) a word of truth concerning El Hejaz, and that fulsome courtiers persuade him that men there tremble at his name. His government, however, is desirous, if report speaks truth, of thrusting El Hejaz upon the Egyptian, who on his side would willingly pay a large sum to avert such a calamity. The Holy Land drains off Turkish gold and blood in abundance, and the lords of the country hold in it a contemptible position. If they catch a thief, they dare not hang him. They must pay black mail, and yet be shot at in every pass. They affect superiority over the Arabs, hate them, and are despised by them. Such in El Hejaz are the effects of the charter of Gulkhanch, a panacea like Holloway's pills for all the evils to which Turkish, Arab, Syrian, Greek, Egyptian, Persian, Armenian, Kurd, and Albanian flesh is heir to. Such the results of the Tanzimat, the silliest copy of Europe's folly – bureaucracy and centralisation – that the pen of empirical statecraft ever traced. Under a strong-handed and strong-hearted despotism, like Mohammed Ali's, El Hejaz, in one generation, might be purged of its pests. By a proper use of the blood feud, by vigorously supporting the weaker against the stronger classes, by regularly defeating every Bedouin who earned a name for himself, and, above all, by the exercise of unsparing, unflinching, justice, the few thousands of half naked bandits, who now make the land a fighting field, would soon sink into utter insignificance. But to effect such end, the Turks require the old stratocracy, which, bloody as it was, worked with far less misery than the charter and the new code. What Milton calls 'The solid rule of civil government' has done wonders for the race that nurtured and brought to perfection an idea spontaneous to their organisation. But the world has yet to learn that the admirable exotic will thrive amongst the country gentlemen of Monomotapa or the ragged nobility of El Hejaz.

Saad, the old man of the mountains, was described to me as a little brown Bedouin, contemptible in appearance, but remarkable for courage and ready wit. He has a keen scent for treachery, and requires to keep it in exercise. A blood feud with Abdel Muttalib, the present Sherif of Meccah, who slew his nephew, and the hostility of several Sultans has rendered his life an eventful one. He lost all his teeth by poison, which would have killed him, had he not in mistake, after swallowing the potion, corrected it by drinking off a large pot-full of clarified butter. Since that time he has lived entirely upon fruits, which he gathers for himself, and coffee which he prepares with his own hand. In Sultan Mahmud's time he received from Constantinople a gorgeous purse, which he was told to open himself, as it contained something for his private inspection. Suspecting treachery, he gave it for this purpose to a slave, bidding him carry it to some distance; the bearer was shot by a pistol cunningly fixed, like Rob Roy's, in the folds of the hag. But whether this well-known story be 'true or only well found', it is certain that Shaykh Saad now fears the Turks, even when they bring gifts. The Sultan sends, or is supposed to send him presents of fine horses, robes of honor, and a large quantity of grain. But the Shaykh, trusting to his hills rather than to steeds, sells them; he gives away the dresses to his slaves, and distributes the grain among his clansmen. Of his character men tell two tales: some praise his charity, and call him the friend of the poor, as certainly as he is a foe to the rich. Others on the contrary describe him as cruel, cold-blooded, and notably, even among Arabs, revengeful and avaricious. The truth probably lies between these two extremes, but I observed that those of my companions who spoke most highly of the robber chief when at a distance seemed to be in the sudori freddi whilst under the shadow of his hills.

El Hamra is the third station from El Medinah in the Darb Sultani – the Sultan's or High Road – the westerly line leading to Meccah along the sea coast. When the robbers permit, the pilgrims prefer this route on account of its superior climate, the facility of procuring water and supplies, the vicinity of the sea, and the circumstance of its passing through 'Bedr', the scene of the Prophet's principal military exploits. After mid-day (on the 21st July), when we had made up our minds that fate had determined we should halt at El Hamra, a caravan arrived from Meccah, and the new travellers had interest, to procure an escort, and permission to proceed towards El Medinah without delay. The good news filled us with joy. A little after 4 p.m. we urged our panting camels over the fiery sands to join the Meccans, who were standing ready for the march, on the other side of the torrent bed, and at 5 we started in an easterly direction.

My companions had found friends and relations in the Meccan caravan – the boy Mohammed's elder brother, about whom more anon, was of the number; – they were full of news and excitement. At sunset they prayed with unction: even Saad and Hamid had not the face to sit their camels during the halt, when all around were washing, sanding themselves, and busy with their devotions. We then ate our suppers, remounted, and started once more. Shortly after night set in, we came to a sudden halt. A dozen different reports rose to account for this circumstance, which was occasioned by a band of Bedouins, who had manned a gorge, and sent forward a 'parliamentary' ordering us forthwith to slop. They at first demanded money to let us pass; but at last, hearing that we were sons of the Holy cities, they granted us transit on the sole Condition that the military, – whom they, like Irish peasants, hate and fear – should return to whence they came. Upon this, our escort, 200 men, wheeled their horses round and galloped back to their barracks. We moved onwards, without, however, seeing any robbers; my camel-man pointed out their haunts, and showed me a small bird hovering over a place where he supposed water trickled from the rock. The fellow had attempted a sneer at my expense when the fray was impending. 'Why don't you load your pistols, Effendi', he cried, 'and get out of your litter, and show light?' 'Because', I replied as loudly, 'in my country, when dogs run at us, we thrash them with sticks'. This stopped Mansur's mouth for a time, but he and I were never friends. Like the lowest orders of Orientals he required to be ill-treated; gentleness and condescension he seemed to consider a proof of cowardice or of imbecility. I began with kindness, but was soon compelled to use hard words at first, and then threats, which, though he heard them with frowns and mutterings, produced manifest symptoms of improvement. 'Oignez vilain, il vous poindra! Poignez vilain, il vous oindra!' says the old French proverb, and the axiom is more valuable in the East even than in the West.

Our night's journey had no other incident. We travelled over rising ground with the moon full in our faces, and about midnight passed through another long straggling line of villages, called Jadaydah, or El Khayf. The principal part of it lies on the left of the road going to El Medinah; it has a fort like that of El Hamra, springs of tolerable drinking water, a Nakhil or date ground, and a celebrated (dead) saint, Abd el Rahim el Burai. A little beyond it lies the Bughaz, or defile, where in A.D. 1811 Tussun Bey and his 8,000 Turks were totally defeated by 25,000 Harbi Bedouins and Wahhabis. This is a famous attacking point of the Beni-Harb. In former times both Jezzar Pacha, the celebrated 'butcher' of Syria, and Abdullah Pacha of Damascus, were baffled at the gorge of Jadaydah; and this year the commander of the Syrian caravan, afraid of risking an attack at a place so ill-omened, avoided it by marching upon Meccah by the desert of Nejd. At 4 a.m., having travelled about twenty-four miles due east, we encamped at Bir Abbas.

CHAP. XIII

From Bir Abbas To
El Medinah

The 22nd of July was a grand trial of temper to our little party. The position of Bir Abbas exactly resembles that of El Hamra, except that the bulge of the hill-girt Fiumara is at this place about two miles wide. There are the usual stone forts and palm-leaved hovels for the troopers, stationed here to hold the place and to escort travellers, with a coffee-shed, and a hut or two, called a bazar, but no village. Our encamping ground was a bed of loose sand, with which the violent Simoom filled the air: not a tree or a bush was in sight; a species of hardy locust and swarms of flies were the only remnants of animal life: the scene was a caricature of Sindh. Although we were now some hundred feet, to judge by the water-shed, above the level of the sea, the mid-day sun scorched even through the tent; our frail tenement was more than once blown down, and the heat of the sand made the work of repitching it painful. Again my companions, after breakfasting, hurried to the coffee-house, and returned one after the other with dispiriting reports. Then they either quarrelled desperately about nothing, or they threw themselves on their rugs, pretending to sleep for very sulkiness. The Lady Maryam soundly rated her surly son, for refusing to fill her chibouque for the twelfth time that morning, with the usual religious phrases, 'Ali direct thee into the right way, O my son!' – meaning that he was going to the bad – and 'O my calamity, thy mother is a lone woman, O Allah!' – equivalent to the European parental plaint about grey hairs being brought down in sorrow to the grave. Before noon a small Caravan which followed us came in with two dead bodies – a trooper shot by the Bedouins, and an Albanian killed by sun-stroke, or the fiery wind. Shortly after mid-day a Cafila, travelling in an opposite direction, passed by us; it was composed chiefly of Indian pilgrims, habited in correct costume, and hurrying towards Meccah in hot haste. They had been allowed to pass unmolested, because probably a pound sterling could not have been collected from a hundred pockets, and Saad the Robber sometimes does a cheap good deed. But our party having valuables with them did not seem to gather heart from this event. In the evening we all went out to see some Arab Shaykhs who were travelling to Bir Abbas in order to receive their salaries. Without such douceurs, it is popularly said and believed, no stone walls could enable a Turk to hold El Hejaz against the hill-men. Such was our system in Afghanistan – most unwise, teaching in limine the subject to despise rulers subject to black-mail. Besides which these highly paid Shaykhs do no good. When a fight takes place or a road is shut, they profess inability to restrain their clansmen, and the richer they are, of course the more formidable they become. The party looked well; they were Harb, dignified old men in the picturesque Arab costume, with erect forms, fierce thin features, and white beards, well armed, and mounted upon high-bred and handsomely equipped dromedaries from El Shark. Preceded by their half-naked clansmen, carrying spears twelve or thirteen feet long, garnished with single or double tufts of black ostrich feathers, and ponderous matchlocks, which were discharged on approaching the fort, they were not without a kind of barbaric pomp.

Immediately after the reception of these Shaykhs, there was a parade of the Arnaut Irregular Horse. About 500 of them rode out to the sound of a Nukus or little kettle-drum, whose puny notes strikingly contrasted with this really martial sight. The men, it is true, were mounted on lean Arab and Egyptian nags, ragged looking as their clothes, and each trooper was armed in his own way, though all had swords, pistols, and matchlocks, or firelocks of some kind. But they rode hard as Galway buckeens, and there was a gallant reckless look about the fellows which prepossessed me strongly in their favour. Their animals, too, though notable 'screws', were well trained, and their accoutrements were intended for use, not show. I watched their manoeuvres with curiosity. They left their cantonments one by one, and, at the sound of the tom-tom, by degrees formed a 'plump' or 'herse' – *column* it could not be called – all huddled together in confusion. Presently the little kettle-drum changed its note and the parade its aspect. All the serried body dispersed as Light Infantry would, continuing their advance, now hanging back, then making a rush, and all the time keeping up a hot fire upon the enemy. At another signal they suddenly put their horses to full speed, and, closing upon the centre, again advanced in a dense mass. After three quarters of an hour parading, sometimes charging singly, often in bodies, now to the right, then to the left., and then straight in front,when requisite halting, and occasionally retreating, Parthian-like, the Arnauts turned en masse towards their lines. As they neared them all broke off and galloped in, ventre à terre, discharging their shotted guns with much recklessness against objects assumed to denote the enemy. But ball cartridge seemed to be plentiful hereabouts; during the whole of this and the next day, I remarked that bullets were fired away in mere fun.

Barbarous as these movements may appear to the Cavalry Martinet of the 'good old school', yet to something of the kind will the tactics of that arm, I humbly opine, return, when the perfect use of the rifle, the revolver, and field artillery shall have made the present necessarily slow system fatal. Also, if we adopt the common-sense opinion of a modern writer, and determine that 'individual prowess, skill in single combats, good horsemanship, and sharp swords render cavalry formidable', these semi-barbarians are wiser in their generation than the civilised, who never practise arms (properly so called), whose riding-drill never made a good rider, whose horses are over-weighted, and whose swords are worthless. They have another point of superiority over us – they cultivate the individuality of the soldier, whilst we strive to make him a mere automaton. In the days of European chivalry, battles were a system of well fought duels. This was succeeded by the age of discipline, when, to use the language of Rabelais, 'men seemed rather a consort of organ-pipes, or mutual concord of the wheels of a clock, than an infantry and cavalry, or army of soldiers'. Our aim should now be to combine the merits of both systems; to make men individually excellent in the use of weapons, and still train them to act naturally and habitually in concert. The French have given a model to Europe in the Chasseurs de Vincennes – a body capable of most perfect combination, yet never more truly excellent than when each man is fighting alone. We, I suppose, shall imitate them at some future time.

A distant dropping of fire-arms ushered in the evening of our first melancholy day at Bir Abbas.

This, said my companions, was a sign that the troops and the hill-men were fighting at no great distance. They communicated the intelligence, as if it ought to be an effectual check upon my impatience to proceed; it acted, however, in the contrary way. I supposed that the Bedouins, after battling out the night, would be less warlike the next day; the others, however, by no means agreed in opinion with me. At Yambu the whole party had boasted loudly that the people of El Medinah could keep their Bedouins in order, and had twitted the boy Mohammed with their superiority in this respect to his townsmen, the Meccans. But now that a trial was impending I saw none of the fearlessness so conspicuous when peril was only possible. The change was charitably to be explained by the presence of their valuables; the 'Sahharahs' like conscience, making cowards of them all. But the young Meccan, who, having sent on his box by sea from Yambu to Jeddah, felt merry, like the empty traveller, would not lose the opportunity to pay off old scores. He taunted the Medinites till they stamped and raved with fury. At last, fearing some violence, and feeling answerable for the boy's safety to his family, I seized him by the nape of his neck and the upper posterior portion of his nether garments, and drove him before me into the tent.

When the hubbub had subsided and all sat smoking the pipe of peace after supper in the cool night air, I rejoined my companions, and found them talking, as usual, about old Shaykh Saad. The scene was appropriate for the subject. In the distance rose the blue peak said to be his eyric, and with fearful meaning the place was pointed out. As it is inaccessible to strangers, report has converted it into another garden of Irem. A glance, however, at its position and formation satisfied me that the bubbling springs, the deep forests, and the orchards of apple trees, quinces and pomegranates, with which my companions furnished it, were a 'myth', whilst some experience of Arab ignorance of the art of defence suggested to me strong doubts about the existence of an impregnable fortress on the hill-top. The mountains, however, looked beautiful in the moonlight, and distance gave them a semblance of mystery well suited to the themes connected with them.

That night I slept within my Shugduf, for it would have been mere madness to lie on the open plain in a place so infested by banditti. The being armed is but a poor precaution near this robbers' den. If a man be wounded in the very act of plundering, an exorbitant sum must be paid for blood-money. If you kill him, even to save your life, then adieu to any chance of escaping destruction. I was roused three or four times during the night by jackals and dogs prowling about our little camp, and thus observed that my companions, who had agreed amongst themselves to keep watch by turns, had all fallen into a sound sleep. However, when we awoke in the morning, the usual inspection of goods and chattels showed that nothing was missing.

The next day was a forced halt, a sore stimulant to the traveller's ill-humour; and the sun, the sand, the dust, the furious Simoom, and the want of certain small supplies, aggravated our grievance. My sore foot had been inflamed by a dressing of onion skin which the Lady Maryam had insisted upon applying to it. Still I was resolved to push forward by any conveyance that could be procured, and offered ten dollars for a fresh dromedary to take me on to El Medinah. Shaykh Hamid also declared he would leave his box in charge of a friend and accompany me. Saad the Devil flew into a passion at the idea of any member of the party escaping the general evil, and he privily threatened Mohammed to cut off the legs of any camel that ventured into camp. This, the boy – who, like a boy of the world as he was, never lost an opportunity of making mischief – instantly communicated to me, and it brought on a furious dispute. Saad was reproved and apologised for by the rest of the party, and presently he himself was pacified, principally, I believe, by the intelligence that no camel was to be hired at Bir Abbas. One of the Arnaut garrison, who had obtained leave to go to El Medinah, came to ask us if we could mount him, as otherwise he should be obliged to walk the whole way. With him we debated the propriety of attempting a passage through the hills by one of the many by-paths that traverse them: the project was amply discussed, and duly rejected.

We passed the day in the usual manner; all crowded together for shelter under the tent. Even Maryam joined us, loudly informing Ali, her son, that his mother was no longer a woman but a man, whilst our party generally, cowering away from the fierce glances of the sun, were either eating or occasionally smoking, or were occupied in cooling and drinking water. About sunset-time came a report that we were to start that night. None could believe that such good was in store for us; before sleeping, however, we placed each camel's pack apart, so as to be ready for loading at a moment's notice, and we took care to watch that our Bedouins did not drive their animals away to any distance. At last about 11 p.m., as the moon was beginning to peep over the eastern wall of rock, was heard the glad sound of the little kettle-drum calling the Albanian troopers to mount and march. In the shortest possible time all made ready, and hurriedly crossing the sandy flat, we found ourselves in company with three or four caravans, forming one large body for better defence against the dreadful Hawamid. By dint of much manoeuvring, arms in hand – Shaykh Hamid and the 'Devil' took the prominent parts – we, though the last comers, managed to secure places about the middle of the line. On such occasions all push forward recklessly, as an English mob in the strife of sight-seeing; the rear, being left unguarded, is the place of danger, and none seek the honor of occupying it.

We travelled that night up the Fiumara in an easterly direction, and at early dawn found ourselves in an ill-famed gorge called Shuab El Hajj (the 'Pilgrim's Pass'). The loudest talkers became silent as we neared it, and their countenances showed apprehension written in legible diameters. Presently from the high precipitous cliff on our left, thin blue curls of smoke – somehow or other they caught every eye – rose in the air, and instantly afterwards rang the loud sharp cracks of the hill-men's matchlocks echoed by the rocks on the right. My Shugduf had been broken by the camels falling during the night, so I called out to Mansur that we had better splice the frame-work with a bit of rope: he looked up, saw me laughing, and with an ejaculation of disgust disappeared. A number of Bedouins were to be seen swarming like hornets over the crests of the rocks, boys as well as men carrying huge weapons, and climbing with the agility of cats. They took up comfortable places on the cut-throat eminence, and began firing upon us with perfect convenience to themselves. The height of the hills and the glare of the rising sun prevented my seeing objects very distinctly, but my companions pointed out to me places where the rock had been scarped, and a kind of breastwork of rough stones – the Sangah of Afghanistan – piled up as a defence, and a rest for the long barrel of the matchlock. It was useless to challenge the Bedouins to come down and light us upon the plain like men; they will do this on the eastern coast of Arabia, but rarely, if ever, in El Hejaz. And it was equally unprofitable for our escort to fire upon a foe ensconced behind stones. Besides which, had a robber been killed, the whole country would have risen to a man; with a force of 3,000 or 4,000, they might have gained courage to overpower a caravan, and in such a case not a soul would have escaped. As it was, the Bedouins directed their fire principally against the Albanians. Some of these called for assistance to the party of Shaykhs that accompanied us from Bir Abbas, but the dignified old men, dismounting and squatting round their pipes in council, came to the conclusion that, as the robbers would probably turn a deaf ear to their words, they had better spare themselves the trouble of speaking. We had therefore nothing to do but to blaze away as much powder, and to veil ourselves in as much smoke, as possible; the result of the affair was that we lost twelve men, besides camels and other beasts of burden. Though the bandits showed no symptoms of bravery, and confined themselves to slaughtering the enemy from their hill-top, my companions seemed to consider this questionable affair a most gallant exploit.

After another hour's hurried ride through the Wady Sayyalah appeared Shuhada, to which we pushed on, 'Like nighted swain on lonely road, When close behind fierce goblins tread'.

Shuhada is a place which derives its name 'The Martyrs', because here are supposed to be buried forty braves that fell in one of Mohammed's many skirmishes. Some authorities consider it the cemetery of the people of Wady Sayyalah. The once populous valley is now barren, and one might easily pass by the consecrated spot without observing a few ruined walls and a cluster of rude Bedouin graves, each an oval of rough stones lying beneath the thorn trees on the left of and a little off the road. Another half hour took us to a favourite halting-place, Bir el Hindi, so called from some forgotten Indian who dug a well there. But we left it behind, wishing to put as much space as we could between our tents and the nests of the Hamidah. Then quitting the Fiumara, we struck northwards into a well-trodden road running over stony rising ground. The heat became sickening; here, and in the East generally, at no time is the sun more dangerous than between 8 and 9 a.m.: still we hurried on. It was not before 11 a.m. that we reached our destination, a rugged plain covered with stones, coarse gravel, and thorn trees in abundance, and surrounded by inhospitable rocks, pinnacle-shaped, of granite below, and in the upper parts fine limestone. The well was at least two miles distant, and not a hovel was in sight: a few Bedouin children belonging to an outcast tribe fed their starveling goats upon the hills. This place is called 'Suwaykah'; it is, I was told, that celebrated in the history of the Arabs. Yet not for this reason did my comrades look lovingly upon its horrors: their boxes were safe, and with the eye of imagination they could now behold their homes. That night we must have travelled about twenty-two miles; the direction of the road was due east, and the only remarkable feature in the ground was its steady rise.

We pitched the tent under a villanous Mimosa, the tree whose shade is compared by poetic Bedouins to the false friend who deserts you in your utmost need. I enlivened the hot dull day by a final dispute with Saad the Devil. His alacrity at Yambu obtained for him the loan of a couple of dollars: he had bought grain at El Hamra, and now we were near El Medinah; still there was not a word about repayment. And knowing that an Oriental debtor discharges his debt as he pays his rent – namely, with the greatest unwillingness – and that, on the other hand, an Oriental creditor will devote the labor of a year to recovering a sixpence, I resolved to act as a native of the country, placed in my position, would, and by dint of sheer dunning and demanding pledges to recover my property. About noon Saad the Devil, after a furious rush, bare-headed, through the burning sun, flung the two dollars down upon my carpet: however, he presently recovered, and, as subsequent events showed, I had chosen the right part. Had he not been forced to repay his debt, he would have despised me as a 'fresh-man', and asked for more. As it was, the boy Mohammed bore the brunt of unpopular feeling, my want of liberality being traced to his secret and perfidious admonitions. He supported his burden the more philosophically, because, as he notably calculated, every dollar saved at El Medinah would be spent under his stewardship at Meccah.

At 4 p.m. we left Suwaykah, all of us in the crossest of humours, and travelled in a N. E. direction. So out of temper were my companions, that at sunset, of the whole party, Umar Effendi was the only one who would eat supper. The rest sat upon the ground, pouting, grumbling, and – they had been allowed to exhaust my stock of Latakia – smoking Syrian tobacco as if it were a grievance. Such a game at naughty children, I have seldom seen played even by Oriental men. The boy Mohammed privily remarked to me that the camel-men's beards were now in his fist – meaning that we were out of their kinsmen, the Harb's, reach. He soon found an opportunity to quarrel with them; and, because one of his questions was not answered in the shortest possible time, he proceeded to abuse them in language which sent their hands flying in the direction of their swords. Despite, however, this threatening demeanour, the youth, knowing that he now could safely go to any lengths, continued his ill words, and Mansur's face was so comically furious, that I felt too much amused to interfere. At last the camel-men disappeared, thereby punishing us most effectually for our sport. The road lay up rocky hill and down stony vale; a tripping and stumbling dromedary had bceu substituted for the usual one: the consequence was that we had either a totter or a tumble once per mile during the whole of that long night. In vain the now fiery Mohammed called for the assistance of the camel-men with the full force of his lungs: 'Where be those owls, those oxen of the oxen, those beggars, those cut-off ones, those foreigners, those Sons of Flight? Withered be their hands! palsied be their fingers! the foul mustachioed fellows, basest, of the Arabs that ever hammered tent-peg, sneaking eats, goats of El Akhfash! Truly I will torture them the torture of the oil, the mines of infamy! the cold of countenance!' The Bedouin brotherhood of the camel-men looked at him wickedly, muttering the while 'By Allah! and by Allah! and by Allah! O boy, we will flog thee like a hound when we catch thee in the Desert!' All our party called upon him to desist, but his temper had got completely the upper hand over his discretion, and he expressed himself in such classic and idiomatic Hejazi, that I had not the heart to stop him. Some days after our arrival at El Medinah, Shaykh Hamid warned him seriously never again to go such perilous lengths, as the Beni-Harb were celebrated for shooting or poniarding the man who ventured to use even the mild epithet 'O jack-ass!' to them. And in the quiet of the city the boy Mohammed, like a sobered man shuddering at dangers braved when drunk, hearkened with discomposure and penitence to his friend's words. The only immediate consequence of his abuse was that my broken Shugduf became a mere ruin, and we passed the night perched like two birds upon the only entire bits of frame-work the cots contained.

The sun had risen before I shook off the lethargic effects of such a night. All around me were hurrying their camels, regardless of rough ground, and not a soul spoke a word to his neighbour. 'Are there robbers in sight?' was the natural question. 'No!' replied Mohammed; 'they are walking with their eyes, they will presently see their homes!'. Rapidly we passed the Wady el Akik, of which, 'O my friend, this is Akik, then stand by it, Endeavouring to be distracted by love, if not really a lover', and a thousand other such pretty things, have been said by the Arab poets. It was as 'dry as summer's dust', and its 'beautiful trees' appeared in the shape of vegetable mummies. Half an hour after leaving the 'Blessed Valley' we came to a huge flight of steps roughly cut in a long broad line of black scoriaccous basalt. This is called the Mudarraj or flight of steps over the western ridge of the so-called El Harratayn. It is holy ground; for the Prophet spoke well of it. Arrived at the top, we passed through a lane of black scoria, with steep banks on both sides, and after a few minutes a full view of the city suddenly opened upon us.

We halted our beasts as if by word of command. All of us descended, in imitation of the pious of old, and sat down, jaded and hungry as we were, to feast our eyes with a view, of the Holy City. 'O Allah! this is the Haram (sanctuary) of thy Prophet; make it to us a protection from hell fire, and a refuge from eternal punishment! O open the gates of thy mercy, and let us pass through them to the land of joy!' and 'O Allah, bless the last of Prophets, the seal of prophecy, with blessings in number as the stars of heaven, and the waves of the sea, and the sands of the waste – bless him, O Lord of Might and Majesty, as long as the corn field and the date grove continue to feed mankind!' And again, 'Live, for ever, O most excellent of Prophets! – live in the shadow of happiness during the hours of night and the times of day, whilst the bird of the tamarisk (the dove) moaneth like the childless mother, whilst the west wind bloweth gently over the hills of Nejd, and the lightning flasheth bright in the firmament of El Hejaz!' Such were the poetical exclamations that rose all around me, showing how deeply tinged with imagination becomes the language of the Arab under the influence of strong passion or religious enthusiasm. I now understood the full value of a phrase in the Moslem ritual, 'And when his (the pilgrim's) eyes fall upon the trees of El Medinah, let him raise his voice and bless the Prophet with the choicest of blessings'. In all the fair view before us nothing was more striking, after the desolation through which we had passed, than the gardens and orchards about the town. It was impossible not to enter into the spirit of my companions, and truly I believe that for some minutes my enthusiasm rose as high as theirs. But presently, when we remounted the traveller returned strong upon me: I made a rough sketch of the town, put questions about the principal buildings, and in fact collected materials for the next chapter.

The distance traversed that night was about twenty miles in a direction varying from easterly to north-easterly. We reached El Medinah on the 25th July, thus taking nearly eight days to travel over little more 130 miles. This journey is performed with camels in four days, and a good dromedary will do it without difficulty in half that time.

CHAP. XIV

A Visit To The Prophet's Tomb

Having performed the greater ablution, and used the tooth-stick as directed, and dressed ourselves in white clothes, which the Prophet loved, we were ready to start upon our holy errand. As my foot still gave me great pain, Shaykh Hamid sent for a donkey. A wretched animal appeared, raw-backed, lame of one leg, and wanting an ear, with accoutrements to match, and pack-saddle without stirrups, and a halter instead of a bridle. Such as the brute was, however, I had to mount it, and to ride through the Misri gate, to the wonder of certain Bedouins, who, like the Indians, despise the ass. 'Honorable is the riding of a horse to the rider, But the mule is a dishonor, and the ass a disgrace.' says their song. The Turkish pilgrims, however, who appear to take a pride in ignoring all Arab points of prejudice, generally mount donkeys when they cannot walk. The Bedouins therefore settled among themselves, audibly enough, that I was an Osmanli, who of course could not understand Arabic, and put the question generally, 'By what curse of Allah they had been subjected to ass-riders?'

But Shaykh Hamid is lecturing me upon the subject of the mosque.

The Masjid El Nabawi, or the Prophet's Mosque, is one of the Haramayn, or the 'two sanctuaries' of El Islam, and is the second of the three most venerable places of worship in the world; the other two being the Masjid El Haram at Meccah (connected with Abraham) and the Masjid El Aksa of Jerusalem (the peculiar place of Solomon). A Hadis or traditional saying of Mohammed asserts, 'One prayer in this my mosque is more efficacious than a thousand in other places, save only the Masjid El Haram.' It is therefore the visitor's duty, as long as he stays at El Medinah, to pray the five times per diem there, to pass the day in it reading the Koran, and the night, if possible, in watching and devotion.

A visit to the Masjid El Nabawi, and the holy spots within it, is technically called 'Ziyarat' or Visitation. An essential difference is made between this rite and Hajj or pilgrimage. The latter is obligatory by Koranic order upon every Moslem once in his life: the former is only a meritorious action. 'Tawaf', or circumambulation of the House of Allah at Meccah, must never be performed at the Prophet's tomb. This should not be visited in the Ihram or pilgrim dress; men should not kiss it, touch it with the hand, or press the bosom against it, as at the Kaabah; or rub the face with dust collected near the sepulchre; and those who prostrate themselves before it, like certain ignorant Indians, are held to be guilty of deadly sin. On the other hand, to spit upon any part of the Mosque, or to treat it with contempt, is held to be the act of an infidel.

Thus learning and the religious have settled, one would have thought, accurately enough the spiritual rank and dignity of the Masjid El Nabawi. But mankind, especially in the East, must always be in extremes. The orthodox school of El Malik holds

El Medinah, on account of the sanctity of, and the religious benefits to be derived from, Mohammed's tomb, more honorable than Meccah. The Wahhabis, on the other hand, rejecting the intercession of the Prophet on the day of judgment, considering the grave of a mere mortal unworthy of notice, and highly disgusted by the idolatrous respect paid to it by certain foolish Moslems, plundered the sacred building with sacrilegious violence, and forbade visitors from distant countries to enter El Medinah. The general consensus of El Islam admits the superiority of the Bayt Allah (House of God) at Meccah to the whole world, and declares El Medinah to be more venerable than every part of Meccah, and consequently all the earth, except only the Bayt Allah.

Passing through muddy streets – they had been freshly watered before evening time – I came suddenly upon the Mosque. Like that at Meccah, the approach is choked up by ignoble buildings, some actually touching the holy 'enceinte', others separated by a lane compared with which the road round St. Paul's is a Vatican square. There is no outer front, no general prospect of the Prophet's Mosque; consequently, as a building, it has neither beauty nor dignity. And entering the Bab el Rahmah – the Gate of Pity – by a diminutive flight of steps, I was astonished at the mean and tawdry appearance of a place so universally venerated in the Moslem world. It is not, like the Meccan Temple, grand and simple – the expression of a single sublime idea: the longer I looked at it, the more it suggested the resemblance of a museum of second-rate art, a curiosity-shop, full of ornaments that are not accessaries, and decorated with pauper splendor.

The Masjid el Nabi is a parallelogram about 420 feet in length by 340 broad, the direction of the long walls being nearly north and south. As usual in El Islam, it is a hypæthral building with a spacious central area, called El Sahn, El Hosh, El Haswah, or El Ramlah, surrounded by a peristyle with numerous rows of pillars like the colonnades of an Italian monastery. Their arcades or porticoes are flat-ceilinged, domed above with the small 'Media Naranja', or half-orange cupola of Spain, and divided into four parts by narrow passages, three or four steps below the level of the pavement. Along the whole inner length of the northern short wall runs the Mejidi Riwak, so called from the reigning Sultan. The western long wall is occupied by the Riwak of the Rahmah Gate; the eastern by that of the Bab el Nisa, the 'Women's Entrance'. Embracing the inner length of the southern short wall, and deeper by nearly treble the amount of columns than the other porticoes, is the main colonnade, called El Rauzah, the adytum containing all that is venerable in the building. These four Riwaks, arched externally, are supported internally by pillars of different shape and material, varying from fine porphyry to dirty plaster; the southern, where the sepulchre or cenotaph stands, is paved with handsome slabs of white marble and marquetry work, here and there covered with coarse matting, and above this by unclean carpets, well worn by faithful feet.

But this is not the time for Tafarruj, or lionizing. Shaykh Hamid warns me with a nudge, that other things are expected of a Zair. He leads me to the Bab el Salam, fighting his way through a troop of beggars, and inquires markedly if I am religiously pure. Then, placing our hands a little below and on the left of the waist, the palm of the right covering the back of the left, in the position of prayer, and beginning with the right feet, we pace slowly forwards down the line called the Muwajihat el Sharifah, or 'the Holy Fronting', which, divided off like an aisle, runs parallel with the southern wall of the Mosque. On my right hand walks the Shaykh, who recites aloud the following prayer, which I repeat after him. It is literally rendered, as, indeed, are all the formulae, and the reader is requested to excuse the barbarous fidelity of the translation.

> 'In the name of Allah and in the Faith of Allah's Prophet! O Lord cause me to enter the entering of Truth, and cause me to issue forth the issuing of Truth, and permit me to draw near to thee, and make me a Sultan Victorious!'

Then follow blessings upon the Prophet, and afterwards: 'O Allah I open to me the doors of thy mercy, and grant me entrance into it, and protect me from the Stoned Devil!'

During this preliminary prayer we had passed down two-thirds of the Muwajihat el Sharifah. On the left hand is a dwarf wall, about the height of a man, painted with arabesques, and pierced with four small doors which open into the Muwajihat. In this barrier are sundry small erections, the niche called the Mihrab Sulaymani, the Mambar, or pulpit, and the Mihrab el Nabawi. The two niches are of beautiful mosaic, richly worked with various coloured marbles, and the pulpit is a graceful collection of slender columns, elegant tracery, and inscriptions admirably carved. Arrived at the western small door in the dwarf wall, we entered the celebrated spot called El Rauzah, or the Garden, after a saying of the Prophet's, 'Between my Tomb and my Pulpit is a Garden of the Gardens of Paradise'. On the north and west sides it is not divided from the rest of the portico; on the south lies the dwarf wall, and on the east it is limited by the west end of the lattice-work containing the tomb. Accompanied by my Muzawwir

I entered the Rauzah, and was placed by him with the Mukabbariyah behind me, fronting Meccah, with my right shoulder opposite to and about twenty feet distant from the dexter pillar of the Prophet's Pulpit. There, after saying the afternoon prayers, I performed the usual two bows in honor of the temple, and at the end of them recited the 109th and the 112th chapters of the Koran – the "Kul ya ayyuha'l Kafiruna', and the 'Surat el Ikhlas', called also the 'Kul Huw' Allah', or the Declaration of Unity; and may be thus translated:

'Say, he is the one God!
The eternal God!
He begets not, nor is he begot,
And unto him the like is not.'

After which was performed a single Sujdah of thanks, in gratitude to Allah for making it my fate to visit so holy a spot. This being the recognised time to give alms, I was besieged by beggars, who spread their napkins before us on the ground sprinkled with a few coppers to excite generosity. But not wishing to be distracted by them, before leaving Hamid's house I had asked change of two dollars, and had given it to the boy Mohammed, who accompanied me, strictly charging him to make that sum last all through the Mosque. My answer to the beggars was a reference to my attendant, backed by the simple action of turning my pockets inside out, and whilst he was battling with the beggars, I proceeded to cast my first coup-d'œil upon the Rauzah.

The 'Garden' is the most elaborate part of the Mosque. Little can be said in its praise by day, when it bears the same relation to a second-rate church in Rome as an English chapel-of-case to Westminster

Abbey. It is a space of about eighty feet in length, tawdrily decorated so as to resemble a garden. The carpets are flowered, and the pediments of the columns are cased with bright green tiles, and adorned to the height of a man with gaudy and unnatural vegetation in arabesque. It is disfigured by handsome branched candelabras of cut crystal, the work, I believe, of a London house, and presented to the shrine by the late Abbas Pacha of Egypt. The only admirable feature of the view is the light cast by the windows of stained glass in the southern wall. Its peculiar background, the railing of the tomb, a splendid filagree-work of green and polished brass, gilt or made to resemble gold, looks more picturesque near than at a distance, when it suggests the idea of a gigantic bird cage. But at night the eye, dazzled by oil-lamps suspended from the roof, by huge wax candles, and by smaller illuminations falling upon crowds of visitors in handsome attire, with the richest and the noblest of the city sitting in congregation when service is performed, becomes less critical. Still the scene must be viewed with a Moslem's spirit, and until a man is thoroughly embued with the East, the last place the Rauzah will remind him of, is that which the architect primarily intended it to resemble – a garden.

Then with Hamid, professionally solemn, I reassumed the position of prayer, as regards the hands; and retraced my steps. After passing through another small door in the dwarf wall that bounds the Muwajihah, we did not turn to the right, which would have led us to the Bab el Salam; our course was in an opposite direction, towards the eastern wall of the temple. Meanwhile we repeated, 'Verily Allah and his Angels bless the Prophet! O ye who believe, bless him, and salute him with honor!' At the end of this prayer, we arrived at the Mausoleum, which requires some description before the reader can understand the nature of our proceedings there.

The Hujrah or 'Chamber' as it is called, from the circumstance of its having been Ayisha's room, is an irregular square of from 50 to 55 feet in the S. E. corner of the building, and separated on all sides from the walls of the Mosque by a passage about 26 feet broad on the S. side, and 20 on the eastern. The reason of this isolation has been before explained, and there is a saying of Mohammed's, 'O Allah, cause not my tomb to become an object of idolatrous adoration! May Allah's wrath fall heavy upon the people who make the tombs of their prophets places of prayer!' Inside there are, or are supposed to be, three tombs facing the south, surrounded by stone walls without any aperture, or, as others say, by strong planking. Whatever this material may be, it is hung outside with a curtain, somewhat like a large four-post bed. The outer railing is separated by a dark narrow passage from the inner, which it surrounds, and is of iron filagree painted of a vivid grass green – with a view to the garden – whilst carefully inserted in the verdure, and doubly bright by contrast, is the gilt or burnished brass work forming the long and graceful letters of the Suls character, and disposed into the Moslem creed, the profession of unity, and similar religious sentences. On the south side, for greater honor, the railing is plated over with silver, and silver letters are interlaced with it. This fence, which connects the columns and forbids passage to all men, may be compared to the baldacchino of Roman churches. It has four gates: that to the south is the Bab el Muwajihah; eastward is the gate of our Lady Fatimah; westward the Bab el Taubah (of repentance), opening into the Rauzah or garden, and to the north, the Bab el Shami or Syrian gate. They are constantly kept closed, except the fourth, which admits, into the dark narrow passage above alluded to, the officers who have charge of the treasures there deposited, and the eunuchs who sweep the floor, light the lamps, and carry away the presents sometimes thrown in here by devotees. In the southern side of the fence are three windows, holes about half a foot square, and placed from four to five feet above the ground; they are said to be between three and four cubits distant from the Prophet's head. The most westerly of these is supposed to front Mohammed's tomb, wherefore it is called the Shubak el Nabi, or the Prophet's window. The next, on the right as you front it, is Abubekr's, and the most easterly of the three is Omar's. Above the Hujrah is the Green Dome, surmounted outside by a large gilt crescent springing from a series of globes. The glowing imaginations of the Moslems crown this gem of the building with a pillar of heavenly light, which directs from three days' distance the pilgrims' steps towards El Medinah. But alas! none save holy men (and perhaps, odylic sensitives), whose material organs are piercing as their vision ia spiritual, are allowed the privilege of beholding this poetic splendor.

Arrived at the Shubak el Nabi, Hamid took his stand about six feet or so out of reach of the railing, and at that respectful distance from, and facing the Hazirah (or presence), with hands raised as in prayer, he recited the following supplication in a low voice, telling me in a stage whisper to repeat it alter him with awe, and fear, and love.

'Peace be upon thee, O Prophet of Allah, and the mercy of Allah and his blessings! Peace be upon thee, O Prophet of Allah! Peace be upon thee, O friend of Allah! Peace be upon thee, O best of Allah's creation! Peace be upon thee, O pure creature of Allah! Peace be upon thee, O chief of Prophets! Peace be upon thee, O seal of the Prophets! Peace be upon thee, O prince of the pious! Peace be upon thee, O Prophet of the Lord of the (three) worlds! Peace be upon thee, and upon thy family, and upon thy pure wives! Peace be upon thee, and upon all thy companions! Peace be upon thee, and upon all the Prophets, and upon those sent to preach Allah's word! Peace be upon thee, and upon all Allah's righteous worshipper! Peace be upon thee, O thou bringer of glad tidings! Peace be upon thee, O bearer of threats! Peace be upon thee, O thou bright lamp! Peace be upon time, O thou Prophet of mercy! Peace be upon time, O ruler of thy faith! Peace be upon thee, O opener of grief! Peace be upon thee! and Allah bless thee! And Allah repay thee for us, O thou Prophet of Allah! the choicest of blessings with which he ever blessed prophet! Allah bless thee as often as mentioners have mentioned thee, and forgetters have forgotten thee! And Allah bless thee among the first and the last, with the best, the highest, and the fullest of blessings ever bestowed on man, even as we escaped error by means of thee, and were made to see after blindness, and after ignorance were directed into the right way. I bear witness that there is no god but Allah, and I testify that thou art his servant, and his prophet, and his faithful follower, and best creature. And I bear witness, O Prophet of Allah! that thou hast delivered thy message, and discharged thy trust, and advised thy faith, and opened grief, and published proofs, and fought valiantly for thy Lord, and worshipped thy God till certainty came to thee (i.e. to the hour of death); and we thy friends, O Prophet of Allah appear before thee travellers from distant lands and far countries, through dangers and difficulties, in the times of darkness, and in the hours of day, longing to give thee thy rights (i.e. to honor thee by benediction and visitation), and to obtain the blessings of thine intercession, for our sins have broken our backs, and thou intercedest with the Healer.' And Allah said, 'And though they have injured themselves, they came to thee, and begged thee to secure their pardon, and they found God an acceptor of penitence, and full of compassion.' O Prophet of Allah, intercession! Intercession! intercession! O Allah, bless Mohammed and Mohammed's family, and give him superiority and high rank, even us thou didst promise him, and graciously allow us to conclude this visitation. I deposit on this spot, and near thee, O Prophet of God, my everlasting profession (of faith) from this our day, to the day of judgment, that there is no god but Allah, and that our Lord Mohammed is his servant, and his Prophet Amen! O Lord of the (three) worlds!'

After which, performing Ziyarat for ourselves, we repeated the Fatihah or 'opening' chapter of the Koran.

'In the name of Allah, the Merciful, the Compassionate!
Praise be to Allah, who the (three) worlds made.
The Merciful, the Compassionate.
The King of the day of Faith.
Thee (alone) do we worship, and of thee (alone) do we ask aid.
Guide us to the path that is straight –
The path of those for whom thy love is great, not those on whom is hate, nor they that deviate.
Amen! O Lord of Angels, Jinns, and men!'

After reciting this mentally with upraised hands, the forefinger of the right hand being extended to its full length, we drew our palms down our faces and did almsdeeds, a vital part of the ceremony. Thus concludes the first part of the ceremony of visitation at the Prophet's tomb.

Hamid then stepped about a foot and a half to the right, and I followed his example, so as to place myself exactly opposite the second aperture in the grating called Abubekr's window. There, making a sign towards the mausoleum, wc addressed its inmate, as follows:

> 'Peace be upon thee, O Abubekr, O thou truthful one! Peace be upon thee, O caliph of Allah's Prophet over his people! Peace be upon thee, O Companion of the Cave, and friend in travel! Peace be upon thee, O thou banner of the Fugitives and the Auxiliaries! I testify thou didst ever stand firm in the right way, and wast a smiter of the Infidel, and a benefactor to thine own people. Allah grant thee through his Prophet weal! We pray Almighty God to cause us to die in thy friendship, and to raise us up in company with his Prophet and thyself, even as he hath mercifully vouchsafed to us this visitation.'

After which we closed one more step to the right, and standing opposite Omar's window, the most easterly of the three, after making a sign with our hands, we addressed the just Caliph in these words:

> 'Peace be upon thee, O Omar! O thou just one! Thou prince of true believers! Peace be upon thee, who spakest with truth, and who madest thy word agree with the Strong Book! (the Koran), O thou Faruk! O thou faithful one! who girdedst thy loins with the Prophet, and the first believers, and with them didst make up the full number forty, and thus causedst to be accomplished the Prophet's prayer, and then didst return to thy God a martyr leaving the world with praise! Allah grant thee, through his Prophet and his Caliph and his followers, the best of good, and may Allah feel in thee all satisfaction!'

Shaykh Hamid, after wrenching a beggar or two from my shoulders, then permitted me to draw near to the little window, called the Prophet's, and to look in. Here my proceedings were watched with suspicious eyes. The Persians have sometimes managed to pollute the part near Abubekr's and Omar's graves by tossing through the aperture what is externally a handsome shawl intended as a present for the tomb. After straining my eyes for a time I saw a curtain, or rather hangings, with three inscriptions in long gold letters, informing readers, that behind them lie Allah's Prophet and the two first caliphs. The exact place of Mohammed's tomb is moreover distinguished by a large pearl rosary, and a peculiar ornament, the celebrated Kaukab el Durri, or constellation of pearls, suspended to the curtain breast high. This is described to be a 'brilliant star set in diamonds and pearls', and placed in the dark in order that man's eye may be able to bear its splendors: the vulgar believe it to be a 'jewel of the jewels of Paradise'. To me it greatly resembled the round stoppers of glass, used for the humbler sorts of decanters, but I never saw it quite near enough to judge fairly of it, and did not think fit to pay an exorbitant sum for the privilege of entering the inner passage of the baldaquin. Altogether the coup d'œil had nothing to recommend it by day. At night, when the lamps hung in this passage shed a dim light upon the mosaic work of the marble floors, upon the glittering inscriptions, and the massive hangings, the scene is more likely to become 'ken-speckle'.

Never having seen the tomb, I must depict it from books—by no means an easy task. Most of the historians are silent after describing the inner walls of the Hajrah. El Kalkashandi declares 'in eo lapidem nobilem continere sepulchra Apostoli, Abubecr et Omar, circumcinctum peribole in modum conclavis fere usque ad tectum assurgente quæ velo serico nigro obligatur'. This author, then, agrees with my Persian friends, who declare the sepulchre to be a marble slab. Ibn Jubayr, who travelled A.H. 580, relates that the Prophet's coffin is a box of ebony (abnus) covered with sandal-wood, and plated with silver; it is placed, he says, behind a curtain, and surrounded by an iron grating. El Samanhudi, quoted by Burekhardt, declares that the curtain covers a square building of black stones, in the interior of which are the tombs of Mohammed and his two immediate successors. He adds that the tombs are deep holes, and that the coffin which contains the Prophet is cased with silver, and has on the top a marble slab inscribed 'Bismiliah! Allahumma salli alayh!' ('In the name of Allah! Allah have mercy upon him!').

The Prophet's body, it should be remembered, lies, or is supposed to lie, stretched at full length on the right side, with the right palm supporting the right cheek, the face fronting Meccah, as Moslems are always buried, and consequently the body lies with the head almost to due West and the feet to due East. Close behind him is placed Abubekr, whose face fronts the Prophet's shoulder, and lastly Omar holds the same position with respect to his predecessor.

It is popularly believed that in the Hujrah there is now spare place for only a single grave, which is reserved for Isa bin Maryam after his second coming. The historians of El Islam are full of tales proving that though many of their early saints, as Osman the Caliph and Hasan the Imam, were desirous of being buried there, and that although Ayisha, to whom the room belonged, willingly acceded to their wishes, son of man has as yet been unable to occupy it.

After the Fatihah pronounced at Omar's tomb, and the short inspection of the Hujrah, Shaykh Hamid led me round the south-east corner of the baldaquin. Turning towards the north we stopped at what is commonly called the Mahbat Jibrail ('Place of the Archangel Gabriel's Descent with the Heavenly Revelations'), or simply El Malaikah – the Angels. It is a small window in the eastern wall of the mosque; we turned our backs upon it, and fronting the Hujrah, recited the following prayer:

'Peace be upon you, ye Angels of Allah, the Mukarrabin (cherubs), and the Musharrifin (scraphs), the pure, the holy, honored by the dwellers in heaven, and by those who abide upon the earth. O beneficent Lord! O long-suffering! O Almighty! O Pitier! O thou Compassionate One! perfect our light, and pardon our sins, and accept penitence for our offences, and cause us to die among the holy! Peace be upon ye, Angels of the Merciful, one and all I And the mercy of God and his blessings be upon you!'

After which I was shown the spot in the Hujrah where Sayyidna Isa shall be buried by Mohammed's side.

Then turning towards the west, at a point where there is a break in the symmetry of the Hujrah, we arrived at the sixth station, the sepulchre or cenotaph of the Lady Fatimah. Her grave is outside the enceinte and the curtain which surrounds her father's remains, so strict is Moslem decorum, and so exalted its opinion of the "Virgin's" delicacy; the eastern side of the Hujrah, here turning a little westward, interrupting the shape of the square, in order to give this spot the appearance of disconnection with the rest of the building. The tomb, seen through a square aperture like those above described, is a long catafalque, covered with a black pall. Though there is great doubt whether the Lady be not buried with her son Hasan in the Bakia cemetery, this place is always visited by the pious Moslem. The following is the prayer opposite the grave of the amiable Falimah:

'Peace be upon thee, daughter of the Messenger of Allah! Peace be upon thee, daughter of the Prophet of Allah! Peace be upon thee, thou daughter of Mustafa! Peace be upon thee, thou mother of the Shurafa! Peace be upon thee, O Lady amongst women! Peace be upon thee, O fifth of the Ahl El IKisa! Peace be upon thee, O Zahra and Batul! Peace be upon thee, O daughter of the Prophet! Peace be upon thee, O spouse of our lord Ali El Murtaza! Peace be upon thee, O mother of Hasan and Husayn, the two moons, the two lights, the two pearls, the two princes of the youth of heaven, and coolness of the eyes of true believers! Peace be upon thee and upon thy sire, El Mustafa, and thy husband, our lord Ali! Allah honor his face, and thy face, and thy father's face in Paradise, and thy two sons the Hasanayn! And the mercy of Allah and his blessings!'

We then broke away as we best could from the crowd of female 'askers', who have established their Lares and Penates under the shadow of the Lady's wing, and, advancing a few paces, we fronted to the north, and recited a prayer in honor of Hamzah, and the martyrs who lie buried at the foot of Mount Ohod. We then turned to the right, and, fronting the easterly wall, prayed for the souls of the blessed whose mortal spirits repose within El Bakia's hallowed circuit.

After this we returned to the southern wall of the Mosque, and, facing towards Meccah, we recited the following supplication:

'O Allah! (three times repeated) O Compassionate! O Beneficent! O Requiter (of good and evil)! O Prince! O Ruler! O ancient of Benefits! O Omniscient! O thou who givest when asked, and who aidest when aid is required, accept this our Visitation, and preserve us from dangers, and make easy our affairs, and expand our chests, and receive our prostration, and. requite us according to our good deeds, and turn not our evil deeds against us, and place not over us one who feareth not thee, and one who pitieth not us, and write safety and health upon us and upon thy slaves, the Hujjaj, and the Ghuzzat, and the Zawwar, and the home-dwellers and the wayfarers of the Moslems, by land and by sea, and pardon those of the faith of our lord Mohammed one and all!'

From the southern wall we returned to the 'Prophet's Window', where we recited the following tetrastich and prayer.

'O Mustafa! verily, I stand at thy door,
A man, weak and fearful, by reason of my sins:
If thou aid me not, O Prophet of Allah!
I die – for, in the world there is none generous as thou art!'
'Of a truth, Allah and his Angels bless the Prophet! O ye who believe, bless him and salute him with salutation! O Allah! verily I implore thy pardon, and supplicate thine aid in this world as in the next! O Allah! O Allah! abandon us not in this holy place to the consequences of our sins without pardoning them, or to our griefs without consoling them, or to our fears, O Allah! without removing them. And blessings and salutation to thee, O Prince of Prophets, Commissioned (to preach the word), and praise to Allah the lord of the (three) worlds!'

We turned away from the Hujrah, and after gratifying a meek-looking but exceedingly importunate Indian beggar, who insisted on stunning me with the Chapter Y, S., we fronted southwards, and taking care that our backs should not be in a line with the Prophet's face, stood opposite the niche called Mihrab Osman. There Hamid proceeded with another supplication.

'O Allah ! (three times repeated), O Safeguard of the fearful, and defender of those who trust in thee, and pitier of the weak, the poor, and the destitute! accept us, O Beneficent! and pardon us, O Merciful! and receive our penitence, O Compassionate! and have mercy upon us, O Forgiver! – for verily none but thou can remit sin! Of a truth thou alone knowest the hidden and veilest man's transgressions: veil, then, our offences, and pardon our sins, and expand our chests, and cause our last words at the supreme hour of life to be the words, "There is no god but Allah, and our lord Mohammed is the Prophet of Allah!" O Allah! cause us to live according to this saying, O thou Giver of life; and make us to die in this faith, O thou ruler of death! And the best of blessings and the completest of salutations upon the sole Lord of Intercession, our Lord Mohammed and his family, and his companions one and all!'

Lastly, we returned to the Garden, and prayed another two-bow prayer, ending, as we began, with the worship of the Creator.

Unfortunately for me, the boy Mohammed had donned that grand embroidered coat. At the end of the ceremony the Aghas, or eunuchs of the Mosque – a race of men considered respectable by their office, and prone to make themselves respected by the freest administration of club law – assembled in El Rauzah to offer me the congratulation 'Ziyaratak Mubarak' – 'Blessed be thy Visitation', and to demand fees. Then came the Sakka, or water-carrier of the Zem Zem, offering a tinned saucer filled from the holy source. And lastly I was beset by beggars – some, mild beggars and picturesque who sat upon the ground immersed in the contemplation of their napkins; others, angry beggars who cursed if they were not gratified; and others noisy and petulant beggars, especially the feminine party near the Lady's tomb, who captured me by the skirt of my garment, compelling me to ransom myself. There were, besides, pretty beggars, boys who held out the right hand on the score of good looks; ugly beggars, emaciated rascals whose long hair, dirt, and leanness entitled them to charity; and lastly, the blind, the halt, and the diseased, who, as sons of the Holy City, demanded from the Faithful that support with which they could not provide themselves. Having been compelled by my companions, highly against my inclination, to become a man of rank, I was obliged to pay in proportion, and my almoner in the handsome coat, as usual, took a kind of pride in being profuse. This first visit cost me double what I had intended – four dollars – nearly one pound sterling, and never afterwards could I pay less than half that sum.

Having now performed all the duties of a good Zair, I was permitted by Shaykh Hamid to wander about and see the sights. We began our circumambulation at the Bab el Salam – the Gate of Salvation – in the south portion of the western long wall of the Mosque. It is a fine archway handsomely incrusted with marble and glazed tiles; the number of gilt inscriptions on its sides give it, especially at night-time, an appearance of considerable splendor. The portcullis-like doors are of wood, strengthened with brass plates, and nails of the same metal. Outside this gate is a little Sabil, or public fountain, where those who will not pay for the water, kept ready in large earthen jars by the 'Sakka' of the Mosque, perform their ablutions gratis. Here all the mendicants congregate in force, sitting on the outer steps and at the entrance of the Mosque, up and through which the visitors must pass. About the centre of the western wall is the Bab el Rahmah – the Gate of Mercy. It admits the dead bodies of the Faithful when carried to be prayed over in the Mosque; there is nothing remarkable in its appearance; in common with the other gates it has huge folding doors, iron-bound, an external flight of steps, and a few modern inscriptions. The Bab Mejidi, or Gate of the Sultan Abd el Mejid, stands in the centre of the northern wall; like its portico, it is unfinished, but its present appearance promises that it will eclipse all except the Bab el Salam. The Bab el Nisa is in the eastern wall opposite the Bab el Rahmah, with which it is connected by the 'Farsh el Hajar', a broad band of stone, two or three steps below the level of the portico, and Blightly raised above the Sahn or the hypæthral portion of the Mosque. And lastly, in the southern portion of the same eastern wall is the Bab Jibrail, the Gate of the Archangel Gabriel. All these entrances are arrived at by short external flights of steps leading from the streets, as the base of the temple, unlike that of Meccah, is a little higher than the foundations of the buildings around it. The doors are closed by the eunuchs in attendance immediately after the night prayers, except during the blessed month El Ramazan and the pilgrimage season, when a number of pious visitors pay considerable fees to pass the night there in meditation and prayer.

The minarets are five in number; but one, the Shikayliyah, at the north-west angle of the building, has been levelled, and is still in process of being re-built. The Munar Bab el Salam stands by the gate of that name: it is a tall handsome tower surmounted by a large ball or cone of brass gilt or burnished. The Munar Bab el Rahmah, about the centre of the western wall, is of more simple form than the others: it has two galleries with the superior portion circular, and surmounted by the conical 'extinguisher' roof so common in Turkey and Egypt. On the north-east angle of the Mosque stands the Sulaymaniyah Munar, so named after its founder, Sultan Sulayman the Magnificent. It is a well-built and substantial stone tower divided into three stages; the two lower portions are polygonal, the upper circular, and each terminates in a platform with a railed gallery carried all round for the protection of those who ascend. And lastly, from the south-east angle of the Mosque, supposed to be upon the spot where Belal, the Prophet's crier, called the first Moslems to prayer, springs the Munar Raisiyah, so called because it is appropriated to the Ruasa or chiefs of the Muezzins. Like the Sulaymaniyah, it consists of three parts: the first and second stages are polygonal, and the circular third is furnished like the lower two with a railed gallery. Both the latter minarets end in solid ovals of masonry, from which project a number of wooden triangles. To these and to the galleries on all festive occasions, such as the arrival of the Damascus caravan, are hung oil lamps – a poor attempt at illumination, which may perhaps rationally explain the origin of the Medinite superstition concerning the column of light which crowns the Prophet's tomb. There is no uniformity in the shape or the size of these four minarets, and at first sight, despite their beauty and grandeur, they appear somewhat bizarre and misplaced. But after a few days I found that my eye grew accustomed to them, and that I had no difficulty in appreciating their massive proportions and lofty forms.

Equally irregular are the Riwaks, or porches, surrounding the hypæthral court. Along the northern wall there will be, when finished, a fine colonnade of granite, paved with marble. The eastern Riwak has three rows of pillars, the western four, and the southern, under which stands the tomb, of course has its columns ranged deeper than all the others. These supports of the building are of different material; some of fine marble, others of rough stone merely plastered over and painted with the most vulgar of arabesques – vermilion and black in irregular patches, and broad streaks like the stage face of a London clown. Their size moreover is different, the southern colonnade being composed of pillars palpably larger than those in the other parts of the Mosque. Scarcely any two shafts have similar capitals; many have no pedestal, aud some of them are cut with a painful ignorance of art. I cannot extend my admiration of the minarets to the columns – in *their* 'architectural lawlessness' there is not a redeeming point.

Of these unpraisable pillars three are celebrated in the annals of El Islam, for which reason their names are painted upon them, and five others enjoy the honor of distinctive appellations. The first is culled El Mukhallak, because, on some occasion of impurity, it was anointed with a perfume called Khaluk. It is near the Mihrab el Nabawi, on the right of the place where the Imam prays, and notes the spot where, before the invention of the pulpit, the Prophet, leaning upon the Ustuwanat el Hannanah – the Weeping Pillar – used to recite theKhutbah or Friday sermon. The second stands third from the pulpit, and third from the Hujrah. It is called the Pillar of Ayisha, also the Ustuwanat el Kurah, or the Column of Lots, because the Prophet, according to the testimony of his favourite wife, declared that if men knew the value of the place, they would cast lots to pray there: in some books it is known as the Pillar of the Muhajirin or Fugitives, and others mention it as El Mukhallak – the Perfumed. Twenty cubits distant from Ayisha's Pillar, and the second from the Hujrah and the fourth from the pulpit, is the Pillar of Repentance, or of Abu Lubabah. It derives its name from the following circumstance. Abu Lubabah was a native of El Medinah, ono of the Auxiliaries and a companion of Mohammed, originally it is said a Jew, according to others of the Beni Amr bin Auf of the Aus tribe. Being sent for by his kinsmen or his allies, the Beni Kurayzah, at that time capitulating to Mohammed, he was consulted by the distracted tribe: men, women and children throw themselves at his feet, and begged of him to intercede for them with the offended Prophet. Abu Lubabah swore he would do so: at the same time, he drew his hand across his throat, as much as to say, 'Defend yourselves to the Lost, for if you yield, such is your doom'. Afterwards repenting, he bound himself with a huge chain to the date-tree in whose place the column now stands, vowing to continue there until Allah and the Prophet accepted his penitence – a circumstance which did not take place till the tenth day, when his hearing was gone and he had almost lost his sight. The less celebrated pillars are the Ustuwanat Sarir, or Column of the Cot, where the Prophet was wont to sit meditating on his humble couch-frame of date-sticks. The Ustuwanat Ali notes the spot where the fourth caliph used to pray and watch his father-in-law at night. At the Ustuwanat el Wufud, as its name denotes, the Prophet received envoys, couriers, and emissaries from foreign places. The Ustuwanat el Tahajjud now stands where Mohammed, sitting upon his mat, passed the night in prayer. And lastly is the Makam Jibrail (Gabriel's place), for whose other name, Mirbaat el Bair, 'the Pole of the Beast of Burden', I have been unable to find an explanation.

The four Riwaks, or porches, of theMedinah Mosque open upon a hypæthral court of parallelogrammic shape. The only remarkable object in it is a square of wooden railing enclosing a place full of well-watered earth, called the Garden of our Lady Fatimah. It now contains a dozen date-trees – in Ibn Jubayr's time there were fifteen. Their fruit is sent by the eunuchs as presents to the Sultan and the great men of El Islam; it is highly valued by the vulgar, but the Olema do not think much of its claims to importance. Among the palms are the venerable remains of a Sidr, or Lote tree, whose produce is sold for inordinate sums. The enclosure is entered by a dwarf gate in the, south-eastern portion of the railing, near the well, and one of the eunuchs is generally to be seen in it: it is under the charge of the Mudir, or chief treasurer. These gardens are not uncommon in Mosques, as the traveller who passes through Cairo can convince himself. They form a pretty and an appropriate feature in a building erected for the worship of Him 'who spread the earth with carpets of flowers and drew shady trees from the dead ground.' A tradition of the Prophet also declares that 'acceptable is devotion in the garden and in the orchard'. At the south-east angle of the enclosure, under a wooden roof supported by pillars of the same material, stands the Zem Zem, generally called the Bir el Nabi, or 'the Prophet's well'. My predecessor declares that the brackishness of its produce has stood in th way of its reputation for holiness. Yet a well educated man told me that it was as 'light' water as any in El Medinah – a fact which he accounted for by supposing a subterraneous passage which connects it with the great Zem Zem at Meccah. Others, again, believe that it is filled by a vein of water springing directly under the Prophet's grave: generally, however, among the learned it is not more revered than our Lady's Garden, nor is it ranked in books among the holy wells of El Medinah. Between this Zem Zem and the eastern Riwak is the Stoa, or Academia, of the Prophet's city. In the cool mornings and evenings the ground is strewed with professors, who teach, as an eminent orientalist hath it, the young idea how to shout rather than to shoot. A few feet to the south of the palm garden is a moveable wooden planking painted green, and about three feet high; it serves to separate the congregation from the Imam when he prays here; and at the north-eastern angle of the enclosure is a Shajar Kanadil, a large brass chandelier which completes the furniture of the court.

After this inspection, the shadows of evening began to gather round us. We left the Mosque, reverently taking care to issue forth with the left foot and not to back out of it as is the Sunnat – practice derived from the Prophet – when taking leave of the Meccan Temple.

To conclude this long chapter. Although every Moslem, learned and simple, firmly believes that Mohammed's remains are interred in the Hujrah at El Medinah, I cannot help suspecting that the place is at least as doubtful as that of the Holy Sepulchre at Jerusalem. It must be remembered that a tumult followed the announcement of the Prophet's death, when the people, as often happens, believing him to be immortal, refused to credit the report, and even Omar threatened destruction to anyone that asserted it. Moreover the body was scarcely cold when the contest about the succession arose between the fugitives of Meccah and the auxiliaries of El Medinah: in the ardor of which, according to the Shiahs, the house of Ali and Fatimah – within a few feet of the spot where the tomb of the Prophet is now placed – was threatened with fire, and Abubekr was elected caliph that same evening. If any one find cause to wonder that the last resting-place of a personage so important was not fixed for ever he may find many a parallel case in El Medinah. To quote no other, three several localities claim the honor of containing the Lady Fatimah's mortal spoils, although one might suppose that the daughter of the Prophet and the mother of the Imams would not be laid in an unknown grave. My reasons for incredulity are the following:

From the earliest days the shape of the Prophet's tomb has never been generally known in El Islam. For this reason it is that graves are made convex in some countries, and flat in others: had there been a Sunnat, such would not have been the case.

The accounts of the learned are discrepant. El Samanhudi, perhaps the highest authority, contradicts himself. In one place he describes the coffin; in another he expressly declares that he entered the Hujrah when it was being repaired by Kaid Bey, and saw in the inside three deep graves, but no traces of tombs. Either, then, the mortal remains of the Prophet had – despite Moslem superstition – mingled with the dust (a probable circumstance after nearly 900 years' interment) or, what is more likely, they had been removed by the Shiah schismatics who for centuries had charge of the sepulchre.

And lastly, I cannot but look upon the tale of the blinding light which surrounds the Prophet's tomb, current for ages past and still universally believed upon the authority of the attendant eunuchs, who must know its falsehood, as a priestly gloss intended to conceal a defect.

I here conclude the subject, committing it to some future and more favored investigator. In offering the above remarks, I am far from wishing to throw a doubt upon an established point of history. But where a suspicion of fable arises from popular 'facts', a knowledge of man and of his manners teaches us to regard it with favoring eye.

CHAP. XV

A Ride To The
Mosque Of Kuba

The principal places of pious visitation in the vicinity of El Medinah, are the Mosques of Kuba, the Cemetery El Bakia, and the martyr Hamzah's tomb, at the foot of Mount Ohod. These the Zair is directed by all the Olema to visit, and on the holy ground to pray Allah for a blessing upon himself, and upon his brethren of the faith.

Early one Saturday morning, I started for Kuba with a motley crowd of devotees. Shaykh Hamid, my Muzawwir, was by my side, mounted upon an ass more miserable than I had yet seen. The boy Mohammed had procured for me a Meccan dromedary, with splendid trappings, a saddle with burnished metal peaks before and behind, covered with a huge sheepskin dyed crimson, and girthed over fine saddle-bags, whose enormous tassels hung almost to the ground. The youth himself, being too grand to ride a donkey, and unable to borrow a horse, preferred walking. He was proud as a peacock, being habited in a style somewhat resembling the plume of that gorgeous bird, in the coat of many colours – yellow, red, and golden flowers, apparently sewed on a field of bright green silk – which cost me so dear in the Haram. He was armed, as indeed all of us were, in readiness for the Bedouins, and he anxiously awaited opportunities of discharging his pistol. Our course lay from Shaykh Hamid's house in the Munakkah, along and up the Fiumarn, 'El Sayh,' and tlrough the Bab Kuba, a little gate in the suburb wall, where, by the bye, my mounted companion was nearly trampled down by a rush of half wild camels. Outside the town, in this direction, southward, is a plain of clay, mixed with chalk, and here and there with sand, whence protrude blocks and little ridges of basalt. As far us Kuba, and the Harrah ridge to the west, the earth is sweet and makes excellent gugglets. Immediately outside the gate I saw a kiln, where they were burning tolerable bricks. Shortly after leaving the suburb, an Indian, who joined our party upon the road, pointed out on the left of the way what he declared was the place of the celebrated Khandak, or Moat, the Torres Vedras of Arabian History.

Presently the Nakhil, or palm plantations, began. Nothing lovelier to the eye, weary with hot red glare, than the rich green waving crops and cool shade – for hours I could have sat and looked at it, requiring no other occupation – the 'food of vision,' as the Arabs call it, and 'pure water to the parched throat.' The air was soft and balmy, a perfumed breeze, strange luxury in El Hejaz, wandered amongst the date fronds; there were fresh flowers and bright foliage, in fact, at midsummer, every beautiful feature of spring. Nothing more delightful to the ear than the warbling of the small birds, that sweet familiar sound, the splashing of tiny cascades from the wells into the wooden troughs, and the musical song of the water-wheels. Travellers – young travellers – in the East talk of the 'dismal grating,' the 'mournful monotony,' and the 'melancholy creaking of these dismal machines.'

To the veteran wanderer their sound is delightful from association, reminding him of green fields, cool water-courses, hospitable villagers, and plentiful crops. The expatriated Nubian, for instance, listens to the water-wheel with as deep emotion as the Ranz des Vaches ever excited in the hearts of Switzer mercenary at Naples, or 'Lochaber no more,' among a regiment of Highlanders in the West Indies.

The date-trees of El Medinah merit their celebrity. Their stately columnar stems, here, seem higher than in other lands, and their lower fronds are allowed to tremble in the breeze without mutilation. These enormous palms were loaded with ripening fruit, and the clusters, carefully tied up, must often have weighed upwards of eighty pounds. They hung down between the lower branches by a bright yellow stem, as thick as a man's ancle. Books enumerate 139 varieties of trees; of these between sixty and seventy are well-known, and each is distinguished, as usual among Arabs, by its peculiar name. The best kind is El Shelebi; it is packed in skins, or in flat round boxes covered with paper, somewhat in the manner of French prunes, and sent as presents to the remotest parts of the Moslem world. The fruit is about two inches long, with a small stone, and what appeared to me a peculiar aromatic flavour and smell; it is seldom eaten by the citizens on account of the price, which varies from two to ten piastres the pound. The tree, moreover, is rare, and said to be not so productive as the other species. The Ajwah is eaten, but not sold, because a tradition of the Prophet declares, that who so breaketh his fast every day with six or seven of the Ajwah-date need fear neither poison, nor magic. The third kind, El Hilwah, also a large date, derives a name from its exceeding sweetness: of this tree the Moslems relate that the Prophet planted a stone, which in a few minutes grew up and bore fruit. Next comes El Birni, of which was said, 'It causeth sickness to depart, and there is no sickness in it.' The Wahshi on one occasion bent its head, and salamed to Mohammed as he ate its fruit, for which reason even now its lofty tuft turns earthwards. The Sayhani is so called, because when the founder of El Islam, holding Ali's hand, happened to pass beneath, it cried, 'This is Mohammed the Prince of Prophets, and this is Ali the Prince of the Pious, and the progenitor of the immaculate Imams.' Of course the descendants of so intelligent a vegetable hold high rank in the kingdom of palms, and the vulgar were in the habit of eating the Sayhani and of throwing the stones about the Haram. The Khuzayriyah is called so, because it preserves its green colour, even when perfectly ripe; it is dried and preserved as a curiosity. The Jebeli is that most usually eaten: the poorest kinds are the Laun and the Hilayah, costing from 4 to 7 piastres per mudd.

I cannot say that the dates of El Medinah are finer than those of Meccah, although it be highly heretical to hold such tenet. The produce of the former city was the favorite food of the Prophet, who invariably broke his fast with this food: a circumstance which invests it with a certain degree of relic-sanctity. The citizens delight in speaking of dates as an Irishman does of potatoes, with a manner of familiar fondness: they eat them for medicine as well as food: 'Rutab,' or wet dates, being held to be the most saving. It is doubtless the most savoury of remedies. The fruit is prepared in a great variety of ways: perhaps the most favorite dish is a broil with clarified butter, extremely distasteful to the European palate. The date is also left upon the tree to dry, and then called 'Balah:' this is eaten at dessert as the 'Nukliyat' – the 'quatre mendiants' of Persia.

Amongst peculiar preparations must be mentioned the Kulladat el Sham. The unripe fruit is dipped in boiling water to preserve its gamboge color, strung upon a thick thread and hung out in the air to dry. These strings are worn all over El Hejaz as necklaces by children, who seldom fail to munch the ornament when not in fear of slappings; and they are sent as presents to distant countries.

January and February are the time for the masculation of the palm. The 'Nakhwali,' as he is called, opens the female flower, and having inserted the inverted male flowers, binds them together: this operation is performed, as in Egypt, upon each cluster. The fruit is ripe about the middle of May, and the gathering of it forms the Arabs' 'vendemmia.' The people make merry the more readily because their favorite fruit is liable to a variety of accidents: droughts injure the tree, locusts destroy the produce, and the date crop, like most productions which men are imprudent enough to adopt singly as the staff of life, is subject to failure. One of the reasons for the excellence of Medinah dates is the quantity of water they obtain: each garden or field has its well, and even in the hottest weather the Persian wheel floods the soil every third day. It has been observed that the date-tree can live in dry and barren spots; but it loves the beds of streams and places where moisture is procurable. The palms scattered over the other parts of the plain, and depending solely upon rain water, produce less fruit, and that too of an inferior quality.

Verdure is not usually wholesome in Arabia, yet invalids leave the close atmosphere of El Medinah to seek health under the cool shades of Kuba. The gardens are divided by what might almost be called lanes, long narrow lines with tall reed fences on both sides. The graceful branches of the Tamarisk, pearled with manna, and cottoned over with dew, and the broad leaves of the castor plant, glistening in the sun, protected us from the morning rays.

The ground on both sides of the way was sunken, the earth being disposed in heaps at the foot of the fences, an arrangement which facilitates irrigation, by giving a fall to the water, and in some cases affords a richer soil than the surface. This part of the Medinah plain, however, being higher than the rest, is less subject to the disease of salt and nitre. On the way here and there the earth crumbles and looks dark under the dew of morning, but nowhere has it broken out into that glittering efflorescence which notes the last stage of the attack. The fields and gardens are divided into small oblongs separated from one another by little ridges of mould which form diminutive water-courses. Of the cereals there are luxuriant maize, wheat, and barley, but the latter two are in small quantities. Here and there patches of 'Barsim,' or Egyptian clover, glitter brightly in the sun. The principal vegetables are Badanjan (Egg plant), the Bamiyah (a kind of esculent hibiscus, called Bhendi in India), and Mulukhiyah (Corchoris olitorius), a mucilaginous spinage common throughout this part of the East. These three are eaten by citizens of every rank; they are in fact the greens and the potatoes of Arabia. I remarked also onions and leeks in fair quantities, a few beds of carrots and beans, some Fiji (radishes), Lift (turnips), gourds, cucumbers, and similar plants. Fruit trees abound. There are five descriptions of vines, the best of which is El Sherifi, a long white grape of a flavour somewhat resembling the produce of Tuscany. Next to it, and very similar, is El Birni. The Hejazi is a round fruit, sweet, but insipid, which is also the reproach of the Sawadi, or black grapes. And lastly, the Raziki is a small white fruit, with a diminutive stone. The Nebek, or Jujube, is here a fine large tree with a dark green loaf, roundish and polished like the olive; it is armed with a short, curved, and sharp thorn, and bears a pale straw-colored berry, about the size of a gooseberry, with red streaks on the side next the sun. Little can be said in favor of the fruit, which has been compared successively by disappointed 'Lotus eaters' to a bad plum, an unripe cherry, and an insipid apple. It is, however, a favorite with the people of El Medinah, who have reckoned many varieties of the fruit: Hindi (Indian), Baladi ('native'), Tamri (date-like), &c. There are a few peaches, hard like the Egyptian, and almost tasteless, fit only for stewing, but greedily eaten in a half-ripe state, large coarse bananas, lime trees, a few water melons, figs, and apples, but neither apricots nor pears. There are three kinds of pomegranates: the best is the Shami (Syrian); it is red outside, very sweet, and costs one piastre; the Turki is large, and of a white color; and the Misri has a greenish rind, and a somewhat sub-acid and harsh flavour: the latter are sold four times as cheap as the best. I never saw in the East, except, at Meccah, a finer fruit than the Shami: almost stoneless, like those of Muscat, they are delicately perfumed, and as large as an infant's head. El Medinah is celebrated, like Taif, for its 'Rubb Rumman,' a thick pomegranate syrup, drunk with water during the hot weather, and esteemed cooling and wholesome.

After threading our way through the gardens, an operation requiring less time than to describe them, we saw, peeping through the groves, Kuba's simple minaret. Then we came in sight of a confused heap of huts and dwelling-houses, chapels and towers with trees between, and foul lanes, heaps of rubbish, and barking dogs – the usual material of a Hejazi village. Having dismounted, we gave our animals in charge of a dozen infant Bedouins, the produce of the peasant gardeners, who shouted 'Bakhshish' the moment they saw us. To this they were urged by their mothers, and I willingly parted with a few paras for the purpose of establishing an intercourse with fellow-creatures so fearfully and wonderfully resembling the tail-less baboon. Their bodies, unlike those of Egyptian children, were slim and straight, but their ribs stood out with a curious distinctness, the color of the skin was that oily lamp-black seen upon the face of a European sweep, and the elf-locks, thatching the coconut heads, had been stained by the sun, wind, and rain to that reddish-brown hue which Hindu romances have appropriated to their Rakshasas or demons. Each anatomy carried in his arms a stark-naked miniature of himself, fierce-looking babies with faces all eyes, and the strong little wretches were still able to extend the right hand and exert their lungs with direful clamor. Their mothers were fit progenitors for such progeny: long, gaunt, with emaciated limbs, wall-sided, high-shouldered, and straight-backed, with pendulous bosoms, spider-like arms, and splay feet. Their long elf-locks, wrinkled faces, and high cheek-bones, their lips darker than the epidermis, hollow staring eyes, sparkling as if to light up the extreme ugliness around, and voices screaming as if in a perennial rage, invested them with all the 'charms of Sycorax.' These 'Houris of Zetannum' were habited in long night-gowns dyed blue to conceal want of washing, and the squalid children had about a yard of the same material wrapped round their waist for all toilette. This is not an overdrawn portrait of the farmer race of Arabs, the most despised by their fellow-countrymen, and the most hard-favored, morally as well as physically, of all the breed.

Before entering the Mosque of El Kuba it will be necessary to cull to mind some passages of its past history. When the Prophet's she-camel, El Kaswa, as he was approaching El Medinah after the flight from Meccah, knelt down here, he desired his companions to mount the animal. Abubekr and Omar did so; still she sat upon the ground, but when Ali obeyed the order, she arose. The Prophet bade him loose her halter, for she was directed by Allah, and the Mosque walls were built upon the line over which she trod. It was the first place of public prayer in El Islam. Mohammed laid the lirst brick, and with an 'Anzah' or iron-shod javelin, marked out the direction of prayer, each of his successors followed his example. According to most historians, the land belonged to Abu Ayyub the Ansari; for which reason the 'Bayt Ayyub,' his descendants, still perform the service of the Mosque, keep the key, and share with the Bawwabs or porters the alms and fees here offered by the Faithful. Others declared that the ground was the property of one Linah, a woman who was in the habit of tethering her ass there. The Prophet used to visit it every Saturday on foot, and always made a point of praying (lie dawn-prayer there on the 17th Ramazan. A number of traditions testify to its dignity: of these two are especially significant. The first assures all Moslems that a prayer at Kuba is equal to a Lesser Pilgrimage at Meccah in religious efficacy; and the second declares that such devotion is more acceptable to the Deity than prostrations at the Bayt el Mukaddas (Jerusalem). Moreover sundry miracles took place here, and a verset of the Koran descended from heaven. For which reasons the Mosque was much respected by Omar, who, once finding it empty, swept it himself with a broom of thorns, and expressed his wonder at the lukewarmness of Moslem piety. It was originally a square building of very small size; Osman enlarged it in the direction of the minaret, making it sixty-six cubits each way. It is no longer 'mean and decayed' as in Burckhardt's time: the Sultan Abd el Hamid, father of Mahmud, erected a neat structure of cut stone, whose crenelles make it look more like a place of defence than of prayer. It has, however, no pretensions to grandeur. The minaret is of the Turkish shape. To the south a small and narrow Riwak, or raised hypo-style, with unpretending columns, looks out northwards upon a little open area simply sanded over; and this is the whole building.

The large Mastabah or stone bench at the entrance of the Mosque, was crowded with sitting people: we therefore lost no time, after ablution and the Niyat ('the Intention') peculiar to this visitation, in ascending the steps, in pulling off our slippers, and in entering the sacred building. We stood upon the Musalla el Nabi (the Prophet's place of prayer): after Shaykh Nur and Hamid had forcibly cleared that auspicious spot of a devout Indian, and had spread a rug upon the dirty matting, we performed a two-bow prayer, in front of a pillar into which a diminutive marble Mihrab or niche had been inserted by way of memento. Then came the Dua, or suplication, which was as follows:

'O Allah! Bless and preserve, and increase, and perpetuate, and benefit, and be propitious to, our lord Mohammed, and to his family, and to his companions, and be thou their Preserver! O Allah! This is the Mosque Kuba, and the place of the Prophet's prayers. O Allah! Pardon our sins, and veil our faults, and place not over us one who feareth not thee, and who pitieth not us, and pardon us, and the true believers, men and women, the quick of them and the dead; for verily thou, O Lord, art the hearer, the near to us, the answerer of our supplications.'

After which we recited the Testification and the Fatihah, and we drew our palms as usual down our faces.

We then moved away to the south-eastern corner of the edifice, and stood before a Mihrab in the southern wall. It is called 'Takat el Kashf' or 'Niche of Disclosure,' by those who believe that as the Prophet was standing undecided about the direction of Meccah, the Archangel Gabriel removed all obstructions to his vision. There again we went through the two-bow prayer, the Supplication, the Testification, and the Fatihah, under difficulties, for people crowded us excessively. During our devotions, I vainly attempted to decipher a Cufic inscription fixed in the wall above and on the right of the Mihrab – my regret, however, at this failure was transitory, the character not being of an ancient date. Then we left the Riwak, and despite the morning sun which shone fiercely witli a sickly heat, we went, to the open area where stands the 'Mabrak el Nakuh,' or the 'Place of kneeling of the she Dromedary.' This, the exact spot where El Kaswa sat down, is covered with a diminutive dome of cut stone, supported by four stone pillars: the building is about eight feet high and a little less in length and breadth. It has the appearance of being modern. On the floor, which was raised by steps above the level of the ground, lay, as usual, a bit of dirty matting, upon which we again went through the ceremonies above detailed.

Then issuing from the canopy into the sun, a little outside the Riwak and close to the Mabrak, we prayed upon the 'Makan el Ayat,' or the'Place of Signs.' Here was revealed to Mohammed a passage in the Koran especially alluding to the purity of the place and of the people of Kuba, 'a temple founded in purity from its first day;' and again; 'there men live who love to be cleansed, and verily Allah delights in the clean.' The Prophet exclaimed in admiration, 'O ye sons of Amr! What have ye done to deserve all this praise and beneficence?' when the people offered him an explanation of their personal cleanliness which I do not care to repeat. The temple of Kuba from that day took a fresh title – Masjid el Takwa, or the 'Mosque of Piety.'

Having finished our prayers and ceremonies at the Mosque of Piety, we fought our way out through a crowd of importunate beggars, and turning a few paces to the left, halted near a small chapel adjoining the south-west angle of the larger temple. We there stood at a grated window in the western wall, and recited a supplication looking the while most reverently at a dark dwarf archway under which the Lady Fatimah used to sit grinding grain in a hand mill. The Mosque in consequence bears the name of Sittna Fatimah. A surly-looking Khadim, or guardian, stood at the door demanding a dollar in the most authoritative Arab tone – we therefore did not enter. At El Medinah and at Meccah the traveller's hand must be perpetually in his pouch: no stranger in Paris or London is more surely or more severely taken in. Already I began to fear that my eighty pounds would not suffice for all the expenses of sight-seeing, and the apprehension was justified by the sequel. My only friend was the boy Mohammed, who displayed a fiery economy that brought him into considerable disrepute with his countrymen. They saw with emotion that he was preaching parsimony to me solely that I might have more money to spend at Meccah under his auspices. This being palpably the case, I threw all the blame of penuriousness upon the young Machiavel's shoulders, and resolved, as he had taken charge of my finances at El Medinah, so at Meccah to administer them myself.

After praying at the window, to the great disgust of the Khadim, who openly asserted that we were 'low fellows,' we passed through some lanes lined with beggars and Bedouin children, till we came to a third little Mosque situated due south of the larger one. This is called the Masjid Arafat, and is created upon a mound also named Tall Arafat, because on one occasion the Prophet, being unable to visit the Holy mountain at the pilgrimage season, stood there, saw through the intervening space, and in spirit performed tho ceremony. Here also we looked into a window instead of opening the door with a silver key, and the mesquin appearance of all within prevented my regretting the necessity of economy. In India or Sindh every village would have a better mosque. Our last visit was to a fourth chapel, the Masjid Ali, so termed because the Prophet's son-in-law had a house upon this spot. After praying there – and terribly hot the little hole was! – We repaired to the last place of visitation at Kuba – a large deep well called the Bir El Aris, in a garden to the west of the Mosque of Piety, with a little oratory adjoining it. A Persian wheel was going drowsily round, and the cool water fell into a tiny pool, whence it whirled and bubbled away in childish mimicry of a river. The music sounded sweet in my ears, I stubbornly refused to do any more praying – though Shaykh Hamid, for form's sake, reiterated, with parental emphasis, 'how very wrong it was,' – and sat down, as the Prophet himself did not disdain to do, with the resolution of enjoying on the brink of the well a few moments of unwonted 'Kayf.' The heat was overpowering, though it was only nine o'clock, the sound of the stream was soothing, that water wheel was creaking a lullaby, and the limes and pomegranates, gently rustling, shed voluptuous fragrance through the morning air. I fell asleep – and wondrous the contrast! – dreamed that I was once more standing

'By the wall whereon liangcth the crucified vine,'

looking upon the valley of the Lianne, with its glaucous seas and grey skies, and banks here and there white with snow.

The Bir el Aris, so called after a Jew of El Medinah, is one which the Prophet delighted to visit. He would sit upon its brink with his bare legs hanging over the side, and his companions used to imitate his example. This practice caused a sad disaster; in the sixth year of his caliphate, Osman, according to Abulfeda and Yakut, dropped from his finger Mohammed's seal ring, which, engraved in three lines with 'Mohammed – Apostle – (of) Allah,' had served to seal the letters sent to neighboring kings, and had descended to the first three successors! The precious article was not recovered after three days' search, and the well was thenceforward called Bir el Khatim – of the Seal Ring. It is also called the Birel Taflat – of Saliva – because the Prophet honoured it by expectoration, which, by the bye, he seems to have done to almost all the wells in El Medinah. The effect of the operation upon the Bir el Aris, say the historians, was to sweeten the water, which before was salt. Their testimony, however, did not prevent my detecting a pronounced medicinal taste in the luke-warm draught drawn for me by Shaykh Hamid. In Mohammed's day the total number of wells is recorded to have been twenty: most of them have long since disappeared; but there still remain seven, whose waters were drunk by the Prophet, and which, in consequence, the Zair is directed to visit. They are known by the classical title of Saba Abar, or the seven wells, and their names are included in this couplet,

'Aris and Ghars, and Rumah and Buznat
And Busat, with Bayruha and Bin.'

After my sleep, which was allowed to last until a pipe or two of Latakia had gone round the party, we remounted our animals. On the left of the village returning towards El Medinah, my companions pointed out to me a garden, called El Madshuniyah. It contains a quarry of the yellow loam or bole-earth, called by the Arabs Tafl, the Persians Gil i Sarshui and the Sindhians Met. It is used as soap in many parts of the East, and, mixed with oil, it is supposed to cool the body, and to render the skin fresh and supple. It is related that the Prophet cured a Bedouin of the Beni Haris tribe of fever by washing him with a pot of Tafl dissolved in water, and hence the earth of El Medinah derived its healing fame. As far as I could learn from the Madani, this clay is no longer valued by them, either medicinally or cosmetically; the only use they could mention was its being eaten by the fair sex, when in the peculiar state described by 'chlorosis.'

The Visitation Of Hamzah's Tomb

On the morning of Sunday, the twenty-third Zu'l Kaadah (28th August, 1853), arrived the great Caravan from El Sham or Damascus. It is popularly called Hajj El Shami, the 'Damascus pilgrimage,' as the Egyptian Cafila is El Misri, or the Cairo pilgrimage. It is the main stream which carries off all the small currents that at this season of general movement flow from central Asia towards the great centre of the Islamic world, and in 1853 amounted to about 7000 souls. It was anxiously expected by the people for several reasons. In the first place, it brought with it a new curtain for the Prophet's Hujrah, the old one being in a tattered condition; secondly, it had charge of the annual stipends and pensions of the citizens; and thirdly, many families expected members returning under its escort to their homes. The popular anxiety was greatly increased by the disordered state of the country round about; and, moreover, the great caravan had been one day late, generally arriving on the morning of the 22nd Zu'l Kaadah.

During the night three of Shaykh Hamid's brothers, who had entered as Muzawwirs with the Hajj, came suddenly to the house: they leaped off their camels, and lost not a moment in going through the usual scene of kissing, embracing, and weeping bitterly for joy. I arose in the morning, and looked out from the windows of the Majlis: the Barr el Munakhah, from a dusty waste dotted with a few Bedouins and hair tents, had assumed all the various shapes and the colors of a kaleidescope. The eye was bewildered by the shifting of innumerable details, in all parts totally different from one another, thrown confusedly together in one small field; and, however jaded with sightseeing, it dwelt with delight upon the vivacity, the variety, and the intense picturesqueness of the scene. In one night had sprung up a town of tents of every size, color, and shape – round, square and oblong – open and closed – from the shawl-lined and gilt-topped pavilion of the Pacha, with all the luxurious appurtenances of the Harem, to its neighbour the little dirty green 'rowtie' of the tobacco-seller. They were pitched in admirable order: here ranged in a long line, where a street was required; there packed in dense masses, where thoroughfares were unnecessary. But how describe the utter confusion in the crowding, the hustling, and the vast variety and volume of sound? Huge white Syrian dromedaries, compared with which those of El Hejaz appeared mere pony-camels, jingling large bells, and hearing Shugdufs like miniature green tents, swaying and tossing upon their backs; gorgeous Takh-trawan, or litters carried between camels or mules with scarlet and brass trappings; Bedouins bestriding naked-backed 'Daluls,' and clinging like apes to the hairy humps; Arnaut, Turkish, and Kurd Irregular Cavalry, fiercer looking in their mirth than Roman peasants in their rage; fainting Persian pilgrims, forcing their stubborn dromedaries to kneel, or dismounted grumbling from jaded donkeys; Kahwajis, sherbet sellers, and ambulant tobacconists crying their goods; country-people driving flocks of sheep and goats with infinite clamor through lines of horses fiercely snorting and rearing; townspeople seeking their friends; returned travellers exchanging affectionate salutes; devout Hajis jolting one another, running under the legs of camels, and tumbling over the tents' ropes in their hurry to reach the Haram; cannon roaring from the citadel; shopmen, watercarriers and fruit vendors fighting over their bargains; boys bullying heretics with loud screams; a well-mounted party of fine old Arab Shaykhs of Hamidah clan, preceded by their varlets, performing the Arzah or war dance – compared with which the Pyrenean bear's performance is grace itself – firing their duck-guns upwards, or blowing the powder into the calves of those before them, brandishing their swords, leaping frantically the while, with their bright-colored rags floating in the wind, tossing their long spears tufted with ostrich feathers high in the air, reckless where they fall; servants seeking their masters, and masters their tents with vain cries of Ya Mohammed; grandees riding mules or stalking on foot, preceded by their crowd-beaters, shouting to clear the way; – here the loud shrieks of women and children, whose litters are bumping and rasping against one another; – there the low moaning of some poor wretch that is seeking a shady corner to die in: – add a thick dust which blurs the outlines like a London fog, with a flaming sun that draws sparkles of fire from the burnished weapons of the crowd, and the brass balls of tent and litter; and – I doubt, gentle reader, that even the length, the jar, and the confusion of this description is adequate to its subject, or that any 'word-painting' of mine can convey a just idea of the scene.

This was the day appointed for our visiting the martyrs of Ohod. After praying the dawn-prayers as directed at the Haram, we mounted our donkeys, and, armed with pistols and knives, set out from the city. Our party was large. Saad the Devil had offered to accompany us, and the bustle around kept him in the best of humours; Umar Effendi was also there, quiet-looking and humble as usual, leading his ass to avoid the trouble of dismounting every second minute. I had the boy Mohammed and my 'slave,' and Shaykh Hamid was attended by half a dozen relations. To avoid the crush of the Barr el Munakhah, we made a detour westwards, over the bridge and down the course of the torrent-bed 'el Sayh.' We then passed along the southern wall of the castle, traversed its eastern outwork, and issued from the Bab el Shami. During the greater part of the time we were struggling through a living tide; and among dromedaries and chargers a donkey is by no means a pleasant monture. With some difficulty, but without any more serious accident than a fall or two, we found ourselves in the space beyond and northward of the city. This also was covered with travellers and tents, amongst which, on an eminence to the left of the road, rose conspicuous the bright green pavilion of the Emir El Hajj, the commandant of the Caravan. Hard by, half its height surrounded by a Kanat or tent wall, stood the Syrian or Sultan's Mahmal, all glittering with green and gilding and gold, and around it were pitched the handsome habitations of the principal officers and grandees of the pilgrimage. On the right hand lay extensive palm plantations, and on the left, strewed over the plain, were signs of wells and tanks, built to supply the Hajj with water. We pass two small buildings – one the Kubbat El Sabak, or Dome of Precedence, where the Prophet's warrior friends used to display their horsemanship; the second the Makan, or burial-place of Sayyidna Zaki el Din, one of Mohammed's multitudinous descendants. Then we fall into a plain, resembling that of Kuba, but less fertile. While we are jogging over it, a few words concerning Mount Ohod may not be misplaced. A popular distich says,

> 'Verily there is healing to the eye that looks
> Unto Ohod and the two Harrahs near.'

And of this holy hill the Prophet declared, 'Ohod is a mountain which loves us and which we love: it is upon the gate of Heaven'; adding, 'and Ayr is a place which hates us and which we hate: it is upon the gate of Hell.' The former sheltered Mohammed in the time of danger, therefore, on Resurrection Day it will be raised to Paradise: whereas Jebel Ayr, its neighbour, having been so ill-judged as to refuse the Prophet water on an occasion while he thirsted, will be cast incontinently into Hell. Moslem divines, be it observed, ascribe to Mohammed miraculous authority over animals, vegetables, and minerals, as well as over men, angels, and jinns. Hence the speaking wolf, the weeping post, the oil-stone, and the love and hate of these two mountains. It is probably one of the many remains of ancient paganism pulled down and afterwards used to build up the edifice of El Islam. According to the old Persians, the sphere hath an active soul. Some sects of Hindus believe 'mother earth,' upon whose bosom we little parasites crawl, to be a living being. This was a dogma also amongst the ancient Egyptians, who denoted it by a peculiar symbol – the globe with human legs. Hence the 'Makrokosmos' of the plagiaristic Greeks, the animal on a large scale, whose diminutive was the 'Mikrokosmos' – man. 'Tota natura,' repeats Malpighi, 'existit in minimis.' Amongst the Romans,

Tellus or Terra was a female deity, anthropomorphised according to their syncretic system, which furnished with strange gods their Pantheon, but forgot to append the scroll explaining the inner sense of the symbol. And some modern philosophers, Kepler, Blackmore, and others, have not scrupled to own their belief in a doctrine which as long as 'Life' is a mere word on man's tongue, can neither be disproved nor proved. The Mohammedans, as usual, exaggerate the dogma – a Hadis related by Abu Hurayrah casts on the day of judgment the sun and the moon into hell fire.

Jebel Ohod owes its present reputation to a cave which sheltered the Prophet when pursued by his enemies, to certain springs of which he drank, and especially to its being the scene of a battle celebrated in El Islam. On Saturday, the 11th Shawwal, in the 3rd year of the Hijrah (26th January AD 625) Mohammed with 700 men engaged 3000 infidels under the command of Abu Sufiyan, ran great personal danger, and lost his uncle Hamzah, the 'Lord of Martyrs.' On the topmost pinnacle, also, is the Kubbat Harun, the dome erected over Aaron's remains. It is now, I was told, in a ruinous condition, and is placed upon the 'pinnacle of seven hills' in a position somewhat like that of certain buildings on St. Angelo in the bay of Nuples. Alluding to the toil of reaching it, the Madani quote a facetious rhyme inscribed upon the wall by one of their number who had wasted his breath; –

'Malun ibn Malun
Man talaa Kubbat Harun!'

Anglicè, 'The man must be a ruffian who climbs up to Aaron's Dome.' Devout Moslems visit Ohod every Thursday morning after the dawn devotions in the Haram, pray for the Shuhada of Ohod, and, after going through the ceremonies, return to the Haram in time for mid-day worship. On the 12th of Rajab, Zairs come out in large bodies from the city, encamp here for three or four days, pass the time in feasting, jollity, and devotion, as usual at saints' festivals and pilgrimages in general.

After half an hour's ride we came to the Mustarah or resting place, so called because the Prophet sat here for a few minutes on his way to the battle of Ohod. It is a newly-built square enclosure of dwarf whitewashed walls, within which devotees pray. On the outside fronting El Medinah is a seat like a chair of rough stones. Here I was placed by my Muzawwir, who recited an insignificant supplication to be repeated after him. At its end with the Fatihah and accompaniments, we remounted our asses and resumed our way. Travelling onwards, we came in sight of the second Harrah or ridge. It lies to the right and left of the road, and resembles lines of lava, but I had not on opportunity to examine it narrowly. Then we reached the gardens of Ohod, which reflect in miniature those of Kuba, and presently we arrived at what explained the presence of verdure and vegetable life – a deep Fiumara full of loose sand and large stones denoting an impetuous stream. It flows along the southern base of Ohod, said to be part of the Medinah plain, and collects the drainage of the high lands to the S. and S. E. The bed becomes impassable after rain, and sometimes the torrents overflow the neighbouring gardens. By the direction of this Fiumara I judged that it must supply the Ghabbah or 'basin' in the hills north of the plain. Good authorities, however, informed me that a large volume of water will not stand there, but flows down the beds that wind through the Ghauts westward of El Medinah and falls into the sea near the harbour of Wijh. To the south of the Fiumara is a village on an eminence, containing some large brick houses now in a ruinous state; these are the villas of opulent and religious citizens who visited the place for change of air, recreation, and worship at Hamzah's tomb. Our donkeys sank fetlock-deep in the loose sand of the torrent-bed. Then reaching the northern side and ascending a gentle slope, we found ourselves upon the battlefield.

This spot, so celebrated in the annals of El Islam, is a shelving strip of land, close to the southern base of Mount Ohod. The army of the Infidels advanced from tho Fiumara in crescent shape, with Abu Sufiyan, the general, and his idols in the centre. It is distant about three miles from El Medinah, in a northerly direction. All the visitor sees is hard gravelly ground, covered with little heaps of various colored granite, red sandstone, and hits of porphyry, to denote the different places where the martyrs fell, and were buried. Seen from this point, there is something appalling in the look of the Holy Mountain. Its seared and jagged flanks rise like masses of iron from the plain, and the crevice into which the Moslem host retired, when the disobedience of the archers in hastening to plunder enabled Khalid bin Walid to fall upon Mohammed's rear, is the only break in the grim wall. Reeking with heat, its surface produces not one green shrub or stunted tree; not a bird or beast appeared upon its inhospitable sides, and the bright blue sky glaring above its bald and sullen brow, made it look only the more repulsive. I was glad to turn my eyes away from it.

To the left of the road N. of the Fiumara, and leading to the mountains, stands Hamzah's Mosque, which, like the Haram of El Medinah, is a mausoleum as well as a fane. It is a small square strongly-built edifice of hewn stone, with a dome covering the solitary hypostyle to the south, and the usual minaret. The westward wing is a Zawiyah or oratory, frequented by the celebrated Sufi and Saint Mohammed el Samman, the 'clarified butter-seller,' one of whose blood, the reader will remember, stood by my side in the person of Shaykh Hamid. On the eastern side of the building a half wing projects, and opens to the south, with a small door upon a Mustabah or stone bench five or six feet high, which completes the square of the edifice. On the right of the road opposite Hamzah's Mosque, is a large erection, now in ruins, containing a deep hole leading to a well, and huge platforms for the accommodation of travellers, and beyond, towards the mountains, are the small edifices presently to be described.

Some Turkish women were sitting veiled upon the shady platform opposite the Martyrs' Mosque. At a little distance their husbands, and the servants holding horses and asses, lay upon the ground, and a large crowd of Bedouins, boys, girls, and old women, had gathered around to beg, draw water, and sell dry dates. They were awaiting the guardian, who had not yet acknowledged the summons. After half an hour's vain patience, we determined to proceed with the ceremonies. Ascending by its steps the Mastabah subtending half the eastern wall, Shaykh Hamid placed me so as to front the tomb. There, standing in the burning sun, we repeated the following prayer: 'Peace be upon thee, O our lord Hamzah! O paternal uncle of Allah's messenger! O paternal uncle of Allah's Prophet! Peace be upon thee, O paternal uncle of Mustafa! Peace be upon thee, O Prince of the Martyrs! O Prince of the Happy! Peace be upon thee, O Lion of Allah! O Lion of his Prophet!'

After which, we asked Hamzah and his companions to lend us their aid, in obtaining for us and ours pardon, worldly prosperity, and future happiness. Scarcely had we finished when, mounted on a high-trotting dromedary, appeared the emissary of Mohammed Khalifah, descendant of El Abbas, who keeps the key of the Mosque, and receives the fees and donations of the devout. It was to be opened for the Turkish pilgrims. I waited to see the interior. The Arab drew forth from his pouch, with abundant solemnity, a bunch of curiously made keys, and sharply directed me to stand away from and out of sight of the door. When I obeyed, grumblingly, he began to rattle the locks, and to snap the padlocks, opening them slowly, shaking them, and making as much noise as possible. The reason of the precaution – it sounded like poetry if not sense – is this. It is believed that the souls of martyrs, leaving the habitations of their senseless clay, are fond of sitting together in spiritual converse, and profane eye must not fall upon the scene. What grand pictures these imaginative Arabs see! Conceive the majestic figures of the saints – for the soul with Mohammedans is like the old European spirit, a something immaterial in the shape of the body – with long grey beards, earnest faces, and solemn eyes, reposing beneath the palms, and discussing events now buried in the darkness of a thousand yours.

I would fain be hard upon this superstition, but shame prevents. When in Nottingham, eggs may not be carried out after sunset; when Ireland hears Banshees, or apparitional old women, with streaming hair, and dressed in blue mantles; when Scotland sees a shroud about a person, showing his approaching death; when France has her loup-garous, revenants, and poules du Vendredi Saint (i.e. hens hatched on

Good Friday supposed to change color every year): as long as the Holy Coat cures devotees at Trèves, Madonnas wink at Rimini, San Gennaro melts at Naples, and Addolorate and Estatiche make converts to hysteria at Rome – whilst the Virgin manifests herself to children on the Alps, whilst Germany sends forth Psychography, whilst Europe, the civilised, the enlightened, the sceptical, dotes over such puerilities as clairvoyance and table-turning; and whilst even hard-headed America believes in 'mediums,' in 'snail-telegraphs,' and 'spirit- rappings,' – I must hold the men of El Medinah to be as wise, and their superstition to be as respectable as others.

But the realities of Hamzah's Mosque have little to recommend them. The building is like that of Kuba, only smaller, and the hypostyle is hung with oil lamps and ostrich eggs, the usual paltry furniture of an Arab mausoleum. On the walls are a few modern inscriptions and framed poetry, written in a caligraphic hand. Beneath the Riwak lies Hamzah, under a mass of black basaltic stone, resembling that of Aden, only more porous and scoriaceous, convex at the top, like a heap of earth, without the Kiswah, or cover of a saint's tomb, and railed round with wooden bars. At his head, or westward, lies Abdullah bin Jaysh, a name little known to fame, under a plain whitewashed tomb, also convex; and in the courtyard is a similar pile, erected over the remains of Shammas bin Usman, another obscure companion. We then passed through a door in the northern part of the western wall, and saw a diminutive palm plantation and a well. After which we left the Mosque, and I was under the 'fatal necessity' of paying a dollar for the honor of entering it. But the guardian promised that the chapters Y. S. and El Ikhlas should be recited for my benefit – the latter forty times – and if their efficacy be one-twentieth part of what men say it is, the reader cannot quote against me a certain popular proverb, concerning an order of men easily parted from their money.

Issuing from the Mosque, we advanced a few paces towards the mountain. On our left we passed by – at a respectful distance, for the Turkish Hajis cried out that their women were engaged in ablution – a large Sehrij or tank, built of cut stone with steps, and intended to detain the overflowing waters of the torrent. The next place we prayed at was a small square, enclosed with dwarf whitewashed walls, containing a few graves denoted by ovals of loose stones thinly spread upon the ground. This is primitive Arab simplicity. The Bedouins still mark the places of their dead with four stones planted at the head, the feet, and the sides; in the centre the earth is either heaped up Musannam (i.e. like the hump of a camel), or more generally left Musattah – level. I therefore suppose that the latter was the original shape of the Prophet's tomb. Within the enclosure certain martyrs of the holy army were buried. After praying there, we repaired to a small building still nearer to the foot of the mountain. It is the usual cupola springing from four square walls, not in the best preservation. Here the Prophet prayed, and it is called the Kubbat el Sanaya, 'Dome of the Front Teeth,' from the following circumstance. Five Infidels were bound by oath to slay Mohammed at the battle of Ohod: one of these, Ibn Kumayyah, threw so many stones, and with such good will that two rings of the Prophet's helmet were driven into his cheek, and blood poured from his brow down his mustachios, which he wiped with a cloak to prevent the drops falling to the ground. Then Utbah bin Abi Wakkas hurled a stone at him, which, splitting his lower lip, knocked out one of his front teeth. On the left of the Mihrab, inserted low down in the wall, is a square stone, upon which Shaykh Hamid showed me the impression of a tooth: he kissed it with peculiar reverence, and so did I. But the boy Mohammed being by me objurgated – for I remarked in him a jaunty demeanour combined with neglectfulness of ceremonies – saluted it sulkily, muttering the while hints about the holiness of his birthplace exempting him from the trouble of stooping. Already he had appeared at the Haram without his Jubbah, and with ungirt loins – in waistcoat and shirt sleeves. Moreover he had conducted himself indecorously by nudging Shaykh Hamid's sides during divine service. Feeling that the youth's 'moral man' was, like his physical, under my charge, and determined to arrest a course of conduct which must have ended in obtaining for me, the master, the reputation of a 'son of Belial,' I insisted upon his joining us in the customary two-bow prayers. And Saad the Devil taking my side of the question with his usual alacrity when a disturbance was in prospect, the youth found it necessary to yield. After this little scene, Shaykh Hamid pointed out a sprawling inscription blessing the companions of the Prophet. The unhappy Abubekr's name had been half effaced by some fanatic Shiah, a circumstance which seemed to arouse all the evil in my companions' nature, and looking close at the wall I found a line of Persian verse to this effect:

'I am weary of my life (Umr), because it bears the name of Umar.'

We English wanderers are beginning to be shamed out of our habit of scribbling names and nonsense in noted spots. Yet the practice is both classical and oriental. The Greeks and Persians left their marks everywhere, as Egypt shows, and the paws of the Sphinx bear scratches which, being interpreted, are found to be the same manner of trash as that written upon the remains of Thebes in AD 1853. And Easterns appear never to enter a building with a white wall without inditing upon it platitudes in verse and prose. Influenced by these considerations, I drew forth a pencil and inscribed in the Kubbat el Sanaya, 'Abdullah, the servant of Allah.' (A. H. 12G9.)

Issuing from the dome we turned a few paces to the left, passed northwards, and thus blessed the Martyrs of Ohod:

> 'Peace be upon ye, O Martyrs! Peace be upon ye, O blessed! Ye pious! Ye pure! Who fought upon Allah's path the good fight, who worshipped your Lord until He brought you to certainty. Peace be upon you of whom Allah said (viz. in the Koran) 'Verily repute not them slain on God's path (i.e. warring with Infidels); nay, rather they are alive, and there is no fear upon them, nor are they sorrowful!' Peace be upon ye, O Martyrs of Ohod I one and all, and the mercy of Allah and his blessings.'

Then again we moved a few paces forward and went through a similar ceremony, supposing ourselves to be in the cave that sheltered the Prophet. After which, returning towards the torrent-bed by the way we came, we stood a small distance from a cupola called Kubbat el Masra. It resembles that of the 'Front-teeth,' and notes, as its name proves, the place where the gallant Hamzah fell by the spear of Wahshi the slave. We faced towards it and finished the ceremonies of this Ziyarat by a Supplication, the Testification, and the Fatihah.

In the evening I went with my friends to the Haram. The minaret galleries were hung with lamps, and the inside of the temple was illuminated. It was crowded with Hajis, amongst whom were many women, a circumstance which struck me from its being unusual. Some pious pilgrims, who had duly paid for the privilege, were perched upon ladders trimming wax candles of vast dimensions, others were laying up for themselves rewards in Paradise, by performing the same office to the lamps; many were going through the ceremonies of Ziyarat, and not a few were sitting in different parts of the Mosque apparently overwhelmed with emotion. The boys and the beggars were inspired with fresh energy, the Aghawat were gruffer and surlier than I had ever seen them, and the young men about town walked and talked with a freer and an easier demeanour than usual. My old friends the Persians – there were about 1200 of them in the Hajj caravan – attracted my attention. The doorkeepers stopped them with curses as they were about to enter, and all claimed from each the sum of five piastres, whilst other Moslems are allowed to enter the Mosque free. Unhappy men! they had lost all the Shiraz swagger, their mustachios drooped pitiably, their eyes would not look any one in the face, and not a head bore a cap stuck upon it crookedly. Whenever an 'Ajami,' whatever might be his rank, stood in the way of an Arab or a Turk, he was rudely thrust aside, with abuse muttered loud enough to be heard by all around. All eyes followed them as they went through the ceremonies of Ziyarat, especially as they approached the tombs of Abubekr and Omar – which every man is bound to defile if he can – and the supposed place of Fatimah's burial. Here they stood in parties, after praying before the Prophet's window: one read from a book the pathetic tale of the Lady's life, sorrows, and mourning death, whilst the others listened to him with breathless attention. Sometimes their emotion was too strong to be repressed. 'Ay Fatimah! Ay Mazlumah! Way! way! – O Fatimah! O thou injured one! Alas! alas!' – burst involuntarily from their lips, despite the danger of such exclamations, tears trickled down their hairy cheeks, and their brawny bosoms heaved with sobs. A strange sight it was to see rugged fellows, mountaineers perhaps, or the fierce Iliyat of the plains, sometimes weeping silently like children, sometimes shrieking like hysteric girls, and utterly careless to conceal a grief so coarse and grisly, at the same time so true and real, that we knew not how to behold it. Then the Satanic scowls with which they passed by or pretended to pray at the hated Omar's tomb! With what curses their hearts are belying those mouths full of blessings! How they are internally canonising Fayruz, and praying for his eternal happiness in the presence of the murdered man! Sticks and stones, however, and not unfrequently the knife and the sabre, have taught them the hard lesson of disciplining their feelings, and nothing but a furious contraction of the brow, a roll of the eye, intensely vicious, and a twitching of the muscles about the region of the mouth, denotes the wild storm of wrath within. They generally, too, manage to discharge some part of their passion in words. 'Hail Omar thou hog!' exclaims some fanatic Madani as he passes by the heretic – a demand more outraging than requiring a red-hot, black-north Protestant to bless the Pope. 'Oh Allah! *Hell* him!' meekly responds the Persian, changing the benediction to a curse most intelligible to, and most delicious in, his fellows' ears.

I found an evening hour in the steamy heat of the Harem equal to half a dozen afternoons; and left it resolved never to revisit it till the Hajj departed from El Medinah. It was only prudent not to see much of the Ajamis; and as I did so somewhat ostentatiously, my companions discovered that the Hajj Abdullah, having slain many of those heretics in some war or other, was avoiding them to escape retaliation. In proof of my generalistic qualities, the rolling down of the water jar upon the heads of the Maghribi pilgrims in the 'Golden Thread' was quoted, and all offered to fight for me à l'outrance. I took care not to contradict the report.

A Visit To The Saints' Cemetery

A splendid comet, blazing in the western sky, had aroused the apprehensions of the Madani. They all fell to predicting the usual disasters – war, famine, and pestilence – it being still an article of Moslem belief that the dread star foreshows all manner of calamities. Men discussed the probability of Abd el Mejid's immediate decease; for here as in Rome,

'When beggars die, there are no comets seen:
The heavens themselves blaze forth the death of prince.'

And in every strange atmospheric appearance about the time of the Hajj, the Hejazis are accustomed to read tidings of the dreaded Rih el Asfar.

Whether the event is attributable to the Zu Zuwabah – the 'Lord of the Forelock,' – or whether it was a case of post hoc ergo propter hoc, I would not commit myself by deciding; but, influenced by some cause or other, the Hawazim and the Hawamid, subfamilies of the Beni-Harb, began to fight about this time with prodigious fury. These tribes are eternally at feud, and the least provocation fans their smouldering wrath into a flame. The Hawamid number, it is said, between 3000 and 4000 fighting men, and the Hawazim not more than 700: the latter, however, are considered a race of desperadoes who pride themselves upon never retreating, and under their fiery Shaykhs, Abbas and Aba Ali, they are a thorn in the sides of their disproportionate foe. On the present occasion a Hamindah happened to strike the camel of a Hazimi which had trespassed; upon which the Hazimi smote the Hamidah, and called him a rough name. The Hamidah instantly shot the Hazimi, the tribes were called out, and they fought with asperity for some days. During the whole of the afternoon of Tuesday the 30th August the sound of firing amongst the mountains was distinctly heard in the city. Through the streets parties of Bedouins, sword and matchlock in hand, or merely carrying quarterstaves on their shoulders, might be seen hurrying along, frantic at the chance of missing the fray. The townspeople cursed them privily, expressing a hope that the wholo race of vermin might consume itself. And the pilgrims were in no small trepidation, fearing the desertion of their camel-men, and knowing what a blaze is kindled in this inflammable land by an ounce of gunpowder. I afterwards heard that the Bedouins fought till night, and separated after losing on both sides ten men.

This quarrel put an end to any lingering possibility of my prosecuting my journey to Muscat as originally intended. I had on the way from Yambu to El Medinah privily made a friendship with one Mujrim of the Beni Harb. The 'Sinful,' as his name, an ancient and classical one amongst the Arabs, means, understood that I had some motive of secret interest to undertake the perilous journey. He could not promise at first to guide me, as his beat lay between Yambu, El Medinah, Meccah, and Jeddah. But he offered to make all inquiries about the route, and to bring me the result at noonday, a time when the household was asleep. He had almost consented at last to travel with me about the end of August, in which case I should have slipped out of Hamid's house and started like a Bedouin towards the Indian Ocean. But when the war commenced, Mujrim, who doubtless wished to stand by his brethren the Hawazim, began to show signs of recusancy in putting off the day of departure to the end of September. At last, when pressed, he frankly told me that no traveller, nay, not a Bedouin, could leave the city in that direction, even as far as Khaybar, which information I afterwards ascertained to be correct. It was impossible to start alone, and when in despair I had recourse to Shaykh Hamid, he seemed to think me mad for wishing to wend northwards when all the world was hurrying towards the south. My disappointment was bitter at first, but consolation soon suggested itself. Under the most favorable circumstances, a Bedouin-trip from El Medinah to Muscat, 1500 or 1600 miles, would require at least ten months; whereas, under pain of losing my commission, I was ordered to be at Bombay before the end of March. Moreover, entering Arabia by El Hejaz, as has before been said, I was obliged to leave behind all my instruments except a watch and a pocket compass, so the benefit rendered to geography by my trip would have been scanty. Still remained to me the comfort of reflecting that possibly at Meccah some opportunity of crossing the Peninsula might present itself. At any rate I had the certainty of seeing the strange wild country of the Hejaz, and of being present at the ceremonies of the Holy City.

I must request the render to bear with a Visitation once more: we shall conclude it with a ride to El Bakia. This venerable spot is frequented by the pious every day after the prayer at the Prophet's Tomb, and especially on Fridays.

Our party started one morning – on donkeys, as usual, for my foot was not yet strong – along the Darb el Jenazah round the southern wall of the town. The locomotives were decidedly slow, principally in consequence of tho tent-ropes which the Hajis had pinned down literally all over the plain, and falls were by no means infrequent. At last we arrived at the end of the Darb, where I committed myself by mistaking the decaying place of those miserable schismatics the Nakhawilah for El Bakia, the glorious cemetery of the Saints. Hamid corrected my blunder with tartness, to which I replied as tartly, that in our country – Afghanistan – we burned tho body of every heretic upon whom we could lay our hands. This truly Islamitic custom was heard with general applause, and as the little dispute ended, we stood at the open gate of El Bakia. Then having dismounted I sat down on a low Dakkah or stone bench within the walls, to obtain a general view and to prepare for the most fatiguing of the visitations.

There is a tradition that 70,000, or according to others 100,000 saints, all with faces like full moons, shall cleave on the last day the yawning bosom of El Bakia. About 10,000 of the Ashab (companions of the Prophet) and innumerable Sayyids are buried here: their graves are forgotten, because, in the olden time, tombstones were not placed over the last dwelling places of mankind. The first of flesh who shall arise is Mohammed, the second Abubekr, the third Omar, then the people of El Bakia (amongst whom is Osman, the fourth Caliph), and then the incolæ of the Jannat el Maala, the Meccan cemetery. The Hadis, 'whoever dies at the two Harams shall rise with the Secure on the Day of Judgment,' has made these spots priceless in value. And even upon earth they might be made a mine of wealth. Like the catacombs at Rome,

El Bakia is literally full of the odour of sanctity, and a single item of the great aggregate here would render any other Moslem town famous. It is a pity that this people refuses to exhume its relics.

The first person buried in El Bakia was Usman bin Mazun, the first of the Muhajirs who died at El Medinah. In the month of Shaaban, A. H. 3, the Prophet kissed the forehead of the corpse and ordered it to be interred within sight of his abode. In those days the field was covered with the tree Gharkad; the vegetation was cut down, the ground was levelled, and Usman was placed in the centre of the new cemetery. With his own hands Mohammed planted two large upright stones at the head and the feet of his faithful follower; and in process of time a dome covered the spot. Ibrahim, the Prophet's infant second son, was laid by Usman's side, after which El Bakia became a celebrated cemetery.

The Burial-place of the Saints is an irregular oblong surrounded by walls which are connected with the suburb at their S.W. angle. The Darb el Jenazah separates it from the enceinte of the town, and the Eastern Desert Road beginning from the Bab el Jumah bounds it on the north. Around it palm plantations seem to flourish. It is small, considering the extensive use made of it: all that die at El Medinah, strangers as well as natives, except only heretics and schismatics, expect to be interred in it. It must be choked with corpses, which it could not contain did not the Moslem style of burial greatly favor rapid decomposition, and it has all the inconveniences of 'intramural sepulture.' The gate is small and ignoble; a mere doorway in the wall. Inside there are no flower plots, no tall trees, in fact none of the refinements which lighten the gloom of a Christian burial-place: the buildings are simple, they might even be called mean. Almost all are the common

Arab Mosque, cleanly whitewashed, and looking quite new. The ancient monuments were levelled to the ground by Saad the Wahhabi and his puritan followers, who waged pitiless warfare against what must have appeared to them magnificent mausolea, deeming as they did a loose heap of stones sufficient for a grave. In Burckhardt's time the whole place was a 'confused accumulation of heaps of earth, wide pits, and rubbish, without a single regular tombstone.' The present erections owe their existence, I was told, to the liberality of the Sultans Abd el Hamid and Mahmud.

A poor pilgrim has lately started on his last journey, and his corpse, unattended by friends or mourners, is carried upon the shoulders of hired buriers into the cemetery. Suddenly they stay their rapid steps, and throw the body upon the ground. There is a life-like pliability about it as it falls, and the tight cerements so define the outlines that the action makes me shudder. It looks almost as if the dead were conscious of what is about to occur. They have forgotten their tools; one man starts to fetch them, and three sit down to smoke. After a time a shallow grave is hastily scooped out. The corpse is packed in it with such unseemly haste that earth touches it in all directions – cruel carelessness among Moslems, who believe this to torture the sentient frame. One comfort suggests itself. The poor man being a pilgrim has died Shahid – in martyrdom. Ere long his spirit shall leave El Bakia,

'And he on honey-dew shall feed,
And drink the milk of Paradise.'

I entered the holy cemetery right foot forwards, as if it were a Mosque, and barefooted, to avoid suspicion of being a heretic. For though the citizens wear their shoes in the Bakia, they are much offended at seeing the Persians follow their example. We began by the general benediction. 'Peace be upon ye, O people of El Bakia! Peace be upon ye, O admitted to the presence of the Most High! Receive ye what ye have been promised! Peace be upon ye, martyrs of El Bakia, one and all! We verily, if Allah please, are about to join ye! O Allah pardon us and them, and the mercy of God, and his blessings!' After which we recited the Chapter El Ikhlas and the Testification, then raised our hands, mumbled the Fatihah, passed our palms down our faces, and went on.

Walking down a rough narrow path, which leads from the western to the eastern extremity of El Bakia, we entered the humble mausoleum of the Caliph Osman – Osman 'El Mazlum,' or the 'ill-treated,' he is called by some Moslem travellers. When he was slain, his friends wished to bury him by the Prophet in the Ilujrah, and Ayisha made no objection to the measure. But the people of Egypt became violent, swore that the corpse should neither be buried nor be prayed over, and only permitted it to be removed upon the threat of Habibah (one of the 'Mothers of the Moslems,' and daughter of Abu Sufiyan) to expose her countenance. During the night that followed his death, Osman was carried out by several of his friends to El Bakia, from which, however, they were driven away, and obliged to deposit their burden in a garden, eastward of and outside the saints' cemetery. It was called Hisn Kaukab, and was looked upon as an inauspicious place of sepulture, till Marwan included it in El Bakia. We stood before Osman's monument, repeating, 'Peace be upon thee, O our Lord Osman, son of Affan! Peace be upon thee, O Caliph of Allah's Prophet! Peace be upon thee, O writer of Allah's book! Peace be upon thee, in whose presence the angels are ashamed! Peace be upon thee, O collector of the Koran! Peace be upon thee, O son-in-law of the Prophet! Peace be upon thee, O Lord of the Two Lights!

Peace be upon thee, who fought the battle of the Faith! Allah be satisfied with thee, and cause thee to be satisfied, and render heaven thy habitation! Peace be upon thee, and the mercy of Allah and his blessing, and praise ho to Allah, Lord of the (three) worlds!' This supplication concluded in the usual manner. After which we gave alms, and settled with ten piastres the demands of the Khadim who takes charge of the tomb: this double-disbursing process had to be repeated at each station.

Then moving a few paces to the north, we faced eastwards, and performed the visitation of Abu Said el Khazari, a Sahib or companion of the Prophet, whose sepulchre lies outside El Bakiu. The third place visited was a dome containing the tomb of our lady Halimah, the Bedouin wet-nurse who took charge of Mohammed: she is addressed thus: 'Peace be upon thee, O Halimah the auspicious! Peace be upon thee, who performed thy trust in suckling the best of mankind! Peace be upon thee, O wet-nurse of El Mustafa! Peace be upon thee, O Wet-nurse of El Mujtaba! May Allah be satisfied with thee, and cause thee to be satisfied, and render Heaven thy house and habitation! and verily we have come visiting thee, and by means of thee drawing near to Allah's Prophet, and through him to God the Lord of the Heavens and the Earths.'

After which, fronting the north, we stood before a low enclosure, containing ovals of loose stones, disposed side by side. These are the martyrs of El Bakia, who received the crown of glory at the hands of El Muslim, the general of the arch-heretic Yezid. The prayer here recited differs so little from that addressed to the martyrs of Ohod, that I will not transcribe it. The fifth station is near the centre of the cemetery at the tomb of Ibrahim, who died, to the eternal regret of El Islam, some say six months old, others in his second year. He was the son of Mariyah, the Coptic girl, sent as a present to

Mohammed by Jarih the Mukaukas or governor of Alexandria. The Prophet with his own hand piled earth upon the grave, and sprinkled it with water – a ceremony then first performed – disposed small stones upon it, and pronounced the final salutation. Then we visited El Nafi Maula, son of Omar, generally called Imam Nafi el Kari, or the Koran chaunter; and near him the great doctor Imam Malik Ibn Anas, a native of El Medinah, and one of the most dutiful of her sons. The eighth station is at the tomb of Ukayl bin Abi Talib, brother of Ali. Then we visited the spot where lie interred all the Prophet's wives, Ayisha included. After the 'Mothers of the Moslems,' we prayed at the tombs of Mohammed's daughters, said to be ten in number.

In compliment probably to the Hajj, the beggars mustered strong that morning at El Bakio. Along the walls and at the entrance of each building squatted ancient dames, all engaged in fervent contemplation of every approaching face, and in pointing to dirty cotton napkins spread upon the ground before them, and studded with a few coins, gold, silver, or copper, according to the expectations of the proprietress. They raised their voices to demand largesse: some promised to write Fatihahs, and the most audacious seized visitors by the skirts of their garments. Fakihs, ready to write 'Y. S.,' or anything else demanded of them, covered the little heaps and eminences of the cemetery, all begging lustily, and looking as though they would murder you, when told how beneficent is Allah. At the doors of the tombs old housewives, and some young ones also, struggled with you for your slippers as you doffed them, and not unfrequently the charge of the pair was divided between two. Inside, when the boys were not loud enough or importunate enough for presents, they were urged on by the adults and seniors, the relatives of the 'Khadims' and hangers on. Unfortunately for me, Shaykh Hamid was renowned for taking charge of wealthy pilgrims: the result was, that my purse was lightened of three dollars. I must add that although at least fifty female voices loudly promised that morning, for the sum of ten parahs each, to supplicate Allah in behalf of my lameness, no perceptible good came of their efforts.

Before leaving El Bakia, we went to the eleventh station, the Kubbat el Abbasiyah, or Dome of Abbas. Originally built by the Abbaside Caliphs in A. H. 519, it is a larger and a handsomer building than its fellows, and is situated on the right-hand side of the gate as you enter in. The crowd of beggars at the door testified to its importance: they were attracted by the Persians who assemble here in force to weep and pray. Crossing the threshold with some difficulty, I walked round a mass of tombs which occupies the centre of the building, leaving but a narrow passage between it and the walls. It is railed round, covered over with several 'Kiswahs' of green cloth, worked with white letters, and looked like a confused heap; but it might have appeared irregular to me by the reason of the mob around. The eastern portion contains the body of El Hasan, the son of Ali and grandson of the Prophet; the Imam Zayn el Abidin, son of El Husayn, and great grandson to the Prophet; the Imam Mohammed El Bakir (fifth Imam), son to Zayn el Abidin; and his son the Imam Jaafar el Sadik – all four descendants of the Prophet, and buried in the same grave with Abbas ibn Abd el Muttalib, uncle to Mohammed. It is almost needless to say that these names are subjects of great controversy. El Masudi mentions that here was found an inscribed stone declaring it to be the tomb of the Lady Fatimah, of Hasan her son, of Ali bin Husayn, of Mohammed bin Ali, and of Jaafar bin Mohammed. Ibn Jubayr, describing El Bakia, mentions only two in this tomb, Abbas and Hasan; the head of the latter, he says, in the direction of the former's feet. Other authors relate that in it, about the ninth century of the Hijrah, was found a wooden box covered with fresh-looking red felt cloth, with bright brass nails, and they believe it to have contained the corpse of Ali, placed here by his son Hasan.

We stood opposite this mysterious tomb, and repeated, with difficulty by reason of the Persians weeping, the following supplication: – 'Peace be upon ye, O family of the Prophet! O lord Abbas, the free from impurity and uncleanness, and father's brother to the best of men! And thou too O lord Hasan, grandson of the Prophet! And thou too O lord Zayn el Abidin! Peace be upon ye, one and all, for verily God hath been pleased to deliver you from all guile, and to purify you with all purity. The mercy of Allah and his blessings be upon you, and verily he is the Praised, the Mighty!' After which, freeing ourselves from the hands of greedy boys, we turned round and faced the southern wall, close to which is a tomb attributed to the Lady Fatimah. I will not repent the prayer, it being the same as that recited in tho Haram.

Issuing from the hot and crowded dome, we recovered our slippers after much trouble, and found that our garments had suffered from the frantic gesticulations of the Persians. We then walked to the gate of El Bakia, stood facing the cemetery upon an elevated piece of ground, and delivered the general benediction:

'O Allah! O Allah! O Allah! O full of mercy! O abounding in beneficence! Lord of length (of days), and prosperity, and goodness! O thou who when asked, grantest, and when prayed for aid, aidest! Have mercy upon the companions of thy Prophet, of the Muhajirin, and the Ansar! Have mercy upon them, one and all! Have mercy upon Abdullah bin Hantal (and so on, specifying their names), and make Paradise their

resting-place, their habitation, their dwelling, and their abode!
O Allah! Accept our Ziyarat, and supply our wants, and
lighten our griefs, and restore us to our homes, and comfort
our fears, and disappoint not our hopes, and pardon us, for on
no other do we rely; and let us depart in thy faith, and after the
practice of thy Prophet, and be thou satisfied with us! O Allah!
forgive our past offences, and leave us not to our (evil) natures
during the glance of an eye, or a lesser time; and pardon us,
and pity us, and let us return to our houses and homes safe (i.e.
spiritually and physically), fortunate, abstaining from what
is unlawful, re-established after our distresses, and belonging
to the good, thy servants upon whom is no fear, nor do they
know distress. Repentance, O Lord! Repentance, O Merciful!
Repentance, O Pitiful! Repentance before death, and pardon
after death! I beg pardon of Allah! Thanks be to Allah! Praise
be to Allah! Amen, O Lord of the (three) worlds!'

After which, issuing from El Bakia, we advanced
northwards, leaving the city gate on the left hand, and
came to a small Kubbah close to the road. It is visited
as containing the tomb of the Prophet's paternal aunts,
especially of Safiyah, daughter of Abd el Muttalib,
sister of Hamzah, and one of the many heroines of
early El Islam. Hurrying over our directions here – for
we were tired indeed – we applied to a Sakka for water,
and entered a little coffeehouse near the gate of the
town, after which we rode home.

I have now described, I fear at a wearying length, the
spots visited by every Zair at El Medinah. The guidebooks
mention altogether between fifty and fifty-five mosques
and other holy places, most of which are now unknown
even by name to the citizens. The most celebrated of these
are the few following, which I describe from hearsay.

About three miles to the N. W. of the town, close to
the Wady el Akik, lies the Mosque called El Kiblatayn –
'The Two Directions of Prayer.' Some give this title to the

Masjid el Takwa at Kuba. Others assert that the Prophet, after visiting and eating at the house of an old woman named Umin Mabshar, went to pray the midday prayer in the Mosque of the Beni Salmah. He had performed the prostration with his face towards Jerusalem, when suddenly warned by revelation he turned southwards and concluded his orisons in that direction. I am told it is a mean dome without inner walls, outer enclosures, or minaret.

The Masjid Beni Zafar (some write the word Tifr) is also called Masjid el Baghlah – of the She-mule – because, according to El Matari, on the ridge of stone to the south of this Mosque are the marks where the Prophet leaned his arm, and where the she-mule, Duldul, sent by the Mukaukas as a present with Mariyah the Coptic Girl and Yafur the donkey, placed her hoofs. At the Mosque was shown a slab upon which the Prophet sat hearing recitations from the Koran; and historians declare that by following his example many women have been blessed with offspring. This Mosque is to the east of El Bakia.

The Masjid el Juraah – of Friday, or El Anikah, of the Sand-heaps – is in the valley near Kuba, where Mohammed prayed and preached on the first Friday after his flight from Meccah.

The Masjid el Fazikh – of Date-liquor – is so called because when Abu Ayyub and others of the Ansar were sitting with cups in their hands, they heard that intoxicating draughts were for the future forbidden, upon which they poured the liquor upon the ground. Here the Prophet prayed six days whilst he was engaged in warring down the Beni Nazir Jews. The Mosque derives its other name, El Shams – of the Sun – because, being erected on rising ground east of and near Kuba, it receives the first rays of morning light.

To the eastward of the Masjid el Fazikh lies the Masjid el Kurayzah, erected on a spot where the Prophet descended to attack the Jewish tribe of that name.

Returning from the Battle of the Moat, wayworn and tired with fighting, he here sat down to wash and comb his hair, when suddenly appeared to him the Archangel Gabriel in the figure of a horseman dressed in a corslet and covered with dust 'The Angels of Allah,' said the preternatural visitor, 'are still in arms, O Prophet, and it is Allah's will that thy foot return to the stirrup. I go before thee to prepare a victory over the Infidels, the sons of Kurayzah.' The legend adds that the dust raised by the angelic host was seen in the streets of El Medinah, but that mortal eye fell upon no horseman's form. The Prophet ordered his followers to sound the battle-call, gave his flag to Ali – the Arab token of appointing a commander-in-chief – and for twenty-five days invested the habitations of the enemy. This hapless tribe was exterminated, sentence of death being passed upon them by Saad ibn Maaz, an Ausi whom they constituted their judge because he belonged to an allied tribe. 600 men were beheaded in the market-place of El Medinah, their property was plundered, and their wives and children were reduced to slavery.

Tantine relligio potuit suadere maloram!

The Masjid Mashrabat Umm Ibrahim, or Mosque of the garden of Ibrahim's mother, is a place where Mariyah had a garden and became the mother of Ibrahim, the Prophet's second son. It is a small building in what is called the Awali, or highest port of the El Medinah plain, to the north of the Masjid Beni Kurayzah, and near the eastern Harrah or ridge.

Northwards of El Bakia is, or was, a small building called the Masjid el Ijabah – of Granting – from the following circumstance. One day the Prophet stopped to perform his devotions at this place, which then belonged to the Beni Muawiyah of the tribe of Aus. He made a long Dua or supplication, and then turning to his companions, exclaimed, 'I have asked of Allah three favors, two hath he vouchsafed to me, but the third was refused!' Those granted were that the Moslems might never be destroyed by famine or by deluge. The third was that they might not perish by internecine strife.

The Masjid el Fath – of Victory – vulgarly called the 'Four Mosques,' ore situated in the Wady El Sayh, which comes from the direction of Kuba, and about half a mile to the east of 'El Kiblatayn.' The largest is called the Masjid el Fath or El Ahzab – of the troops – and is alluded to in the Koran. Here it is said the Prophet prayed for three days during the Battle of the Moat, also called the battle 'El Alizab,' the last fought with the Infidel Kuraysh under Abu Sufiyan. After three days of devotion, a cold and violent blast arose, with rain and sleet, and discomfited the foe. The Prophet's prayer having here been granted, it is supposed by ardent Moslems that no petition put up at the Mosque El Ahzab is ever neglected by Allah. The form of supplication is differently quoted by different authors. When El Shafei was in trouble and fear of Harun el Rashid, by the virtue of this formula he escaped all danger: I would willingly offer so valuable a prophylactory to my readers, only it is of an unmanageable length. The doctors of El Islam also greatly differ about the spot where the Prophet stood on this occasion; most of them support the claims of the Masjid el Fath, the most elevated of the four, to that distinction. Below, and to the south of the highest ground, is the Masjid Salman el Farsi, the Persian, from whose brain emanated the bright idea of the Moat. At the mature age of 250, some say 350, after spending liis life in search of a religion, from a Magus becoming successively a Jew and a Nazarene, he ended with being a Moslem, and a companion of Mohammed. During his eventful career he had been ten times sold into slavery. Below Salman's Mosque is the Masjid Ali, and the smallest building on the south of the hill is called Masjid Abubekr. All these places owe their existence to El Walid the Caliph: they were repaired at times by his successors.

The Masjid el Rayah – of the Banner – was originally built by El Wulid upon a place where the Prophet pitched his tent during the War of the Moat. Others call it El Zubab, after a hill upon which it stands. El Rayah is separated from the Masjid el Fath by a rising ground called Jebel Sula or Jebel Sawab: the former being on the eastern, whilst the latter lies upon the western declivity of the hill. The position of this place is greatly admired, os commanding the fairest view of the Haram.

About a mile and a half south-east of El Bakia is a dome called Kuwwat Islam, the Strength of El Islam. Here the Prophet planted a dry palm-stick, which grew up, blossomed, and bore fruit at once. Moreover, on one occasion when the Moslems were unable to perform the pilgrimage, Mohammed here produced the appearance of a Kaabah, an Arafat, and all the appurtenances of the Hajj. I must warn my readers not to condemn the founder of El Islam for these puerile inventions.

The Masjid Unayn lies south of Hamzah's tomb. It is on a hill called Jebel el Rumat, the Shooters' Hill, and here during the battle of Ohod stood the archers of El Islam. According to some the Prince of Martyrs here received his death-wound; others place that event at the Masjid el Askar or the Masjid el Wady.

Besides these fourteen, I find the names, and nothing but the names, of forty Mosques. The reader loses little by my unwillingness to offer him a detailed list of such appellations as Masjid Beni Abd el Ashhal, Masjid Beni Harisah, Masjid Beni Horam, Masjid el Fash, Masjid el Sukiya, Masjid Beni Bayazah, Masjid Beni Hatmah.

From El Medinah To
El Suwayrkiyah

Four roads lead from El Medinah to Meccah. The 'Darb el Sultani,' or 'Sultan's Way,' follows the line of coast: this general passage has been minutely described by my great predecessor. The 'Tarik el Ghabir,' a mountain path, is avoided by the Mahmal and the great Caravans, on account of its rugged passes; water abounds along the whole line, but there is not a single village; and the Sobh Bedouins, who own the soil, are inveterate plunderers. The route called 'Wady el Kura' is a favorite with Dromedary-Caravans; on this road are two or three small settlements, regular wells, and free passage through the Beni Amr tribe. The Darb el Sharki, or 'Eastern road,' down which I travelled, owes its existence to the piety of Zubaydah Khatun, wife of Ilarun el Rashid. That estimable princess dug wells from Baghdad to El Medinah, and built, we are told, a wall to direct pilgrims over the shifting sands. There is a fifth road, or rather mountain-path, concerning which I can give no information.

At 8 a.m. on Wednesday, the 26th Zu'l Kaaduh (31st August, 1853), as we were sitting at the window of Hamid's house after our early meal, suddenly appeared, in hottest haste, Masud, our camel-Shaykh. He was accompanied by his son, a bold boy about fourteen years of age, who fought sturdily about the weight of each package as it was thrown over the camel's back; and his nephew, an ugly pock-marked lad, too lazy even to quarrel. We were ordered to lose no time in loading; all started into activity, and at 9 a.m. I found myself standing opposite the Egyptian Gate, surrounded by my friends, who had accompanied me thus far on foot, to take leave with due honor. After affectionate embraces and parting mementos, we mounted, the boy Mohammed and I in the litter, and Shaykh Nur in his cot. Then, in company with some Turks and Meccans, for Masud owned a string of nine camels, we passed through the little gate near the castle, and shaped our course towards the north. On our right lay the palm-groves, which conceal this part of the city; far to the left rose the domes of Hamzah's Mosques at the foot of Mount Ohod; and in front a band of road, crowded with motley groups, stretched over a barren stony plain.

After an hour's slow march, bending gradually from N. to N.E., we fell into the Nejd highway and came to a place of renown called El Ghadir, or the Basin. This is a depression conducting the drainage of the plain towards the Northern Hills. The skirts of Ohod still limited the prospect to the left. On the right was the Bir Rashid (Well of Rashid), and the little whitewashed dome of Ali el Urays, a descendant from Zayn el Abidin: – the tomb is still a place of visitation. There we halted and turned to take farewell of the Holy City. All the pilgrims dismounted and gazed at the venerable minarets and the Green Dome – spots upon which their memory would ever dwell with a fond and yearning interest.

Remounting at noon we crossed a Fiumara which runs, according to my camel-Shaykh, from N. to S.;

we were therefore emerging from the Medinah basin. The sky began to be clouded, and although the air was still full of Simoom, cold draughts occasionally poured down from the hills. Arabs fear this 'bitter change/Of fierce extremes, extremes by change more fierce,' and call that a dangerous climate which is cold in the hot season and hot in the cold. Travelling over a rough and stony path, dotted with thorny Acacias, we arrived about 2 p.m. at the bed of lava heard of by Burckhardt. The aspect of the country was volcanic, abounding in basalts and scoriffi, more or less porous: sand veiled the black bed whose present dimensions by no means equal the descriptions of Arabian historians. I made diligent inquiries about the existence of active volcanoes in this port of El Hejaz, and heard of none.

At 5 p.m., travelling towards the East, we entered a Bughaz, or Pass, which follows the course of a wide Fiumara, walled in by steep and barren hills – the portals of a region too wild even for Bedouins. The torrent-bed narrowed where the turns were abrupt, and the drift of heavy stones, with a water-mark from 6 to 7 feet high, showed that after rains a violent stream runs from E. and S.E. to W. and N.W. The fertilising fluid is close to the surface, evidenced by a spare growth of Acacia, camel-grass, and at some angles of the bed by the Daum, or Theban palm. I remarked what are technically called 'Hufrah,' holes dug for water in the sand; and my guide assured me that somewhere near there is a spring flowing from the rocks.

After the long and sultry afternoon, beasts of burden began to sink in considerable numbers. The fresh carcasses of asses, ponies, and camels dotted the way-side: those that had been allowed to die were abandoned to the foul carrion-birds, the Rakham (vulture), and the yellow Ukab; and all whose throats had been properly cut, were surrounded by troops of Takruri pilgrims. These half-starved wretches cut steaks from the choice portions, and slung them over their shoulders till an opportunity of cooking might arrive. I never saw men more destitute. They carried wooden bowls, which they filled with water by begging; their only weapon was a small knife, tied in a leathern sheath above the elbow; and their costume an old skull-cap, strips of leather like sandals under the feet, and a long dirty shirt, or sometimes a mere rag covering the loins. Some were perfect savages, others had been fine-looking men, broad-shouldered, thin-flanked and long-limbed; many were lamed by fatigue and thorns; and looking at most of them, I saw death depicted in their forms and features.

After two hours' slow marching up the Fiumara eastwards, we saw in front of us a wall of rock, and turning abruptly southwards, we left the bed, and ascended rising ground. Already it was night; an hour, however, elapsed before we saw, at a distance, the twinkling fires, and heard the watch-cries of our camp. It was pitched in a hollow, under hills, in excellent order; the Pacha's pavilion surrounded by his soldiers and guards disposed in tents, with sentinels, regularly posted, protecting the outskirts of the encampment. One of our men, whom we had sent forward, met us on the way, and led us to an open place, where wo unloaded the camels, raised our canvas home, lighted fires, and prepared, with supper, for a good night's rest. Living is simple on such inarches. The pouches inside and outside the Shugduf contain provisions and water, with which you supply yourself when inclined. At certain hours of the day, ambulant vendors offer sherbet, lemonade, hot coffee, and water-pipes admirably prepared. Chibouques may be smoked in the litter; but few care to do so during the Simoom. The first thing, however, called for at the halting-place is the pipe, and its delightfully soothing influence, followed by a cup of coffee, and a 'forty winks' upon the sand, will awaken an appetite not to be roused by other means. How could Waterton, the Traveller, abuse a pipe? During the night-halt, provisions are cooked: rice, or Kichri, a mixture of pulse and rice, are eaten with Chutnee and lime-pickle, varied, occasionally, by tough mutton and indigestible goat.

We arrived at Ja el Sherifah at 8 p.m., after a march of about twenty-two miles. This halting-place is the rendezvous of caravans; it lies 50° S.E. of El Medinah, and belongs rather to Nejd than to El Hejaz.

At 3 a.m., on Thursday, we started up at the sound of the departure-gun, struck the tent, loaded the camels, mounted, and found ourselves hurrying through a gloomy Pass, in the hills, to secure a good place in the Caravan. This is an object of some importance, as, during the whole journey, marching order must not be broken. We met with a host of minor accidents, camels falling, Shugdufs bumping against one another, and plentiful abuse. Pertinaciously we hurried on till 6 a.m., at which hour we emerged from the black pass. The large crimson sun rose upon us, disclosing, through purple mists, a hollow of coarse yellow gravel, based upon a hard whitish clay. It is about five miles broad by twelve long, collects the waters of the high grounds after rain, and distributes the surplus through an exit towards the N.E., a gap in the low undulating hills around. Entering it, we dismounted, prayed, broke our fast, and after half an hour's halt proceeded to cross its breadth. The appearance of the Caravan was most striking, as it threaded its slow way over the smooth surface of the Khabt. To judge by the eye, the host was composed of at least 7000 souls, on foot, on horseback, in litters, or bestriding the splendid camels of Syria. There were eight gradations of pilgrims. The lowest hobbled with heavy staves. Then came the riders of asses, camels, and mules. Respectable men, especially Arabs, mounted dromedaries, and the soldiers had horses: a led animal was saddled for every grandee, ready whenever he might wish to leave his litter. Women, children, and invalids of the poorer classes sat upon a 'Haml Musattah,' – rugs and cloths spread over the two large boxes which form the camel's load. Many occupied Shibriyahs, a few, Shugdufs, and only the wealthy and the noble rode in Takhtrawan (litters), carried by camels or mules. The morning beams fell brightly upon the glancing arms which surrounded the stripped Mahmal, and upon the scarlet and gilt litters of the grandees. Not the least beauty of the spectacle was its wondrous variety of detail: no man was dressed like his neighbour, no camel was caparisoned, no horse clothed in uniform, as it were. And nothing stranger than the contrasts; – a band of half-naked Takruri marching with the Pacha's equipage, and long-capped, bearded Persians conversing with Turbushed and shaven Turks.

The plain even at an early hour reeked with vapors distilled by the fires of the Simoom: about noon, however, the air became cloudy, and nothing of color remained, save that milky white haze, dull, but glaring withal, which is the prevailing day-tint in these regions. At mid-day we reached a narrowing of the basin, where, from either sides, 'Irk,' or low hills, stretch their last spurs into the plain. But after half a mile, it again widened to upwards of two miles. At two p.m. we turned towards the S.W., ascended stony ground, and found ourselves one hour afterwards in a desolate rocky flat, distant about twenty-four miles of unusually winding rood from onr last station. 'Mahattah Ghurab,' or the Ravens Station, lies 10° S.W. from Ja el Sharifah, in the irregular masses of hill on the frontier of El Hejaz, where the highlands of Nejd begin.

After pitching the tent, we prepared to recruit our supply of water; for Masud warned me that his camels had not drunk for ninety hours, and that they would soon sink under the privation. The boy Mohammed, mounting a dromedary, set off with the Shaykh and many water bags, giving me an opportunity of writing out my journal. They did not return home till after nightfall, a delay caused by many adventures. The wells are in a Fiumara, as usual, about two miles distant from the halting-place, and the soldiers, regular as well as irregular, occupied the water and exacted hard coin in exchange for it. The men are not to blame; they would die of starvation, but for this resource. The boy Mohammed had been engaged in several quarrels; but after snapping his pistol at a Persian pilgrim's head, he came forth triumphant with two skins of sweetish water, for which we paid ten piastres. He was in his glory. There were many Meccans in the Caravan, among them his elder brother and several friends: the Sherif Zayd had sent, he said, to ask why he did not travel with his compatriots. That evening he drank so copiously of clarified butter, and ate dates mashed with flour and other abominations to such an extent, that at night he prepared to give up the ghost. We passed a pleasant hour or two before sleeping. I began to like the old Shaykh Masud, who, seeing it, entertained me with his genealogy, his battles, and his family affairs. The rest of the party could not prevent expressing contempt when they heard me putting frequent questions about torrents, hills, Bedouins, and the directions of places. 'Let the Father of Mustachios ask and learn,' said the old man; 'he is friendly with the Bedouins, and knows better than you all.' This reproof was intended to be bitter as the poet's satire –

'All fools have still an itching to deride,
And fain would be upon thr laughing side.'

It called forth, however, another burst of merriment, for the jeerers remembered my nickname to have belonged to that pestilent heretic, Saud the Wahhabi.

On Saturday, the 3rd September, that hateful signal-gun awoke us at one a.m. In Arab travel there is nothing more disagreeable than the Sariyah or night-march, and yet the people arc inexorable about it. 'Choose early darkness (Daljah) for your wayfarings,' said the Prophet, 'as the calamities of the earth – serpents and wild beasts – appear not at night.' I can scarcely find words to express the weary horrors of a long night's march, during which the hapless traveller, fuming, if a European, with disappointment in his hopes of 'seeing the country,' is compelled to sit upon the back of a creeping camel. The day sleep too is a kind of lethargy, and it is all but impossible to preserve an apetite during the hours of heat.

At half-past five a.m., after drowsily stumbling through hours of outer darkness, we entered a spacious basin at least six miles broad, and limited by a circlet of low hill. It was overgrown with camel-grass and Acacia trees – mere vegetable mummies – in many places the water had left a mark; and here and there the ground was pitted with mud-flakes, the remains of recently dried pools. After an hour's rapid march we toiled over a rugged ridge, composed of broken and detached blocks of basalt and scoriæ, fantastically piled together, and dotted with thorny trees; Shaykh Masud passed the time in walking to and fro along his line of camels, addressing us with a Khallikum guddam, 'to the front (of the litter)!' as we ascended, and a Khallikum wara 'to the rear!' during the descent. It was wonderful to see the animals stepping from block to block with the sagacity of mountaineers; assuring themselves of their forefeet before trusting all their weight to advance. Not a camel fell, either here or on any other ridge: they moaned, however, piteously, for the sudden turns of the path puzzled them; the ascents were painful, the descents were still more so; the rocks were sharp, deep holes yawned between the blocks, and occasionally an Acacia caught the Shugduf, almost overthrowing the hapless bearer by the suddenness and the tenacity of its clutch. This passage took place during daylight. But we had many at night, which I shall neither forget nor describe.

Descending the ridge, we entered another hill-encircled basin of gravel and clay. In many places basalt in piles and crumbling strata of hornblende schiste, disposed edgeways, green within, and without blackened by sun and rain, cropped out of the ground. At half-past ten we found ourselves in an 'Acacia-barren,' one of the things which pilgrims dread. Here Shugdufs are bodily pulled off the camel's back and broken upon the hard ground; the animals drop upon their knees, the whole line is deranged, and every one, losing his temper, attacks his Moslem brother. The road was flanked on the left by an iron wall of block basalt. Noon brought us to another ridge, whence we descended into a second wooded basin surrounded by hills.

Here the air was filled with those pillars of sand so graphically described by Abyssinian Bruce. They scudded on the wings of the whirlwind over the plain – huge yellow shafts, with lofty heads, horizontally bent backwards, in the form of clouds; – and on more than one occasion camels were overthrown by them. It required little stretch of fancy to enter into the Arabs' superstition. These sand-columns are supposed to be Genii of the Waste, which cannot be caught – a notion arising from the fitful movements of the wind-eddy that raises them – and, as they advance, the pious Moslem stretches out his finger, exclaiming, 'Iron! O thou ill-omened one!'

During the forenoon we were troubled with Simoom, which, instead of promoting perspiration, chokes up and hardens the skin. The Arabs complain greatly of its violence on this line of road. Here I first remarked the difficulty with which the Bedouins bear thirst. 'Ya Latif' – O! merciful Lord – they exclaimed at times, and yet they behaved like men. I had ordered them to place the water-camel in front, so as to exercise due supervision. Shaykh Masud and his son made only an occasional reference to the skins. But his nephew, a short, thin, pockmarked lad of eighteen, whose black skin and woolly head suggested the idea of a semi-African and ignoble origin, was always drinking; except when he climbed the camel's back and, dozing upon the damp load, forgot his thirst. In vain we ordered, we taunted, and we abused him: he would drink, he would sleep, but he would not work.

At one p.m. we crossed a Fiumara; and an hour afterwards we pursued the course of a second. Masud called this the Wady el Khunak, and assured me that it runs from the E. and the S.E. in a N. and N.W. direction, to the Medinah plain. Early in the afternoon we readied a diminutive flat, on the Fiumara bank. Beyond it lies a Mahjar or stony ground, black as usual in El Hejaz, and over its length lay the road, white with dust and the sand deposited by the camels' feet. Having arrived before the Pacha, we did not know where to pitch; many opining that the Caravan would traverse the Mahjar and halt beyond it. We soon alighted, however, pitched the tent under a burning sun, and were imitated by the rest of the party. Masud called the place Hijriyah. According to my computation it is twenty-five miles from Ghurab, and its direction is S.E. 22°.

Late in the afternoon the boy Mohammed started with a dromedary to procure water from the higher part of the Fiumara. Here are sonic wells, still called Bir Harun, after the great Caliph. The youth returned soon with two bags filled at an expense of nine piastres. This being the twenty-eighth Zu'l Kaadah, many pilgrims busied themselves rather fruitlessly with endeavours to sight the crescent moon. They failed; but we were consoled by seeing through a gap in the western hills a heavy cloud discharge its blessed load, and a cool night was the result.

We loitered on Sunday, the 4th of September, at El Hijriyah, although the Shaykh forewarned us of a long march. But there is a kind of discipline in these great Caravans. A gun sounds the order to strike the tents, and a second bids you march off with all speed. There are short halts of half an hour each at dawn, noon, the afternoon, and sunset, for devotional purposes, and these are regulated by a cannon or a culverin. At such times the Syrian and Persian servants, who are admirably experts in their calling, pitch the large green tents, with gilt crescents, for the dignitaries and their hareems. The last resting-place is known by the hurrying forward of these 'Farrash,' who are determined to be the first on the ground and at the well. A discharge of three guns denotes the station, and when the Caravan moves by night, a single cannon sounds three or four halts at irregular intervals.

The principal officers were the Emir el Hajj, one Ashgar Ali Pacha, a veteran of whom my companions spoke slightingly, because he had been the slave of a slave, probably the pipe-bearer of some grandee, who in his youth had been pipe-bearer to some other grandee. Under him was a Wakil or lieutenant, who managed the executive. The Emir el Surrah – called simply El Surrah, or the Purse – had charge of the Caravan, treasure, and remittances to the Holy Cities. And lastly there was a commander of the forces (Bashat el Askar): his host consisted of about 1000 irregular horsemen, Bashi Buzuks, half bandits half soldiers, each habited and armed after his own fashion, exceedingly dirty, picturesque-looking, brave, and in such a country of no use whatever.

Leaving El Hijriyah at seven a.m., we passed over the grim stone-field by a detestable footpath, and at nine o'clock struck into a broad Fiumara, which runs from the east towards the north-west. Its sandy bed is overgrown with Acacia, the Senna plant, different species of Euphorbia; the wild Capparis and the Daum Palm. Up this line we travelled the whole day. About six p.m., we came upon a basin at least twelve miles broad, which absorbs the water of the adjacent hills. Accustomed as I have been to mirage, a long thin line of salt efflorescence appearing at some distance on the plain below us, when the shades of evening invested the view, completely deceived me. Even the Arabs were divided in opinion, some thinking it was the effects of the rain which fell the day before: others were more acute. Upon the horizon beyond the plain rose dark, fort-like masses of rock which I mistook for buildings, the more readily as the Shaykh had warned me that we were approaching a populous place. At last descending a long steep hill, we entered upon the level ground, and discovered our error by the crunching sound of the camels' feet upon large curling flakes of nitrous salt overlying caked mud. Those civilised birds, the kite and the crow, warned us that we were in the vicinity of man. It was not, however, before eleven p.m., that we entered the confines of El Suwayrkiyah. The fact was made patent to us by the stumbling and the falling of our dromedaries over the little ridges of dried clay disposed in squares upon the fields. There were other obstacles, such as garden walls, wells, and hovels, so that midnight had sped before our weary camels reached the resting place. A rumor that we were to halt here the next day, made us think lightly of present troubles; it proved, however, to be false.

During the last four days I attentively observed the general face of the country. This line is a succession of low plains and basins, here quasi-circular, there irregularly oblong, surrounded by rolling hills and cut by Fiumaras which pass through the higher ground. The basins are divided by ridges and flats of basalt and greenstone averaging from 100 to 200 feet in height. The general form is a huge prism; sometimes there is a table on the top. From El Medinah to El Suwayrkiyah the low beds of sandy Fiumaras abound. From El Suwayrkiyah to El Zaribah, their place is taken by 'Ghadir,' or basins in which water stagnates. And beyond El Zaribah the traveller enters a region of water-courses tending W. and S.W. The versant is generally from the E. and S.E. towards the W. and N.W. Water obtained by digging is good where rain is fresh in the Fiumaras; saltish, so as to taste at first unnaturally sweet, in the plains; and bitter in the basins and lowlands where nitre effloresces and rain has had time to become tainted. The landward faces of the hills are disposed at a sloping angle, contrasting strongly with the perpendicularity of their seaward sides, and I saw no inner range corresponding with, and parallel to, the maritime chain. Nowhere is there a land in which Earth's anatomy lies so barren, or one richer in volcanic and primary formations. Especially towards the south, the hills are abrupt and highly vertical, with black and barren flanks, ribbed with furrows and fissures, with wide aud formidable precipices and castellated summits like the work of man. The predominant formation was basalt, called by the Arabs Hajar Jehannum, or Hell-stone; here and there it is porous and cellular; in some places compact and black; and in others coarse and gritty, of a tarry colour, and when fractured shining with bright points. Hornblende abounds at El Medinah and throughout this part of El Hejaz: it crops out of the ground edgeways, black and brittle. Greenstone, diorite, and actinolite are found, though not so abundantly as those above mentioned. The granites, called in Arabic Suwan, abound. Some are large grained, of a pink color, and appear in blocks, which, flaking off under the influence of the atmosphere, form into oöidal blocks and boulders piled in irregular heaps. Others are grey and compact enough to take a high polish when cut. The syenite is generally coarse, although there is occasionally found a rich red variety of that stone. I have never seen eurite or euritic porphyry except in small pieces, and the same may be said of the petrosilex.

From El Suwayrkiyah To Meccah

We have now left the territory of El Medinah. El Suwayrkiyah, which belongs to the Sherif of Meccah, is about twenty-eight miles distant from Hijriyah, and by dead reckoning ninety-nine miles along the road from the Prophet's burial-place. Its bearing from the last station was S.W. 11°. The town, consisting of about 100 houses, is built at the base and on the sides of a basaltic mass, which rises abruptly from the hard clayey plain. The summit is converted into a rude fortalice – without one no settlement can exist in El Hejaz – by a bulwark of uncut stone, piled up so as to make a parapet. The lower part of the town is protected by a mud wall, with the usual semicircular towers. Inside there is a bazar, well supplied with meat (principally mutton) by the neighbouring Bedouins, and wheat, barley, and dates are grown near the town. There is little to describe in the narrow streets and the mud houses, which are essentially Arab. The fields around are divided into little square plots by earthen ridges and stone walls; some of the palms are fine grown trees, and the wells appeared numerous. The water is near the surface and plentiful, but it has a brackish taste, highly disagreeable after a few days' use, and the effects are the reverse of chalybeate.

The town belongs to the Beni Ilusayn, a race of schismatics mentioned in the foregoing pages. They claim the allegiance of the Bedouin tribes around, principally Mutayr, and I was informed that their fealty to the Prince of Meccah is merely nominal.

The morning after our arrival at El Suwayrkiyah witnessed a commotion in our little party: hitherto they had kept together in fear of the road. Among the number was one Ali bin Ya Sin, a perfect 'old man of the sea.' By profession he was a 'Zem Zemi,' or dispenser of water from the Holy Well, and he had a handsome 'palazeo' at the foot of Abu Kubays in Meccah, which he periodically converted into a boarding bouse. Though post sixty, very decrepit, bent by age, white-bearded, and toothless, he still acted cicerone to pilgrims, and for that purpose travelled once every year to El Medinah. These trips had given him the cunning of a veteran voyager. He lived well and cheaply; his home-made Shugduf, the model of comfort, was garnished with soft cushions and pillows, whilst from the pockets protruded select bottles of pickled limes and similar luxuries; he had his travelling Shishah, and at the halting-place, disdaining the crowded, reeking tent, he had a contrivance for converting his vehicle into a habitation. He was a type of the Arab old man. He mumbled all day and three-quarters of the night, for he had des insomnies. His nerves were so fine, that if any one mounted his Shugduf, the unfortunate was condemned to lie like a statue. Fidgetty and priggishly neat, nothing annoyed him so much us a moment's delay or an article out of place, a rag removed from his water-gugglet, or a cooking pot imperfectly free from soot; and I judged his avarice by observing that he made a point of picking up and eating the grains scattered from our pomegranates, exclaiming that the heavenly seed (located there by Arab superstition) might be one of those so wantonly wasted.

Ali bin Ya Sin, returning to his native city, had not been happy in his choice of a companion this time. The other occupant of the handsome Shugduf was an ignoble-faced Egyptian from El Medinah. This ill-suited pair clave together for awhile, but at El Suwayrkiyah some dispute about a copper coin made them permanent foes. With threats and abuse such as none but as an Egyptian could tamely hear, Ali kicked his quondam friend out of the vehicle. But terrified, after reflection by the possibility that the man now his enemy might combine with two or three Syrians of our party to do him a harm, and frightened by a few black looks, the senior determined to fortify himself by a friend. Connected with the boy Mohammed's family, he easily obtained an introduction to me; he kissed my hand with great servility, declared that his servant had behaved disgracefully, and begged my protection, together with an occasional attendance of my 'slave.'

This was readily granted in pity for the old man, who became immensely grateful. He offered at once to take Shaykh Nur into his Shugduf. The Indian boy had already reduced to ruins the frail structure of his Shibriyah, by lying upon it lengthways, whereas prudent travellers sit in it cross-legged and facing the camel. Moreover, he had been laughed to scorn by the Bedouins, who seeing him pull up his dromedary to mount and dismount, had questioned his sex, and determined him to be a woman of the 'Miyan.' I could not rebuke them; the poor fellow's timidity was a ridiculous contrast to the Bedouin's style of mounting; a pull at the camel's head, the left foot placed on the neck, an agile spring, and a scramble into the saddle. Shaykh Nur, elated by the sight of old Ali's luxuries, promised himself some joyous hours; but next morning he owned with a sigh that he had purchased splendor at the extravagant price of happiness – the senior's tongue never rested throughout the livelong night.

During our half-halt at El Sawayrkiyah we determined to have a small feast; we bought some fresh dates, and paid a dollar and a half for a sheep. Hungry travellers consider 'liver and fry,' a dish to set before a Shaykh. On this occasion, however, our enjoyment was marred by the water; even Soyer's dinners would scarcely charm if washed down with cups of a certain mineral-spring found at Epsom.

We started at 10 a.m. in a south-easterly direction, and travelled over a flat, thinly dotted with desert vegetation. At 1 p.m. we passed a basaltic ridge, and then, entering a long depressed line of country, a kind of valley, paced down it five tedious hours. The Simoom as usual was blowing hard, and it seemed to affect the traveller's temper. In one place I saw a Turk, who could not speak a word of Arabic, violently disputing with an Arab who could not understand a word of Turkish. The pilgrim insisted upon adding to the camel's load a few dry sticks, such as are picked up for cooking. The camel-man as perseveringly threw off the extra burthen. They screamed with rage, hustled each other, and at last the Turk dealt the Arab a heavy blow. I afterwards heard that the pilgrim was mortally wounded that night, his stomach being ripped open with a dagger. On inquiring what had become of him, I was assured that he had been comfortably wrapped up in his shroud and placed in a half-dug grave. This is the general practice in the case of the poor and solitary, whom illness or accident incapacitates from proceeding. It is impossible to contemplate such a fate without horror: the torturing thirst of a wound, the burning sun heating the brain to madness, and – worst of all, for they do not wait till death – the attacks of the jackal, the vulture, and the raven of the wild.

At 6 p.m., before the light of day had faded, we traversed a rough and troublesome ridge. Descending it, our course lay in a southerly direction along a road flanked on the left by low hills of red sandstone and bright porphyry. About an hour afterwards we came to a basalt field, through whose blocks we threaded our way painfully and slowly, for it was then dark. At 8 p.m. the camels began to stumble over the dwarf dykes of the wheat and barley fields, and presently we arrived at our halting-place, a large village called El Sufayna. The plain was already dotted with tents and lights. We found the Baghdad Caravan, whose route here falls into the Darb el Sharki. It consists of a few Persians and Kurds, and collects the people of north-eastern Arabia, Wahhabis and others. They are escorted by the Agayl tribe and the fierce mountaineers of Jebel Shamar. Scarcely was our tent pitched when the distant pattering of musketry and an ominous tapping of the kettle-drum sent all my companions in different directions to inquire what was the cause of quarrel. The Baghdad Cafila, though not more than 2000 in number, men, women, and children, had been proving to the Damascus Caravan, that, being perfectly ready to fight, they were not going to yield any point of precedence. From that time the two bodies encamped in different places. I never saw a more pugnacious assembly: a look sufficed for a quarrel. Once a Wahhabi stood in front of us, and by pointing with his finger, and other insulting gestures, showed his hatred to the chibouque, in which I was peaceably indulging. It was impossible to refrain from chastising his insolence by a polite and smiling offer of the offending pipe.

This made him draw his dagger without a thought; but it was sheathed again, for we all cocked our pistols, and these gentry prefer steel to lead. We had travelled about seventeen miles, and the direction of El Sufayna from our last halting-place was S.E. 5°. Though it was night when we encamped, Shaykh Masud set out to water his moaning camels: they had not quenched their thirst for three days. He returned in a depressed state, having been bled by the soldiery at the well to the extent of forty piastres, or about eight shillings.

After supper we spread our rugs and prepared to rest. And here I first remarked the coolness of the nights, proving, at this season of the year, a considerable altitude above the sea. As a general rule the atmosphere stagnated between sunrise and 10 a.m., when a light wind rose. During the forenoon the breeze strengthened, and it gradually diminished through the afternoon. Often about sunset there was a gale accompanied by dry storms of dust at El Sufayna, though there was no night-breeze and little dew, a blanket was necessary, and the hours of darkness were invigorating enough to mitigate the effect of the sand and Simoom-ridden day. Before sleeping I was introduced to a namesake, one Shaykh Abdullah of Meccah. Having committed his Shugduf to his son, a lad of fourteen, he had ridden forward on a dromedary, and had suddenly fallen ill. His objects in meeting me were to ask for some medicine, and a temporary seat in my Shugduf; the latter I offered with pleasure, as the boy Mohammed was longing to mount a camel. The Shaykh's illness was nothing but weakness brought on by the hardships of the journey: he attributed it to the hot wind, and the weight of a bag of dollars, which he had attached to his waist belt. He was a man about forty, long, thin, pale, and of a purely nervous temperament: and a few questions elicited the fact that he had lately and suddenly given up his daily opium pill. I prepared one for him, placed him in my litter, and persuaded him to stow away his burden in some place where it would be less troublesome. He was my companion for two marches, at the end of which he found his own Shugduf, and I never met amongst the Arab citizens a better bred or better informed man. At Constantinople he had learned a little French, Italian, and Greek; and from the properties of a shrub to the varieties of honey, he was full of 'useful knowledge,' and open as a dictionary. We parted near Meccah, where I met him only once, and then accidentally, in the Valley of Muna.

At half-past 6 a.m., on the 5th of September, we arose refreshed by the cool, comfortable night, and loaded the camels. I had an opportunity of inspecting El Sufayna. It is a village of fifty or sixty mud-walled, flat-roofed houses, defended by the usual rampart. Around it lie ample date-grounds, and fields of wheat, barley, and maize. Its bazar at this season of the year is well supplied: even fowls can be procured.

We travelled towards the south-east, and entered a country destitute of the low runges of hill which from El Medinah southwards had bounded the horizon. After two miles' march, our camels climbed up a precipitous ridge, and then descended into a broad gravel plain.

From 10 to 11 a.m. our course was southerly over a high table-land, and we afterwards traversed for five hours and a half a plain which bore signs of standing water. This day's march was peculiarly Arabia. It was a desert peopled only with echoes – a place of death for what little there is to die in it – a wilderness where, to use my companion's phrase, there is nothing but

He. Nature, scalped, flayed, discovered her anatomy to the gazer's eye. The horizon was a sea of mirage; gigantic sund-columns whirled over the plain; and on both sides of our road were huge piles of bare rock, standing detached upon the surface of sand and clay. Here they appeared in oval lumps, heaped up with a semblance of symmetry; there a single boulder stood, with its narrow foundation based upon a pedestal of low, dome-shaped rock. All are of a pink coarse-grained granite, which flakes off in large crusts under the influence of the atmosphere. I remarked one block which could not measure less than thirty feet in height. Through these scenes we travelled till about halfpast 4 p.m., when the guns suddenly roared a halt. There was not a trace of human habitation around us: a few parched shrubs and the granite heaps were the only objects diversifying the hard clayey plain. Shaykh Masud correctly guessed the cause of our detention at the inhospitable 'halting-place of the Mutayr.' 'Cook your bread and boil your coffee,' said the old man; 'the camels will rest for awhile and the gun sound at nightfall.'

We had passed over about eighteen miles of ground; and our present directum was S.W. 20° of El Sufayna.

At half-past ten that evening we heard the signal for departure, and, as the moon was still young, we prepared for a hard night's work. We took a south-westerly course, through what is called a Waar – rough ground covered with thicket. Darkness fell upon us like a pall. The camels tripped and stumbled, tossing their litters like cockboats in a short sea; at times the Shugdufs were well nigh torn off their backs. When we came to a ridge worse than usual, old Masud would seize my camel's halter, and, accompanied by his son and nephew bearing lights, encouraged the animals with gesture and voice. It was a strange, wild scene. The black basaltic field was dotted with the huge and doubtful forms of spongy-footed camels, with silent tread, looming like phantoms in the midnight air; the hot wind moaned, and whirled from the torches sheets of flame and fiery smoke; whilst ever and anon a swift-travelling Takht-rawan, drawn by mules, and surrounded by runners bearing gigantic Mashals, threw a passing glow of red light upon the dark road and the dusky multitude. On this occasion the rule was 'every man for himself.' Each pressed forward into the best path, thinking only of preceding others. The Syrians, amongst whom our little party had become entangled, proved most unpleasant companions: they often stopped the way, insisting upon their right to precedence. On one occasion a horseman had the audacity to untie the halter of my dromedary, and thus to cast us adrift, as it were, in order to make room for some excluded friend. I seized my sword; but Shaykh Abdullah stayed my hand, and addressed the intruder in terms sufficiently violent to make him slink away. Nor was this the only occasion on which my companion was successful with the Syrians. He would begin with a mild 'Move a little, O my father!' followed, if fruitless, by 'Out of the way, O father of Syria!' and, if still ineffectual, advancing to a 'Begone, O he!' This ranged between civility and sternness. If without effect, it was supported by revilings to the 'Abusers of the Salt,' the 'Yezid,' the 'Offspring of Shimr.' Another remark which I mode about my companion's conduct well illustrates the difference between the Eastern and the Western man. When traversing a dangerous place, Shaykh Abdullah the European attended to his camel with loud cries of 'Hai! Hai!' and an occasional switching.

Shaykh Abdullah the Asiatic commended himself to Allah by repeated ejaculations of 'Ya Sátir! Ya Sattár!'

The morning of Wednesday (Sept. 6th) broke as we entered a wide plain. In many places were signs of water: lines of basalt here and there seamed the surface, and wide sheets of the tufaceous gypsum called by the Arabs 'Sabkhah' shone like mirrors set in the russet frame-work of the flat. This substance is found in cakes, often a foot long by an inch in depth, curled by the sun's rays and overlying clay into which water had sunk. After our harassing night, day came on with a sad feeling of oppression, greatly increased by the unnatural glare; –

> 'In vain the sight, dejected to the ground,
> Stoop'd for relief: thence hot ascending streams
> And keen reflection pain'd.'

We were disappointed in our expectations of water, which usually abounds near this station, as its name, 'El Ghadir,' denotes. At 10 a.m. we pitched the tent in the first convenient spot, and lost no time in stretching our cramped limbs upon the bosom of mother Earth. From the halting place of the Mutayr to El Ghadir is a march of about twenty miles, and the direction S. W. 21°. El Ghadir is an extensive plain, which probably presents the appearance of a lake after heavy rains. It is overgrown in parts with desert vegetation, and requires nothing but a regular supply of water to make it useful to man. On the east it is bounded by a wall of rock, at whose base are three wells, said to have been dug by the Caliph Harun. They are guarded by a Burj, or tower, which betrays symptoms of decay.

In our anxiety to rest we had strayed from the Damascus Caravan into the mountaineers of Shamar. Our Shaykh Masud manifestly did not like the company; for shortly after 3 p.m. he insisted upon our striking the tent and rejoining the Hajj, which lay encamped about two miles distant in the western part of the basin. We loaded, therefore, and half an hour before sunset found ourselves in more congenial society. To my great disappointment, a stir was observable in the Caravan. I at once understood that another night-march was in store for us.

At 6 p.m. we again mounted, and turned towards the eastern plain. A heavy shower was filling upon the western hills, whence came damp and dangerous blasts. Between 9 a.m. and the dawn of the next day we had a repetition of the last night's scenes, over a road so rugged and dangerous, that I wondered how men could prefer to travel in the darkness. But the camels of Damascus were now worn out with fatigue; they could not endure the sun, and our time was too precious for a halt. My night was spent perched upon the front bar of my Shugduf, encouraging the dromedary; and that we had not one fall excited my extreme astonishment. At 5 a.m. we entered a wide plain thickly clothed with the usual thorny trees, in whose strong grasp many a Shugduf lost its covering and not a few were dragged with their screaming inmates to the ground. About five hours afterwards we crossed a high ridge, and saw below us the camp of the Caravan, not more than two miles distant. As we approached it, a figure came running out to meet us. It was the boy Mohammed, who, heartily tired of riding a dromedary with his friend, and possibly hungry, hastened to inform my companion Abdullah that he would lead him to his Shugduf and his son. The Shaykh, a little offended by the fact that for two days not a friend nor an acquaintance had taken the trouble to see or to inquire about him, received Mohammed roughly; but the youth, guessing the grievance, explained it away by swearing that he and all the party had tried to find us in vain. This wore the semblance of truth: it is almost impossible to come upon any one who strays from his place in so large and motley a body.

At 11 a.m. we had reached our station. It is about twenty-four miles from El Ghadir, and its direction is S.E. 10°. It is called El Birkat (the Tank), from a large and now ruinous cistern built of hewn stone by the Caliph Harun. The land belongs to the Utaybah Bedouins, the bravest and most ferocious tribe in El Hejaz; and the citizens denote their dread of these banditti by asserting, that to increase their courage they drink their enemy's blood. My companions shook their heads when questioned upon the subject, and prayed that we might not become too well acquainted with them – an ill-omened speech!

The Pacha allowed us a rest of five hours at El Birkat: we spent them in my tent, which was crowded with Shaykh Abdullah's friends. To requite me for this inconvenience, he prepared for me an excellent water-pipe, a cup of coffee, which, untainted by cloves and cinnamon, would have been delicious, and a dish of dry fruits. As we were now near the Holy City, all the Meccans were busy canvassing for lodgers and offering their services to pilgrims. Quarrels, too, were of hourly occurrence. In our party was an Arnaut, a white bearded old man, so decrepit that he could scarcely stand, and yet so violent that no one could manage him but his African slave, a brazen-faced little wretch about fourteen years of age. Words were bandied between this angry senior and Shaykh Maaud, when the latter insinuated sarcastically, that if the former had teeth he would be more intelligible. The Arnaut in his rage seized a pole, raised it, and delivered a blow which missed the camel-man, but brought the striker headlong to the ground. Masud exclaimed, with shrieks of rage, 'Have we come to this, that every old dastard Turk smites us?' Our party had the greatest trouble to quiet the quarrelers. The Arab listened to us when we threatened him with the Pacha. But the Arnaut, whose rage was 'like red-hot steel,' would hear nothing but our repeated declarations, that unless he behaved more like a pilgrim, we should be compelled to leave him and his slave behind.

On the 7th September, at 4 p.m., we left El Birkat, and travelled eastwards over rolling ground thickly wooded. There was a network of footpaths through the thickets, and clouds obscured the moon; the consequence was inevitable loss of way. About 2 p.m. we began ascending hills in a south-westerly direction, and presently fell into the bed of a large rock-girt Fiumara, which runs from east to west. The sands were overgrown with saline and salsolaccous plants; the Coloquintida, which, having no support, spreads along the ground; the Senna, with its small green leaf; the Rhazya stricta; and a large luxuriant variety of the Asclepias gigantea, cottoned over with mist and dew. At 6 a.m. we left the Fiumara, and, turning to the west, we arrived about an hour afterwards at the station. El Zaribah, 'the valley,' is an undulating plain amongst high granite hills. In many parts it was faintly green; water was close to the surface, and rain stood upon the ground. During the night we had travelled about twenty-three miles, and our present station was S.E. 66° from our last.

Having pitched the tent and eaten and slept, we prepared to perform the ceremony of El Ihram (assuming the pilgrim-garb), as El Zaribah is the Mikat, or the appointed place. Between the noonday and the afternoon prayers a barber attended to shave our heads, cut our nails, and trim our mustochios. Then, having bathed and perfumed ourselves – the latter is a questionable point – we donned the attire, which is nothing but two new cotton cloths, each six feet long by three and-a-half broad, white, with narrow red stripes and fringes; in fact, the costume called 'El Eddeh' in the baths at Cairo. One of these sheets, technically termed the 'Rida,' is thrown over the back, and, exposing the arm and shoulder, is knotted at the right side in the style 'Wishah.' The 'Izar,' is wrapped round the loins from waist to knee, and, knotted or tucked in at the middle, supports itself. Our heads were bare, and nothing was allowed upon the instep. It is said that some classes of Arabs still preserve this religious but most uncomfortable costume: it is doubtless of ancient date, and to this day, in the regions lying west of the Red Sea, it continues to be the common dress of the people.

After the toilette we were placed with our faces in the direction of Meccah, and ordered to say aloud 'I vow this Ihram of Hajj (the pilgrimage) and the Umrah (the little pilgrimage) to Allah Almighty!' Having thus performed a two-bow prayer, we repeated, without rising from the sitting position, these words, 'O Allah! verily I purpose the Hajj and the Umrah, then enable me to accomplish the two, and accept them both of me, and make both blessed to me! Followed the 'Talbiyat,' or exclaiming –

'Here I am! O Allah! here am I –
No partner hast thou, here am I:
Verily the praise and the beneficience are thine, and the kingdom –
No partner hast thou, here am I!'

And we were warned to repeat these words as often as possible, until the conclusion of the ceremonies.

Then Shaykh Abdullah, who acted as director of our consciences, bade us be good pilgrims, avoiding quarrels, bad language, immorality, and light conversation. We must so reverence life that we should avoid killing game, causing an animal to fly, and even pointing it out for destruction; nor should we scratch ourselves, save with the open palm, lest vermin be destroyed, or a hair uprooted by the nail. We were to respect the sanctuary by sparing the trees, and not to pluck a single blade of grass. As regards personal considerations, We were to abstain from all oils, perfumes, and unguents; from washing the head with mallow or lote leaves; from dyeing, shaving, cutting, or vellicating a single pile or hair; and though we might take advantage of shade, and even form it with upraised hands, we must by no means cover our sconces. For each infraction of these ordinances we must sacrifice a sheep; and it is commonly said by Moslems, that none but the Prophet could be perfect in the intricacies of pilgrimage. Old Ali began with an irregularity: he declared that age prevented his assuming the garb, but that, arrived at Meccah, be would clear himself by an offering.

The wife and daughters of a Turkish pilgrim of our party assumed the Ihram at the same time as ourselves. They appeared dressed in white garments; and they had exchanged the Lisam, that coquettish fold of muslin which veils without concealing the lower part of the face, for a hideous mask, made of split, dried, and plaited palm-leaves, with two 'bulk-eyes' for light. I could not help laughing when these strange figures met my sight, and, to judge from the shaking of their shoulders, they were not less susceptible to the merriment which they had caused.

At 3 a.m. we left El Zaribah, travelling towards the S.W., and a wondrously picturesque scene met the eye.

Crowds hurried along, habited in the pilgrim garb, whose whiteness contrasted strangely with their black skins, their newly shaven heads glistening in the sun, and their long black hair streaming in the wind. The rocks rang with shouts of 'Labbayk! Labbayk!' At a pass we fell in with the Wahhabis, accompanying the Baghdad Caravan, screaming 'Here am I;' and, guided by a large loud kettle-drum, they followed in double file the camel of a standard-bearer, whose green flag bore in huge white letters the formula of the Moslem creed. They were wild-looking mountaineers, dark and fierce, with hair twisted into thin Dalik or plaits: each was armed with a long spear, a matchlock, or a dagger. They were seated upon course wooden saddles, without cushions or stirrups, a fine saddle-cloth alone denoting a chief. The women emulated the men; they either guided their own dromedaries, or, sitting in pillion, they clung to their husbands; veils they disdained, and their countenances certainly belonged not to a 'soft sex.' These Wahhabis were by no means pleasant companions. Most of them were followed by spare dromedaries, either unladen or carrying waterskins, fodder, fuel, and other necessaries for the march. The beasts delighted in dashing furiously through our file, which being colligated, was thrown each time into the greatest confusion. And whenever we were observed smoking, we were cursed aloud for Infidels and idolaters.

Looking back at El Zaribah, soon after our departure, I saw a heavy nimbus settle upon the hill tops, a sheet of rain being stretched between it and the plain. The low grumbling of thunder sounded joyfully in our ears. We hoped for a shower, but were disappointed by a dust storm, which ended with a few heavy drops. There arose a report that the Bedouins had attacked a party of Meccans with stones, and the news caused men to look exceeding grave.

At 5 p.m. we entered the wide bed of the Fiumara, down which we were to travel all night Here the country falls rapidly towards the sea, as the increasing heat of the air, the direction of the water-courses, and signs of violence in the torrent-bed show. The Fiumara varies in breadth from 150 feet to three-quarters of a mile; its course, I was told, is towards the south-west, and it enters the sea near Jeddah. The channel is a coarse sand, with here and there masses of sheet rock and patches of thin vegetation.

At about half-past 5 p.m. we entered a suspicious-looking place. On the right was a stony buttress, along whose base the stream, when there is one, flows; and to this depression was our road limited by the rocks and thorn trees, which filled the other half of the channel. The left side was a precipice, grim and barren, but not so abrupt as its brother. Opposite us the way seemed barred by piles of hills, crest rising above crest into the far blue distance. Day still smiled upon the upper peaks, but the lower slopes and the Fiumara bed were already curtained with gray sombre shade.

A damp seemed to fall upon our spirits as we approached this Valley Perilous. I remarked that the voices of the women and children sank into silence, and the loud Labbaykas of the pilgrims were gradually stilled. Whilst still speculating upon the cause of this phenomenon, it became apparent. A small curl of the smoke, like a lady's ringlet, on the summit of the right-hand precipice, caught my eye, and, simultaneous with the echoing crack of the matchlock, a high-trotting dromedary in front of me rolled over upon the sands – a bullet had split his heart – throwing his rider a goodly somerset of five or six yards.

Ensued terrible confusion; women screamed, children shrieked, and men vociferated, each one striving with might and main to urge his animal out of the place of death. But the road being narrow, they only managed to jam the vehicles in a solid immovable mass. At every matchlock shot a shudder ran through the huge body, as when the surgeon's scalpel touches some more sensitive nerve. The irregular horsemen, perfectly useless, galloped up and down over the stones, shouting to and ordering one another. The Pacha of the army had his carpet spread at the foot of the left-hand precipice, and debated over his pipe with the officers what ought to be done. No good genius whispered 'Crown the heights.'

Then it was that the conduct of the Wahhabis found favor in my eyes. They came up, galloping their camels–

'Torrents less rapid, and legs rash –'

with their elf-locks tossing in the wind, and their flaring mulches casting a strange lurid light over their features. Taking up a position, one body began to fire upon the Utaybah robbers, whilst two or three hundred, dismounting, swarmed up the hill under the guidance of the Sherif Zayd. I had remarked this nobleman at El Medinah as a model specimen of the pure Arab. Like all Sherifs, he is celebrated for bravery, and has killed many with his own hand. When urged at El Zaribah to ride into Meccah, he swore that he would not leave the caravan till in sight of the walls; and, fortunately for the pilgrims he kept his word. Presently the firing was heard far in our rear – the robbers having fled; the head of the column advanced, and the dense body of pilgrims opened out. Our forced halt was now exchanged for a flight. It required much management to steer our desert-craft clear of danger; but Shaykh

Masud was equal to the occasion. That many were lost was evident by the boxes and baggage that strewed the shingles. I had no means of ascertaining the number of men killed and wounded: reports were contradictory, and exaggeration unanimous. Tho robbers were said to be 150 in number; their object was plunder, and they would eat the shot camels. But their principal ambition was the boast 'We, the Utaybah, on such and such a night stopped the Sultan's Mahmal one whole hour in the Pass.'

At the beginning of the skirmish I had primed my pistols, and sat with them ready for use. But soon seeing that there was nothing to bo done, and, wishing to make an impression – nowhere does Bobadil now 'go down' but in the East – I called aloud for my supper. Shaykh Nur, exanimate with fear, could not move. The boy Mohammed ejaculated only an 'Oh, sir!' and the people around exclaimed in disgust, 'By Allah, he eats!' Shaykh Abdullah, the Meccan, being a man of spirit, was amused by the spectacle. 'Are these Afghan manners, Effendim?' he inquired from the Shugduf behind me, 'Yes,' I replied aloud, 'in my country we always dine before an attack of robbers, because that gentry is in the habit of sending men to bed supperless.' The Shaykh laughed aloud, but those around him looked offended. I thought the bravado this time mal placé; but a little event which took place on my way to Jeddah proved that it was not quite a failure.

As we advanced, our escort took care to fire every large dry Asclepias, to disperse the shades which buried us. Again the scene became wondrous wild: –

'Full many a waste I've wander'd o'er,
Clomb many a crag, cross'd many a shore,
But, by my halidome,
A scene so rude, so wild as this,

Yet so sublime in barrenness,
Ne'er did my wandering footsteps press,
Where'er I chanced to roam.'

On either side were ribbed precipices, dark, angry, and towering above, till their summits mingled with the glooms of night; and between them formidable looked the chasm, down which our host hurried with shouts and discharges of matchlocks. The torch-smoke and the night-fires of flaming Asclepias formed a canopy, sable above and livid red below, which hung over our heads like a sheet, and divided the cliffs into two equal parts. Here the fire flashed fiercely from a tall thorn that crackled and shot up showers of sparks into the air; there it died away in lurid gleams, which lit up a truly Stygian scene. As usual, however, the picturesque had its inconveniences. There was no path. Rocks, stone-banks, and trees obstructed our passage. The camels, now blind in darkness, then dazzled by a flood of light, stumbled frequently; in some places slipping down a steep descent, in others sliding over a sheet of mud. There were furious quarrels and fierce language between camel-men and their hirers, and threats to fellow-travellers; in fact, we were united in discord. I passed that night crying, 'Hai! Hai!' switching the camel, and fruitlessly endeavoring to fustigate Masud's nephew, who resolutely slept upon the water bags. During the hours of darkness we made four or five halts, when we boiled coffee and smoked pipes, but man and beasts were beginning to suffer from a deadly fatigue.

Dawn found us still travelling down the Fiumara, which here is about 100 yards broad. The granite hills on both sides were less precipitous, and the borders of the torrent-bed became natural quays of stiff clay, which showed a water-mark of from twelve to fifteen feet in height. In many parts the bed was muddy; and the moist places, as usual, caused accidents. I happened to be looking back at Shaykh Abdullah, who was then riding in old Ali bin Ya Sin's fine Shugduf; suddenly the camel's four legs disappeared from under him, his right side flattening the ground, and the two riders were pitched severally out of the smashed vehicle. Abdullah started up furious, and abused the Bedouins, who were absent, with great zest. 'Feed these Arabs,' he exclaimed, quoting a Turkish proverb, 'and they will fire at Heaven!' But I observed that, when Shaykh Masud came up, the citizen was only gruff.

We then turned northward, and sighted El Mazik, more generally known as Wady Laymun, the Valley of Limes. On the right bank of the Fiumara stood the Meccan Sherif's state pavilion, green and gold: it was surrounded by his attendants, and prepared to receive the Pacha of the Caravan. We advanced half a mile, and encamped temporarily in a hill-girt bulge of the Fiumara bed. At 8 a.m. we had travelled about twenty-four miles from El Zaribah, and the direction of our present station was S.W. 50°.

Shaykh Masud allowed us only four hours' halt; he wished to precede the main body. After breaking our fast joyously upon limes, pomegranates, and fresh dates, we sallied forth to admire the beauties of the place. We are once more on classic ground – the ground of the ancient Arab poets –

'Deserted is the village – waste the halting place and home
At Mina, o'er Rijam and Ghul wild beasts unheeded roam,
On Rayyan hill the channel lines have left a naked trace,
Time-worn, as primal *Writ that dints the mountain's flinty face*; –'

and this Wady, celebrated for the purity of its air, has from remote ages been a favorite resort of the Meccans.

Nothing can be more soothing to the brain than the dark-green foliage of the limes and pomegranates; and from the base of the southern hill bursts a bubbling stream, whose

'Chiare, fresche e dolci acque'

flow through the garden, filling them with the most delicious of melodies, the gladdest sound which nature in these regions knows.

Exactly at noon Masud seized the halter of the foremost camel, and we started down the Fiumara. Troops of Bedouin girls looked over the orchard walls laughingly, and children came out to offer us fresh fruit and sweet water. At 2 p.m., travelling south-west, we arrived at a point where the torrent-bed turns to the right, and quitting it, we climbed with difficulty over a steep ridge of granite. Before three o'clock we entered a hill-girt plain, which my companions called 'Sola.' In some places were clumps of trees, and scattered villages warned us that we were approaching a city. Far to the left rose the blue peaks of Taif, and the mountain road, a white thread upon the nearer heights, was pointed out to me. Here I first saw the tree, or rather shrub, which bears the balm of Gilead, erst so celebrated for its tonic and stomachic properties. I told Shaykh Masud to break off a twig, which he did heedlessly. The act was witnessed by our party with a roar of laughter, and the astounded Shaykh was warned that he had become subject to an atoning sacrifice. Of course he denounced me as the instigator, and I could not fairly refuse assistance. The tree has of late years been carefully described by many botanists; I will only say that the bark resembled in color a cherry-stick pipe, the inside was a light yellow, and the juice made my fingers stick together.

At 4 p.m. we came to a steep and rocky Pass, up which we toiled with difficulty. The face of the country was rising once more, and again presented the aspect of numerous small basins divided and surrounded by hills. As we jogged on we were passed by the cavalcade of no less a personage than the Sherif of Meccah. Abd el Muttalib bin Ghalib is a dark, beardless, old man with African features derived from his mother. He was plainly dressed in white garments and a white muslin turban, which made him look jet black; he rode an ambling mule, and the only emblem of his dignity was the large green satin umbrella borne by an attendant on foot. Scattered around him were about forty matchlock-men, mostly slaves. At long intervals, after their father, came his four sons, Riza Bey, Abdullah, Ali and Ahmed, the latter still a child. The three elder brothers rode splendid dromedaries at speed; they were young men of light complexion, with the true Meccan cast of features, showily dressed in bright-colored silks, and armed, to denote their rank, with sword and gold-hilted dagger.

We halted as evening approached, and strained our eyes, but all in vain, to catch sight of Meccah, which lies in a winding volley. By Shykah Abdullah's direction I recited, after the usual devotions, the following prayer. The reader is forewarned that it is difficult to preserve the flowers of Oriental rhetoric in a European tongue.

'O Allah! verily this is thy safeguard (Amn) and thy Sanctuary (Haram)! Into it whose entereth becometh safe (Amin). So deny (Harrim) iny flesh and blood, my bones and skin, to hell-fire. O Allah! Save me from thy wrath on the day when thy servants shall be raised from the dead. I conjure thee by this that thou art Allah, besides whom is none (thou only), the Merciful, the Compassionate. And have mercy upon our lord Mohammed, and upon the progeny of our lord Mohammed, and upon his followers, one and all!' This was concluded with the 'Talbiyat,' and with an especial prayer for myself.

We again mounted, and night completed our disappointment. About 1 a.m. I was aroused by general excitement. 'Meccah! Meccah!' cried some voices; 'The Sanctuary! O the Sanctuary!' exclaimed others; and all burst into loud 'Labbayk,' not unfrequently broken by sobs. I looked out from my litter, and saw by the light of the southern stars the dim outlines of a large city, a shade darker than the surrounding plain. We were passing over the last ridge by an artificial cut, called the Saniyat Kudaa. The 'winding path' is flanked on both sides by watch-towers, which command the 'Darb el Maala,' or road leading from the north into Meccah. Thence we passed into the Maabidah (northern suburb), where the Sherif's palace is built. After this, on the left hand, came the deserted abode of the Sherif bin Aun, now said to be a 'haunted house.' Opposite to it lies the Jannat cl Maala, the holy cemetery of Meccah. Thence, turning to the right, we entered the Sulaymaniyah or Afghan quarter. Here the boy Mohammed, being an inhabitant of the Shamiyah or Syrian ward, thought proper to display some apprehension. These two are on bad terms; children never meet without exchanging volleys of stones, and men fight furiously with quarter-staves. Sometimes, despite the terrors of religion, the knife and sabre are drawn. But these hostilities have their code. If a citizen be killed, there is a subscription for blood-money. An inhabitant of one quarter, passing singly through another, becomes a guest; once beyond the walls, he is likely to be beaten to insensibility by his hospitable foes.

At the Sulaymaniyah we turned off the main road into a by-way, and ascended by narrow lanes the rough heights of Jebel Hindi, upon which stands a small whitewashed and crenellated building called a fort. Thence descending, we threaded dark streets, in places crowded with rude cots and dusky figures, and finally at 2 a.m. we found ourselves at the door of the boy Mohammed's house.

From Wady Laymun to Meccah the distance, according to my calculation, was about twenty-three miles, the direction S.E. 45°. We arrived on the morning of Sunday the 7th Zu'l Hijjah (11th September, 1853), and had one day before the beginning of the pilgrimage to repose and visit the Haram.

I conclude this chapter with a few remarks upon the watershed of El Hejaz. The country, in my humble opinion, has a compound slope, southwards and westwards. I have, however, little but the conviction of the modern Arabs to support the assertion that this part of Arabia declines from the north. All declare the course of water to be southerly, and believe the fountain of Arafat to pass underground from Baghdad. The slope, as geographers know, is still a disputed point Ritter, Jomard, and some old Arab authors, make the country rise towards the south, whilst Wallin and others express an opposito opinion. From the sea to El Musahhal is a gentle rise. The water-marks of the Fiumaras show that El Medinah is considerably above the coast, though geographers may not be correct in claiming for Jebel Radhwa a height of 6000 feet; yet that elevation is not perhaps too great for the plateau upon which stands the Prophet's burial-place. From El Medinah to El Suwayrkiyah is another gentle rise, and from the latter to El Zaribah stagnating water denotes a level. I believe the report of a perennial lake on the eastern boundary of El Hejaz as little as the river placed by Ptolemy between Yambu and Meccah.

No Bedouins could tell me of this feature, which, had it existed, would have changed the whole conditions and history of the country; we know the Greek's river to be a Fiumara, and the lake probably owes its existence to a similar cause, a heavy fall of rain. Beginning at El Zaribah is a decided fall, which continues to the sea. The Arafat torrent sweeps from east to west with great force, sometimes carrying away the habitations, and even injuring the sanctuary.